We Never Had a Hotbed of Crime!

Life in Twentieth-Century South Sydney

Sue Rosen is the director of a history and heritage consultancy based in Sydney. She has an MA from Macquarie University and is currently undertaking a PhD at the University of Western Sydney and preparing for publication a history of Old Government House and its Domain at Parramatta.
Her previous publications include Losing Ground: An Environmental History of the Hawkesbury-Nepean Catchment *and* Bankstown: A Sense of Identity. *Sue is committed to shifting perceptions of history as being merely a vehicle for nostalgia to an acceptance of it as an essential tool for understanding the present and addressing the future.*

We Never Had a Hotbed of Crime!

Life in Twentieth-Century South Sydney

Sue Rosen

In association with the South Sydney City Council

First published in 2000.

Typeset and designed by
Bowra+Bowra, Bowral NSW 2576

Printed and bound by
Colorcraft, Hong Kong

For the publisher
Hale & Iremonger Pty Ltd
PO Box 205, Alexandria NSW 2015
www.haleiremonger.com

National Library of Australia
Cataloguing-in-Publication entry:
Rosen, Sue. 1956-.
We never had a hotbed of crime!: Life in twentieth-century
South Sydney.

ISBN 0 86806 687 7 (pbk)
ISBN 0 86806 701 6 (hbk)

1. Interviews - New South Wales - Sydney. 2. Sydney (N.S.W.) - Social conditions - 20th century. 3. Sydney (N.S.W.) - History - 20th century. 1.Title

994.4104

Contents

- The police were supreme!
- I'd say the majority of people took SP Booking and two-up as a national pastime, but you had to be careful not to get caught, that's all
- If you had dyed red hair and red fingernails you were a wanton woman
- It was The Rocks that had the bad reputation!
- We're the Surry Hills mob, the Surry Hills mob are we
- So we done all these silly stupid awful things to people
- I was a terrible kid!

- My aunt won a black bottom contest at the Hub
- We were glued to it, your ear practically stuck to the thing
- And then His Master's Voice put out a phonogram
- People were in an uproar about rock and roll
- Me father drank, me mother went to church and I went to the pictures
- Once we had the TV it was a big event
- We'd go to the Royal Easter Show and you used to get your show bags free
- That night was like a Wonderland to kids

- We'd be out everywhere
- To this day, if I ever smell coconut oil, I remember Bondi Beach
- All the Unions and the Councils used to have picnics once a year
- We went on family outings
- Going for a drive was the big thing
- It was a palace of wonders for me
- We used to rent a cottage at Kincumber for six shillings a week

Acknowledgements

This work has truly been a co-operative undertaking and many people have contributed to its success. Firstly, I would like to acknowledge Jacqueline Kent's *In the Half Light: Life as a child in Australia, 1900–1970,* which inspired me to respond to the Council's call for 'Expressions of Interest' in the history project. Any attempt to capture the cultural, social and economic diversity of South Sydney and present some kind of coherent history of a city that had had a number of geographical incarnations was, I thought, impossible unless one could use as a binding theme the one thing that all residents of South Sydney have in common: that is, they were all children once. Inspired by *In the Half Light,* but feeling convinced that no council steering committee would go for this 'childhood stuff', I was delighted when a very enlightened committee (Chris Harcourt, John Fowler and Anne-Maree Whitaker) accepted the proposal. In the early stages I had assistance from Council's Community Arts Officer Susan Gibbeson and later from Jenny Trinca. Liam Gash and the Media Unit have also advised on publicity and publication.

Past the interview stage, transcription was undertaken by Gail Eglington and Marilyn Karit. Initial editing of the transcripts was performed by Rosemary Kerr, Beverley Johnson and Robin Porter. Maureen Bark undertook picture and general background research. Rosemary was also involved in later stages of editing and in the preparation of the final manuscript. Throughout the project it was a relief to have Shirley Fitzgerald to call on for an 'objective' opinion; her students, particulary Patricia Jacobsen, in the Master of Letters course at the University of Sydney, also made a valuable contribution to the explanatory notes. Bruce Baskerville of the South Sydney Heritage Society and Brenda Humble, local artist and community activist, reviewed the manuscript and provided much-needed sounding boards. My family — David, Jocelyn and Zoe — should also be thanked for accepting their coercion into this capacity and for convincingly saying 'Of course it's wonderful' and 'No, you haven't lost the plot' at all the right moments.

The most important people in the project were, however, the interviewees and I owe a great debt to all of them for their openness, their trust and their hospitality. This book is dedicated to you and your families and particularly to the memories of Dario Lo Schiavo and Paul Herlinger who did not live to see its publication.

Introduction

This menu cover shows many of the sites referred to by South Sydney residents as being important to them.

We *Never Had a Hotbed of Crime! Life in Twentieth-Century South Sydney* is one of the outcomes of the South Sydney Social History Project, which was commissioned by the City Council in 1993. Since that time 70 people have been interviewed about their experience of life, politics, economics and fun in South Sydney when they were growing up. The oldest, Keith Mulhearn, was born in 1904 and, together with his sister Claire, who was born in 1906, they reveal what life was like in Newtown from about 1912 until the early 1920s. Grace Schwebel also lived in Fitzroy Street, Newtown, and her experience, which focuses on the later half of the '20s and the '30s completes almost a thirty-year coverage of that immediate neighbourhood. The youngest interviewee was Dean Ingram, who was born in 1975 and grew up in Waterloo. A complete list of the interviewees, together with their year of birth and the name of the suburb on which their account focuses, is provided on page 238. Most were able to recount from the time they were eight years old through to their late teens.

We Never Had a Hotbed of Crime! presents edited extracts from these interviews with the intent of not only documenting events but also with the strong hope of conveying a sense of what it was like to live through the events and experiences of twentieth-century South Sydney. It is strongly recommended that should a particular reference strike the interest of the reader that the original transcript be consulted for additional material on the topic. As reflected in this work, all aspects of life were pried into and recorded. The resulting audio tapes and their transcripts are available in the City of South Sydney library system. It is hoped that residents might choose to expand on the project by adding to the collection or by drawing out and developing areas of interest.

The interviewees were all volunteers located through community organisations, advertising and at the South Sydney community festivals. All were required to sign a copyright release so that the material could be made publicly available. All were sent copies of the tapes and given the opportunity to check the transcripts for errors and approve of the edited extracts presented here. This work, which is some 90,000 words in length, is a distillation of somewhere in excess of 1.5 million words of transcribed material and clearly there are many valuable stories that were culled from the original material. There is scope for several other works that could focus on specific areas, have a biographic emphasis or explore any number of specific themes, including domestic life, schooling, or rites of passage.

Rather than present the material biographically, it was decided to adopt a thematic approach that, within the constraints of that methodology, was also chronologically arranged. Chapter 1, 'There's a war on', deals with the lead up to World War I, the war period itself and its aftermath, including the influenza epidemic of 1919. Chapter 2, 'Nobody was allowed to go there, but everybody did', deals with the theme of 'fun and games'; it has been placed in this position to provide some relief from the sadness of the preceding war period and to give you the strength for Chapter 3, 'My father lost his job', which looks at the effects of the Great Depression, and Chapter 4, 'The Japanese could have come straight in', which covers life in World War II. Chapter 5, 'My parents talked politics all the time', addresses political activity (almost a universal sport in the area) and issues across the century, some of which refer back to the preceding chapters on the wars and the Depression;

likewise Chapter 6, 'I'd work me arse out too!', which examines working life, has many cross-references to other chapters. In fact, it was very difficult to determine thematic boundaries as in reality life does not function in discrete thematic or chronological compartments, and the effects of events sometimes stretch across generations. Chapter 7, 'You can pay the coppers, or use your influence', deals with 'law and order' issues and is, by today's standards, both amusing and horrifying. Chapter 8, 'There'd be a bit of a song and dance in the parlour', is essentially a chapter on entertainment, and Chapter 9, 'I had a freedom for which I was very grateful', looks at where South Sydney's citizens roamed within and beyond the city, with an emphasis on places that were important to them.

The underlying principle of this project has been to facilitate the telling of the history of South Sydney by its residents as they saw it. *We Never Had a Hotbed of Crime!* reveals the rich and varied experience of living in South Sydney. It was an experience that was sometimes unique, but which at other times is reflective of broader Australian stories that have relevance for us all.

Newtown Boy

Sit'n' on the gas box,
wait'n' for me dad.
He's at the pub.
Friday he celebrates
and puts on a funny voice.

Joy Pithers across the street,
she's in kindergarten too.
I'll bet her dad is home.
Never seen him, but.

Dawn Miller's father, the funeral man,
he's rich.
They're gunna get a television
soon as they switch it on from America.
First thing will be Mickey Mouse.
I'll be seven then.

Joy Pithers kissed me, sit'n' on the gas box,
but I love Christine Parker
'cause she's got long brown hair down to her
    bottom.
When she sits on the scripture mat
I make plaits for her and look at her red ribbon.

On Fridays Dad gets drunk and wobbles his bike
    down the side
but he always brings us fish and scallops,
Fruit Tingles, Steam Rollers, Choo Choo Bars and
    Cherry Ripes.
I fight my sister for the green Fruit Tingles.

Other days,
Dad puts me on his handlebars—
he made a seat for me—
and rides me up to the very end of the street,
across the big road
and we watch the trains go past.
I wave to the guards
and they wave back.

Sit'n' on the gas box
I can see into Salmon Park
where the Dutch Boy who called me a 'bloody
    basket',
threw half a brick and split my head open.
I didn't have to go to hospital, but.
I shouldn't have called him 'Diego'.

The street light just came on,
Now those big flying ants
will bump against the globe until they're fried.

Yesterday my tortoise died
after Mr Morris ran over it in his semi-trailer.

Here's my last green one,
I've been saving it for a week.
Fizzing in my mouth, tickling under my tongue,
I wish a car would come past.

Hey, I can smell fish and scallops.
I'm standing on the gas box, waving.
It's my dad, and the old green bike.

–Brendan Doyle

1

There's a war on

" I had a cousin who joined the Light Horse Brigade."

Defence considerations had been an issue prior to Federation, but the 1899–1902 Boer War, which ultimately saw some 16,000 Australians fight for Britain in South Africa, acted as a militaristic catalyst. The Russo-Japanese War of 1904–05, involving the destruction of the Russian Fleet by the Japanese, was a further impetus for the establishment of an Australian Navy in 1909 and in 1910 compulsory military training for boys was introduced.[1]

When I woke up in the morning after the war started life was different all together.[2] My father come home and told me, 'There's a war on, a big war, but it's a long way away, it's in Europe, and we won't know anything about it'. But the police come along and arrested the man next door, they were Germans, 'German Charlie' I think they called him. And German Charlie he was in a concentration camp the night the war started. And they picked them all up — we had a German teacher, and when we went to school he wasn't there.[3] The police had picked him up and interned him. When we were going to school I remember little groups of women talking, there was a lot of tension. Suddenly we became very German-conscious, but when the other, the big second world war came nothing happened like that at all. I didn't see anybody making any commotion and it was on our doorstep.

As a kid, we were conscripts from age twelve to twenty-four. In the militia — the junior cadets, senior cadets, and militia. We used to drill two nights a month, and two Saturday afternoons a month, and every quarter a full day which went from eight o'clock in the morning till five o'clock at night. We'd all march out to the rifle range at Long Bay from the Alexandria drill hall. And after eighteen, we went to Liverpool for a ten-day camp. And there was a drill hall in the stadium up the road, it wasn't there very long before it burnt down. They ran out of

money when I was getting twenty-four, but we did twelve years. At drill we sang the national anthem, raised the flag and saluted it in the morning. You'd first parade and go back for breakfast, then you'd come out in full dress, the whole lot and do the different sorts of drill and there was fatigue parties to clean up the place. Keith Mulhearn

My older brother, Harry, who was then about eighteen was in 'home protection' during the war, they were kind of called up. He was out at South Head and we used to laugh and say, 'Harry was protecting our shores'. Harry used to say they put their fingers in their ears when any guns went off, and that was our closest connection with the Great War. There they were watching and waiting for the Germans to come. But nothing happened, there was nothing at all. The uniforms were terrible. I remember they had to have puttees, they were like a bandage. They probably wore knickerbockers, and they had these puttees wound around their legs, there was quite an art in putting puttees on, and people used to get in a terrible tangle with them. Zena Sachs

1 Stuart McIntyre, *The Oxford History of Australia — The Succeeding Age 1901–1942*, Oxford University Press, Melbourne, 1993, p. 140.
2 5 August 1914.
3 The treatment of enemy aliens is discussed in Pam Maclean, 'War and Australian Society', in Joan Beaumont (ed.), *Australia's War 1914–19*, Allen & Unwin, 1995, pp. 84–88.

Above: The Light Horse passing along Macquarie Street in preparation for embarkation from Cowper Wharf. (National Library)

Below: A Kindergarten military camp, Empire Day, 1915. (State Records)

Iolanthe, at Number 1 Victoria Street, overlooked the wharves at Woolloomooloo. It was high up. When the soldiers went to the First World War they were marched down to Woolloomooloo Bay and embarked into troopships at that wharf.[4] It was a great place for viewing soldiers marching up and down, being embarked and disembarked at Woolloomooloo in the First World War and Second World War. GLAD WILLIS

—

I had a cousin who joined the Light Horse Brigade and we went down to Cowper Wharf to see them off when they went to Gallipoli. The march seemed to be endless, I mean, I couldn't say the number, because I was only about five. But there seemed to be enough to fill a boat. They all marched around Cowper Wharf Road, right round past the Finger Wharf and then right round what they used to call 'the Burma Road'. But that's not its official name. It was only given that name in World War II. And it's the road that leads up to Victoria Street.[5] Usually, when they dressed, they had leggings and cocked hats, and they had this big feather. They looked absolutely fantastic. The adults were dreadfully emotional. My aunty, whose son it was that was going away, howled all the time, cried for weeks. He wasn't very old, I think he was only about 19. He viewed it as something that he should do, because he was an Australian and the Mother Country needed him. Everybody was very patriotic, there was no hanging back, you didn't have to force them to go. They all applied as soon as the war broke out you know. JOYCE HIGGINS

4   In 1914, the first contingent of volunteers of the Australian Imperial Forces consisted of three brigades of infantry and one of light horse. They sailed for the Gallipoli campaign against the Turks, embarking from Sydney's Finger Wharf, in November. See F.G. Clarke, *Australia: A Concise Political and Social History,* Harcourt Brace Janovich, Marrickville, 1992, pp. 195–196.

5   Many older residents of the area still refer to the 'Burma Road'. See 'Growing up in the Cross', in *Memories — Kings Cross 1936–1946,* Kings Cross Community Aid and Information Services, Potts Point, 1981, p. 31.

(National Library)

all-in!

"They gave me the ballot paper,
The grim death-warrant of doom,
And I smugly sentenced the man to death,
In that dreadful little room.

Above and opposite: When the Government's appeals to patriotism and manliness failed to attract ever more enlistments, two referenda on enforced conscription for overseas service were held. In the vitriolic campaigns preceding the vote, women were particular targets of the propaganda war. (National Library)

My father enlisted and they came down to the house and when the recruiter saw the nine kids, the officer said, 'You've done your duty there', and wouldn't take him. BILL SCHWEBEL

—

Although the war was essentially a European conflict and men flocked to serve the 'Mother Country', because New Guinea, Samoa and the Bismarck Archipelago were all German colonies there was also a Pacific aspect to the hostilities.

So the war was on, and my people were saw milling up in Dorrigo, and I used to go there for three months every year for my colonial experience with the bullock drivers and what have you. And we used to have to go by boat then, there was no railway, and the *Emden*, the first year started to play up, and that was around.[6] My father says, 'Well you've got nothing to fear, you'll be going up on the *Orara*, it's the fastest boat on the coast, it'd run away from the *Emden*, so I went up quite safe, nothing could happen to us, we could wave goodbye. When Gallipoli was on, there was all the excitement, you know, in the papers and everything else like that, we were in a great to-do about it, then it was over, and then all the cousins and everyone else came down and they joined the army and went first to Egypt, then later to France, so it was very interesting. The war hushed everything, you know, you had to be worried about the war. The war done this and that and the other, you couldn't do this because the war was on. And of course the people, so many people, were concerned because they had relatives in it. This one was getting killed, that one was wounded and what have you, and there was tension all the time... KEITH MULHEARN

"WE NEVER HAD A HOTBED OF CRIME"

THE BLOOD VOTE

" Oh, the poor Anzacs!"

The horrific casualties of the Gallipoli campaign galvanised public opinion roughly into two camps: one that supported an increased war effort; and the other group which opposed the conscription of men for overseas military service and who were highly critical of the British. The referenda campaigns were the most divisive in Australian history with the largely working-class and politically aware communities of South Sydney in the 'No!' camp.

My parents voted twice to oppose conscription when it was put as a referendum; they spoke about it for years.[7] The Catholic community carried the weight of the votes, and conscription never, ever got off the ground, even though there were two referenda.

GRACE SCHWEBEL

—

My father was very much against the war. He was particularly angry about Gallipoli, because he didn't have much opinion of Winston Churchill. Dad could

---

6   The *Emden* was sunk in the Indian Ocean in November 1914.

7   There were two bitterly contested referendums to allow for compulsory overseas service during World War I, on both occasions the proposition was rejected.

talk politics till the cows came home, and he said that Gallipoli was one of Churchill's inspirations that fell flat. Apparently when I was very little I used to pick up a newspaper and say, 'Oh, the poor Anzacs!'. Dad used to, oh, he used to get so worked up and angry about Gallipoli, because everybody put such a gloss over it all, it was this great show of heroism and so on, which it was, but it was also unnecessary, and badly organised, and badly thought out. I can remember, but not just from those years, Dad went on and on and on. ZENA SACHS

"Dad added something to Monash's charisma I s'pose."

Dad was at Gallipoli and he was injured in France when he was a machine gunner and then he was a pilot. Dad was very tall and handsome, and Monash chose him in Egypt to ride with him if he could because Dad looked good, added something to Monash's charisma I s'pose. He was only a private. But anyhow when he left Gallipoli and they went to France, he was injured and he was in hospital in France and the Prince of Wales was coming, so they chose Dad to open the door for the Prince of Wales, mind you, again because he was tall and handsome, and of course the Prince of Wales gave him a signed photograph, and those were the days when the monarchy was really something, and the Sister on the ward dearly wanted this signed photo of the Prince of Wales, and Dad said, 'Well, I'll give you the photo if you get me into the Air Corp', which happened. He said flying was marvellous. They used to repair their planes with pieces of string and wire. He said it was very lonely and he used to have special songs to sing to himself when he was flying. Most pilots were killed in landing because the plane used to flip back and they died of a broken neck, or broken back. He spoke about his luck. He'd be sitting there he said, they would all be sitting on the log, chatting, everybody else would be killed but him, this sort of thing. I'm sorry I didn't ask him more. One story was that he

was disgusted with the English because at Gallipoli somehow when they made those roads up the side of the mountains, if the Ghurkhas and the English troops were coming down, the Ghurkhas would have to slide down because the English refused to walk on the same path as the Ghurkhas. And I remember Dad telling us this, and how disgusted he was, 'cause they were all just soldiers together fighting. BRENDA HUMBLE

Because my father had his job to do here, to keep him going and all that kind of thing he didn't go because you didn't have to go to the war if you had a job, and was doing something for the community. I don't think my mother and father were interested that much in the conscription campaign, they were getting on with their own life, see. I had no brothers or anything that went to the war, if you can understand. I remember they were going to have riots and everything, because of Billy Hughes.[8] One person in the family, you know, came back from the war, came home and then went back again and was killed. And he had a wife, he was presumed missing. My mother took me down to the railway station when the war was over when they surrendered, I remember standing down there and watching all the people, screaming and laughing and going on. IRENE WEBBER

---

8   Joan Beaumont, 'The Politics of a Divided Society', in Joan Beaumont (ed.), *Australia's War 1914–18*, Allen & Unwin, St Leonard's, 1995, pp. 43–54.

Opposite: 'A Call from the Dardanelles' (National Library)

" **They were heroes but we thought they were mad.**"

With a population of approximately five million the impact of the war can be assessed by comparing the casualty rate with those experienced during World War II. Of the 330,000 Australian troops who served overseas, the almost 60,000 deaths and overall casualties of 226,000 was double that of World War II when the population had grown to about seven million. The casualty rate of 68.5 per cent was 10 per cent higher than in any other country of the 'Empire'.[9]

I remember the end of the war because all the kids were given peace medals except the kids in kindergarten, but my brother who would have been in primary school gave me his peace medal. I must have pinned it on and I was standing at the front of the shop and I can remember some awful boy coming along and grabbing it. I never saw it again. I was so upset. I can remember also the rather narrow streets in Newtown being decorated with 'Welcome Home' signs, right down Hordern Street from one balcony to the other, right across the street were these banners and flags flying with 'Welcome Home' on them. ZENA SACHS

When the boys were coming back in the train, they'd hang out the windows waving khaki handkerchiefs, because I was about eight, nine, and as they were waving we were grabbing the handkerchiefs as the diggers were going past, you know, dozens of us. Well then up on Newtown bridge, motorcars had little flags, Australian flags up as their mascot in front of their car, little stick and the flags would be silk, about six inches by four inches, and they were tooting their horns, you know, joy for peace and all that, and we'd jump in front of the cars and grab these flags. BILL SCHWEBEL

9 *Australian Encyclopaedia*, Vol. 9, The Grolier Society of Australia, Sydney, 1963, p. 395.

Left: Sir John Monash (National Library)

Opposite: 'The Anti's Creed' (National Library)

"WE NEVER HAD A HOTBED OF CRIME"

THE ANTI'S CREED

I believe the men at the Front should be sacrificed.
I believe we should turn dog on them.
I believe that our women should betray the men who are
    fighting for them.
I believe in the sanctity of my own life.
I believe in taking all the benefit and none of the risks.
I believe it was right to sink the *Lusitania.*
I believe in murder on the high seas.
I believe in the I.W.W.
I believe in Sinn Fein.
I believe that Britain should be crushed and humiliated.
I believe in the massacre of Belgian priests.
I believe in the murder of women, and baby-killing.
I believe that Nurse Cavell got her deserts.
I believe that treachery is a virtue.
I believe that disloyalty is true citizenship.
I believe that desertion is ennobling.
I believe in Considine, Fihelly, Ryan, Blackburn, Brookfield,
    Mannix, and all their works.
I believe in egg power rather than man power.
I believe in holding up transports and hospital ships.
I believe in general strikes.
I believe in burning Australian haystacks.
I believe in mine-laying in Australian waters.
I believe in handing Australia over to Germany.
I believe I'm worm enough to vote No.

Those who DON'T Believe in the above Creed
will **VOTE YES**

Authorised by the Reinforcements Referendum Council. CLAUDE McKAY, Publicity Secretary,
808 Collins Street, Melbourne.
D. W. PATERSON Co. PTY. LTD., Printers, 495 Collins Street, Melbourne.

No. 27.

My uncles were pretty wild blokes, they all went to the war. Pat died of gas, that was in the First World War, he came home and died later. Phil went. Phil was a very heavy drinker, a single bloke. His mother used to go to church every day. They sent him back from overseas because there was a blue over there and he killed an Egyptian in a fight. TERRY MURPHY

—

Then, when they were all coming home again some of them were sick and what have you, some didn't come at all. I had a cousin, lived here for sometime, and he was very shell-shocked, and he used to go down to the Military Hospital… now the Prince of Wales Hospital at Randwick.[10] That was a children's home, deaf and dumb, and they made a soldier's hospital of it, and he used to have to go out there every day for treatment, therapy. He was very funny for a while and then he got alright, and went home to his own place. He lived in the country. KEITH MULHEARN

—

When all the soldiers came back from the war most of them landed down in Woolloomooloo. And people said, 'Oh they're mad', all the stories about the bayonets and things like that — either bomb happy or mad; we were terrified of them. Well, the way they bayoneted all the Germans over there, 'cold steel' they called it. We said anyone that could do that would have to be mad, you don't mind shooting with a gun but when you go into them with a bayonet and 'bang, bang, bang' and cut them to pieces. Yeah, they were heros but we thought they were all mad. And anyone that got a bit drunk, they'd say, 'Oh he's bomb happy!', you'd see an old digger come back and he'd go off his head in the pub, another bomb happy. They were too, they really were. They had a bad time when they came back from the First World War, they just came back and got nothing, they just said the war's over, ta ta. They didn't go on a pension or anything, they just said thanks for what you've done, and ta ta. Half the people down in the soup kitchen sleeping up in The Domain, were old ex-diggers. It's unbelievable, how the poverty was in Sydney in '22 to up to about '32, it was unbelievable. BILLY PASCOE

Veterans were everywhere; they'd have one leg and with their trousers tucked over it, just the stump, and they had one arm. And a lot of them were street people who had no job because they were a cripple. And they'd be playing, singing in the street with a hat in front of them. And mother would always say, 'They are men from the First World War, isn't that sad.' People felt they'd made the supreme sacrifice really, and their lives were horrible because of that. And they didn't see themselves as heroes. They didn't feel they were men; there was always that macho attitude. PAT ROSE

—

I don't think there was very much sympathy for returned servicemen. I saw a fella, he had trench feet from years in the mud out at Flanders and France and he was probably shell-shocked, you'd see him shuffling along. Even the bosses wouldn't employ 'em if they saw service in the war because they were looked upon as mentally damaged, and they couldn't manage to work the modern machinery. During the Influenza Plague we had to wear a mask with bits of camphor in it. It was supposed to be a germ they'd brought back from France. There was a fella down from where we lived in John Street, Erskineville, when he came back apparently he was in the Light Horse Brigade, he kept his horse, and the only job he could get was to buy a cart, and go out and sell fruit and vegetables, there was no job for him. BILL SCHWEBEL

---

10 The Military Hospital at Randwick occupied the old Catherine Hayes Hospital, which had been used since the late 19th century as a Home for Destitute Children. The building still survives on the site of the Prince of Wales Hospital. See Brain Gandevia, *Tears Often Shed: Child Health and Welfare in Australia from 1788,* Pergamon Press, Rushcutters Bay, 1978, pp. 106, 107.

Opposite: "Yes or No — Which?" poster for the referendum on forced enlistments. (National Library)

YES OR NO

WHICH?

❝ They were dying like flies!"

Shortly after the return of the troopships Sydney experienced an influenza epidemic and in late 1921 an outbreak of bubonic plague hit. Although there has been some debate concerning whether there was plague or not, both outbreaks did occur with influenza being the more widespread, but many residents confuse the two and speak of them interchangeably.[11]

I think everyone in Woolloomooloo had the flu, all schools were stopped, practically everything stopped. If you walked outside you had to have a mask on, and there was no cure, they used to have vinegar and brown paper. Soaked in vinegar and put on your forehead and you laid in bed and nearly died, I think it was ten days before you got over it. They were dying like flies! They had trams running up Oxford Street with a great big red cross on them, hospitals were all full and they took them out to the

11 See Proceedings of the Sydney City Council, 28 September 1921 and 26 May 1922; Peter Curson and Kevin McCraken, *Plague in Sydney: The Anatomy of an Epidemic,* NSWU Press, Sydney, n.d.; Humphrey McQueen, 'The Spanish Influenza Pandemic in Australia, 1918–1919', in Jill Roe (ed.), *Social Policy in Australia: Some Perspectives 1901–1975,* Cassell Australia Ltd., Stanmore, 1976. *Sydney Morning Herald,* 18 and 19 January 1919.

Above: A peace demonstration in Newtown, 1918
(State Records)

Opposite: The wearing of nose-and-mouth masks in public was
made compulsory at the height of the 1919 influenza pandemic.
Red Cross workers were mobilised to alleviate shortages in supplies.
(ACP)

showground, put them there where horses and cattle and all that was, that's where they all finished up. Well, we just hadn't been over that six months then the Bubonic Plague came, that was with all the rats, all come back through the war too. There was more killed with the flu than was killed in the war. They were killed in hundreds and thousands! Every street you'd hear poor old so and so's gone. Everyone got it. Everyone in the house had it, I think everyone in the street had it, it went for three months. It was terrible. BILLY PASCOE

When they came back, they came back to the Finger Wharf. And we all went down, the whole bang lot of us. And I wouldn't go on the wharf, because there were rats — literally as big as cats — that had come back with the boats. They would just run in and out of the boats and all over the wharf. So there was no way I was going on there, and one of my brothers wouldn't go on either. So we both stood outside the Finger Wharf, on the other side of the road. I wouldn't even stand outside the gates. Everybody was pleased to see the men home but, I mean, a lot of them had dreadful things wrong with them. My cousin was lucky, he had nothing wrong with him. Oh they came out on wheelchairs, and were carried out on stretchers.

We had the bubonic plague after the men arrived back. They took my brother away, they came down and said, 'Well, he's gotta go'. So a horse and cart arrived, with about another four patients in it, he was just put in, and then they were all taken away. I never really knew where they went to. But my mother struggled out of bed and went and saw him through the glass doors. And that was it, she never saw him again. I mean, you couldn't see them after they'd died because they'd been all done up and made ready for burial. All except the two of us that didn't go on the wharf got the plague, whole families had it. Everybody had to be inoculated and my mother argued with the man, that he wasn't going to put it in my arm. He had this great big needle, she made him put in my knee. But we had a cousin that

worked at Grace Brothers, and they'd gone into the Grace Brothers store at Broadway to inoculate all the workers, and the doctor must've used the same needle ten times. I mean, everything was so crude. But they had no choice because it hit so suddenly. Rex was about six years older than me and we looked after the others. He carried what I couldn't manage, and I carried what I could manage. It was as simple as that. Well, luckily my mother only had a slight attack. My father was very ill with it. Only my mother went to Leonard's funeral, none of us went. The only thing we were told was he wasn't coming home again. I think she still thought about him all the time, 'cause she used to go to Rookwood. He was buried with my grandfather, and I think that my mother paid off the funeral expenses by instalments. JOYCE HIGGINS

When the war finished there was really a serious flu, it was the black death, and the Deaf and Dumb Hostel opposite the university at the start of where City Road joins King Street was taken over and that became a hospital. And the Palais Royal at the showground, on the corner there, that became a hospital and there was a lot of hospitals around about and people were dying left and right. I went to several funerals, I remember one in particular ... Tony Maloney's aunt had died some time previous to that, you know, and then her husband, he died of the flu, and when they went out to Rookwood to bury him, it was all covered in water and they had only half dug the grave, and the mourners had to finish diggin' the grave, and before they could put the coffin down it filled with water and as they pushed the coffin down in the water it was 'gurgle, gurgle, gurgle'. The funerals were on, people were going as fast as they could dig graves and make coffins. It was a very serious type of influenza, but there was a

Opposite: Brenda Humble. Her tall and handsome dad rode beside Monash in Egypt, fought at Gallipoli, was wounded in France and met the Prince of Wales while in hospital there. He used the Prince's autographed photo to bribe his way into the Air Corp and lived to undertake military service again in World War II, albeit on the home front. (Courtesy of Brenda Humble)

"WE NEVER HAD A HOTBED OF CRIME"

couple of types of it. The 'bubonic plague' they called one, and the soldiers brought it back, something had started it in the latter end of the war and it came back and a lot of those died on the way and were sick when they got back and had to have hospitalisation. They were on at the same time, the flu and bubonic plague. And people tell me when people died they went black, discoloured much quicker. The schools were closed up and we all had to wear a mask, like the hospitals do now, and so when we went out, everybody went out with a mask on their face. KEITH MULHEARN

I often heard my mother proudly say that none of us got the Spanish Flu, and that this was in spite of the fact that she had continually sold mourning clothes to customers who had just lost family members. In those days women went into deep mourning, all black clothing for, I think, six months, and for some women, later into half mourning, grey or mauve. And men wore black arm bands. An emergency hospital was set up at the showground because the hospitals could not cope with the numbers of cases. The health authorities ordered that masks should be worn. I believe the masks were discontinued, when it was thought that they in fact harboured germs! ZENA SACHS

They used to salt the kilns at the pottery when they were putting the glaze on the earthenware pipes, water pipes and let a certain amount of chlorine in the air. Dad always reckoned that was a good thing for the district because when the pneumonic flu hit just after the First World War, Erskineville had a lower death rate than practically every other suburb in Sydney. HENRY BROWN

" The impact goes on for generations."

The immediate post-war period was one of instability. Pent-up union demands for improved wages and conditions; reconciliation after the conscription referenda, and the reintegration of troops into civilian life were all issues confronting government. On a more personal level, repeated in households across South Sydney and Australia, there were the consequences of such a large proportion of the male population experiencing armed combat over a sustained period of time.

My mother and sister, who was ten years older than me, lived in Berlin during the First World War and that was a terrible time. They were starving because England blockaded Germany, and they lived for a whole week on apricot jam and nothing else; no bread, nothing. So I mean, they had a dreadful time during the war. But nobody was nasty to them. But funny, when they came out to Australia, my mother's own place, people really hated the Germans and I felt so sorry for my sister, she was fourteen or fifteen. My parents applied to come out here, and my grandmother was going to pay for them until my father got a job. But the Australian Government would have my mother and me because I was born here, but they wouldn't have my father because he was German, or my sister because she was born in Germany. My grandmother pulled strings to get her here and we left my father in Germany. So it was really awful, and their whole lives were ruined by that. My mother never stopped loving my father, and she pined her life out here and looked after her two daughters. PAT ROSE

My father had a lot of illness because he was in the First World War and he did a lot of suffering from that. He was always in the Repatriation Hospital, that stopped him in his work and his job. I can always remember the joy when my dad was coming home. Before the war he was working as a clerk, but when he came out he had to scrape around for a living because his health was so bad. He got gassed and he was blinded, although he was only blind for nine months and then he got his sight back. But he also suffered with all the dampness and the gas had affected his lungs as well. He was in the Ambulance Corp, he would go out into the fields and bring back the wounded. I'm very, very proud of my father and I just loved him. He was nominated for the Victoria Cross. What I am prouder of, is that he never told me, he never boasted, you know. He was fifty-four when he died in the Repatriation Hospital in Randwick. He tried to join up when the Second World War came but he was only in there for less than a year. They had him out there at Victoria Barracks. He was very patriotic. JEAN HENDY

▬

I think the reason my father was so strict and a bit cold and distant could've have been due to his war experience, because we found out that he had been gassed, and he had gas in his system from the war. He used to come out in a red rash all over his body, his arms and legs, and it was on his body permanently. Dad used to wear flannels, like a flannel material and that was made into those grandfather shirts, and wear a flannel belt around his stomach all the time, he wore those all his life. I think he used to go down to the Repat, but all they used to give them was stuff for it, tablets I suppose, and I think that was the cause of his drinking. He was very irritable, you used to know when to keep away from him. BETTY MOULDS

▬

He had bits of lead in him and things and I'm sure the war affected him terribly, because he was, to me he was, a very hard man. When my mother died, I paid for the headstone. For some reason my sister thought it was a good thing for me to do, I was eighteen at the time so I had to save up for it and send this money to an auntie, and I remember asking Dad if he wanted to contribute, and he said, 'Oh sure, here's a penny'. And I was horrified, but that was sort of, I think that was just the view he had because death became meaningless. He was a good man, but I didn't kiss him until I was about thirty-five, you never showed any affection, and I'm very

like that myself now, because of it in a way. So the impact goes on, for generations, really. BRENDA HUMBLE

▬

They had memorial gates down there where they went through, and every Anzac day we used to have a parade from Plunkett Street School around to the gates where people came down and put their flowers. We always had a memorial service at three o'clock. And that went on for years and years and years. But now the Navy own all that wharf. Nobody goes on it at all. They put a fountain opposite the gates as commemoration, but they moved that to somewhere else and put in a car park.[12] I mean, so much for tradition! JOYCE HIGGINS

---

12 In 1921 a memorial tablet was erected by the Women of New South Wales under the auspices of the Centre for Soldiers' Wives and Mothers 'To Commemorate the place of farewell to the soldiers who passed through the gateposts for the Great War, 1914–1918'. The City Council accepted responsibility for it in 1934. There is now a huge car park on the site, but a memorial fountain and the plaque have been preserved and maintained on the opposite side of Cowper Wharf Road. See Sydney City Council, *Fountains, Obelisks, Statues & Memorials — the City of Sydney*, n.d., Sydney City Council.

2

Nobody was allowed to go there, but everybody did

Children and their billycart in Buckland
Street, Newtown, in 1918.
(SCCA 51/8/706)

You'd get a belting every couple of days because you were up on the railway line."

In the early years of this century, parts of Newtown were occupied by families, like the Mulhearns, where the father was in steady employment on the railways. While not wealthy, these children were well provided for in terms of toys and general family support.

Your father or your uncles or someone used to make a lot of toys for you, wooden toys. We'd have scooters and all that sort of thing, they weren't able to buy them. Then bikes, a couple of sizes of three-wheeler bikes as you grew up, and you passed them onto somebody else and you got another one. KEITH MULHEARN

I had a big dresser he made for me. Dad made cradles and dolls' beds, my sisters both had those kind of things. I always had a china doll.
CLAIRE MULHEARN

"WE NEVER HAD A HOTBED OF CRIME"

Woolloomooloo Bay was a favourite swimming spot in the 1930s.
(SLNSW)

NOBODY WAS ALLOWED TO GO THERE, BUT EVERYBODY DID

After World War I and as the 'twenties rolled on, material wealth, as reflected in toys and other 'indulgences' of childhood, diminished. While there are many recollections of fun and community involvement from this period, they are within a greatly restrained financial context.

We played with scooters and billycarts. There used to be a cottage half way over in John Street, Erskineville, that had a bamboo blind outside and we used to get in and sneak these bamboos to make kites with string and flour and water to put paper on, and old rags for a tail on. Sometimes somebody could make a good one, you'd see a mile up in the air. Christmas time you might get little cork boats and things like that, and tin train sets made in Germany and if they lasted twenty-four hours, you'd have to have them in your drawer wrapped up in cotton wool, they'd fall to pieces straight away. You saved the match box covers, Federal Match, and Mays. And we'd walk along the gutter picking them up. Of course we were bare footed with big patches on the seat of our trousers. We'd race our billycarts. Then we might have a wheel from a bicycle and take out all the spikes and have a stick; run it like that and chase the wheel. BILL SCHWEBEL

It was mostly little small lanes around
Woolloomooloo, terrible, the frontage of houses was about twenty foot and there'd always be a lane in front of it only about ten or fifteen foot wide, well that's where you sat in the gutter and played marbles and chasey. You had billycarts, they were the go, everyone seemed to have a billycart. Make them yourself, if you caught an old pram that got thrown out, you got the wheels off it, or them little steel ones. Another thing we'd make were canoes, out of old sheets of tin, doesn't matter what, everyone seemed to make one, and you went down the harbour. Oh God, we did that every day. We took them about thirty yards off the wharf, that's all. We never swam in the harbour down here because that was alive with sharks. It was alive with the fish, the harbour, alive with fish. You would go down to any wharf with a harpoon and you could get anything from twenty to fifty leather jackets, you'd get a bucket full. You didn't have to be a good shot. BILLY PASCOE

We'd walk around to Lady Macquarie's Chair
and we went to the Ladies' Baths and the Men's Baths. I wasn't much good at it, but everybody had to learn to swim. When I went to Plunkett Street School, fourth class, everybody went swimming. And those that couldn't swim, had to stand there on the edge of the walkway or whatever they called it, and the girls that could swim had to go in the water, and then while the teacher was telling us all about how to swim, she just pushed each one in. The ones that could swim had each been assigned a girl to look after, and, if you didn't come up, they'd dive down and get you. That's how we all learnt to swim. My mother got my costumes at a jumble sale and I was so upset to think that I had to wear this costume that somebody else had worn. It was very heavy and weighed more than I did probably at that stage. Went almost to my knees.[1] JOYCE HIGGINS

In summer we played hopscotch on the streets
there until it got dark. When I was about eight we used to take the old tin trays that Mum had to Moore Park, and we'd sit on them and slide down all those hills. I'd come home and I'd have the behind out of me pants, and I'd get belted — holey pants! Oh yeah, we had fun over there on that hill. That park was a godsend, because we used to play vigoro over there, and go and watch the football of a Sunday. ANN RAMSAY

I had a barrow that all the other kids used to like.
Dad had built it out of an oil drum, timber and a crate and he made an engine for me with six wheels on it. We'd get on the top of Devine Street and come down the hill, round the corner in it. Erskineville was very good for kids. HENRY BROWN

---

1 When the Sydney City Council built the new baths at the Domain in 1908, they incorporated separate bathing areas for men and women, as had been the practice at the previous baths in Woolloomooloo Bay.

Edith Moon and Laura Yates in Boundary Street, Chippendale. The boys are playing marbles in the gutter, c. 1944. (Courtesy of Edith Moon)

The worst things that we done, was go up to the brick pits, now known as Sydney Park, where they used to make all the bricks. They left great big holes, and that's where we learnt to swim, a hell of a lot of kids got drowned up there. And there was a place over here just at the back of Waterloo called Burroughs Wellcome, they used to make chemicals and medicines, and we used to swim there, if you got a mouthful, you were sick for a month. When the police come you'd grab your pants, you always swam in the raw, and you were running off with your pants in your hand and the cops screaming out at you. Burroughs Wellcome was polluted but at the brick pits it was mostly only mud and clay, the residual run-off and that sort of thing, it wasn't bad. CLIFF NOBLE

—

We used to play rounders, and have imaginary concerts, we'd play cricket, skipping and throwing the bottle tops, little flat stones, played jacks and 'Knock Down Ginger'; my mother used to get real

frustrated, over that.* We used to play in the street 'cause we weren't allowed to walk down to the park. LORETTO THURGOOD

* 'Knock down Ginger' was played throughout the century. Children would either knock on doors and run away or use a piece of cotton to lift a door knocker and release it as the increasingly annoyed occupant answered.

—

Funnily enough we didn't smoke very much in those days, but we had the odd smoke. I was caught smoking, and got a belting. We were mostly interested in running and playing cricket in the street. So we'd kick the ball around Moore Park or Redfern Park. We'd roam anywhere, really, parents wouldn't know. Coogee was a favourite spot. We'd go and watch the cricket at the Sydney Cricket Ground; we would sneak in there, and there were always ways to get in there without paying. But there was nothing that we were deprived of. We would go down to Coronation Playground, which is in Prince Alfred Park, when the

Young nudists being chased by the ranger from the Centennial Park Ponds. (PIX 23 November 1938)

playgrounds were formed. And where the swimming pool is now in Prince Alfred Park, there was a building there, the Exhibition Building, and we used to go roller skating, which was a lot of fun. I was knocked over by cars three times, and had a few injuries running across the street, trying to be smart. Nothing major, dislocated collarbones and scratches and bruises. Then the sports arena opened and we used to go up there when the cycling was on. That was a big event. Then later on they had boxing there. And there were gymnasiums: Dick Kerr's gym up in Baptist Street. We used to go up to the gym a bit and box. And we'd go and swim at Centennial Park. I recall us swimming there when the trams went by and we would all jump out in the nude! I was a great one for scaling trams. I could even jump off backwards, we all learnt those things. Sir Nicholas Shehadie

You had skipping and hopscotch, and one was winter and one was summer, and you had all these counting rhymes. And then in hopscotch the things we kicked along the ground were called taws, and I had a piece of marble which was very good, and so I was quite successful because I had this very good taw. There weren't that many kids in the top part of Goulburn Street. We played a lot of chasey, variations of chasings games, counting out and rhymes and things. There was a game called 'Stag On', and 'Sheep, sheep come home'. We didn't have a lot of toys; you'd get one thing for Christmas and that'd be it. I always wanted a tea set and I didn't get it, I woke up first on Christmas morning and my sister had the tea set so I swapped it over, and I was amazed and outraged when my parents made me give it back to her, because I couldn't understand how they knew. Portia Fitzsimmons

NOBODY WAS ALLOWED TO GO THERE, BUT EVERYBODY DID

Springfield Avenue, Kings Cross, in 1933. (SCCA 51/17/1586)

The neighbourhood was very important. Playing in the street, in vacant allotments that were remnants from 'slum clearance' policies, in parks, the derelict Elizabeth Bay House in the late 1920s, or in the blackberry labyrinth at Saint Stephen's Cemetery, Newtown, were all activities that are fondly remembered.

We used to sit in the gutter in Balfour Street, and right opposite us on the corner of Queen Street was the Jewish Kadisha, that's like a funeral parlour, and we used to think it was great fun to sit in the gutter and watch these men walking down the street with their funny hats followin' the funeral. We'd go up to the playgrounds in the parks, Victoria Park, Prince Alfred. The mission used to have a bun night, of a Monday night, that was free. You got a hot cross bun and a cup of coffee, and they showed slides, and we went to free concerts. We'd walk down to The Domain, take a cut lunch, and sit in The Domain. Walking was our main

transport, and walking was no trouble, we used to love walking. The whole family would go out together. We went down to Hyde Park when the Archibald Fountain was opened. JANE LANYON

—

In Springfield Avenue, there was never enough children to really play in the streets. We'd go into each others flats and talk and we'd walk around the area. We used to look at the new buildings that were going on, they were starting to build flats at The Cross.[2] We never walked to Rushcutters Bay because there could be nasty men around Rushcutters Bay, in the park there. But you'd walk down Roslyn Street, Billyard Avenue and you'd go into Elizabeth Bay House which was empty and had not been restored. You could go up the stairs and live in a fantasy world. And then we'd go down to Elizabeth Bay and there was a small walk there, and Alexis Albert owned Boomerang, which was on the left facing north, and when the tide was out, we'd try to walk along the sand and paddle. But there would always

Cover of Meccano. (Courtesy of Gerard Colreavy)

be someone come out from Boomerang to shoo us off. GLAD WILLIS

We'd go to Elizabeth Bay Park at night when my cousins came over, we'd all go down and take off our shoes and paddle in the warm water and wander around. And all the kids I went to school with lived around me, and that's why we used to wander around. It was just summer nights and the stars and the beaches, the harbour, and leafy suburbs, it was all just nice. It was a good place to grow up because there was so much space. Well, our garden in Elizabeth Bay Road, was huge and you could wander around freely. I was not allowed to go down to Surry Hills and I wouldn't have been allowed to go into town at night on my own. I was to keep in my own district at night, which was just around Kings Cross where I bought my comics. You went along Darlinghurst Road but no further than Bayswater Road. But all round Elizabeth Bay and the parks was okay. I used to wander down to Rushcutters Bay park with my friends and we'd go to the baths

swimming in the afternoon and that was hilarious, because some baths were still segregated. The men swam on one side, and the women on the other, and they were locked in. We used to go up to Darling Point and try and peer at the men. I had a friend, Eve Raymont, who also lived in Roslyn Gardens, and Eve's brother was very adventuresome, and he found an old bath when we were wandering around the harbour. So he put the plug in, and he got into the bath and sailed out into the middle of the bay with Eve and I saying, 'Aren't you wonderful!' And he couldn't get back. And so we had to ring his father who was a Captain at the Rushcutters Bay Naval Depot, and he had to come and rescue his son. I think Ken got into trouble, but Eve and I were very admiring, we thought that was wonderful. PAT ROSE

2 See H.J. Humphries, *Kings Cross: The Transformation of a Suburb*, Ch. 4, 'The Apartments, 1919–1939', BA Hons. Thesis, University of NSW, 1990.

NOBODY WAS ALLOWED TO GO THERE, BUT EVERYBODY DID

There was a big vacant block down at the back of Springfield Avenue, I think it's St Neot's Avenue, it had been an old theatre, and there was a stage there, and then the rest of the place was just this great paddock, and we used to go down there and play cricket. There were a lot of children in The Cross in those days. We loved going to Elizabeth Bay House, it was fairly derelict then. They had huge gardens there. The caretaker lived in the kitchen cottage, and he used to take us through the place. He took us down in the dungeons and said that was where the convicts had been chained up and we believed him. PAT NICKS

—

Opposite us used to be the Sydney Stadium which had been burnt down and there was a vacant allotment there.* All the kids played there. It was heaven. They would play cubby houses, skipping, and hopscotch. It was a special, fantastic experience. On summer nights the kids all played outside and the families sat around on their verandahs and on their gas boxes. That Stadium was the Mecca for people, it was quite large and took up a block, there would always be a fair there, a fete, a carnival or political rallies, a small circus or a Baptist group would come in and have a mission with big tents. Our balcony overlooked it and when there was nothing else occupying the place the kids took it over, they came from several streets and played there. GRACE SCHWEBEL

Corner of Fitzroy and King streets, Newtown.

—

We used to love to get into the old cemetery up here at St Stephens, Newtown. And because when you're kids you love to think it's haunted, we reckoned there were ghosts in the tombstones and you could look down and see the bodies. But the greatest fun was that, at one stage, the park was all blackberry bushes, and we made our own tracks in there so when the sexton used to chase us, we'd get into those and he could never find us and we thought that was hilarious. Lots of kids played there. I don't know what the church were so frightened about. I don't know that anybody ever did any damage; that

wasn't the thing to do. From Lennox Street down to Federation Road was all cemetery, it was like a maze and a fascinating place for kids. JEAN HENDY

—

In Redfern they used to have sandstock gutters, and because of people walking on them, they used to wear out hollow. And if there was a little bit of an incline somewhere, we'd race marbles down there for hours and hours and hours. Opposite our place in Walker Street, used to be a big open paddock, that was a vacant block of land, and they used to have big concrete pipes. I suppose, a metre and a half high, you know, and we used to run in and out of them and climb over them, and play hide and seek. We didn't roam very far. I got a horse when I was twelve or thirteen. We had a big stable, all the houses running off Walker Street went right through to a laneway, towards Elizabeth Street. I used to stable a horse in the big long shed in the back; I'd ride over to Centennial Park. TED McDERMOTT

—

There wasn't much traffic around then, but we weren't allowed out in the front on account of the trams, but we were always over in Erskineville Park, because that was just across the road. In Erskineville Park there used to be a big water tower there, and that's where my two brothers used to go swimming. You had to climb these iron rungs to get up there, it was the water supply for the trams and the horse and carts. We also used to go down the back of Euston Road, there used to be a canal, it runs right down the back of the Australian Glass works that used to be there, and down the back of Slazenger's. Of a Sunday we used to go over to race little pieces of wood down as boat races. But men use to go over there too and race their boats and they'd bet on them. We had a lot of friends and all my aunties and uncles all lived around Alexandria, and we used to go and visit them. Every Saturday we'd go up to my Nan's in Botany Road where she had the undertaker's shop and lived at the back of the premises, Shine and Field, and that was our Saturday afternoon's visit. They used to bury you for seven pound. It was a sort of gathering with the cousins, and we used to hide in the coffins and think it

Girls at Woolloomooloo playground during the hula-hoop craze of the late 1950s. (SSCC)

was a great joke. My second eldest brother got in one and my grandmother had a Chinaman embalmed to go to China in it and he nearly had a fit when he saw it there. He never got in another coffin. BETTY MOULDS

—

We used to play cards with the cigarette cards up against the wall, win and lose cards. I don't know how it came about, but if they come up one side you'd win it, and if it come up the other side you'd lose it. One side had the history of, say, American gangsters like John Dilinger, Pretty Boy Floyd and Dutch Schultz ... ask me about American gangsters and I know all about them because we read about them when we were kids. And then they used to have such things like cricket cards, with all the cricketers

of the day on them. And on the other side of the card was probably, maybe a logo of the cigarette company. MAUREEN OLIVER

—

As a family we used to play housie, darts or cards and my dad was the greatest cheat you've ever seen at fiddlesticks. We used to play table tennis on this massive big kitchen table. We always had books and the usual run of toys, guns and bob sets, a sailing boat. We used to muck about over the park, in the school holidays and play cricket, Centennial Park. We knew every tree. We all had to come home for lunch, so we'd just hide all the cricket gear in one of the trees. We'd go out to the beach, scale the trams, and get shot if your mother found out. KEVIN RYAN

Behind the Rosebery Hotel was a big pool. It had been a brick pit. And it's depth was unknown, and it was a hundred and fifty yards to two hundred and fifty yards across, a semi-circular thing and alongside it was a place called Burroughs Wellcome, a chemical company. When they were down digging the bricks up, hundreds and hundreds of feet down, they struck a spring. And one man and his horse never got out. It was so deep that by the time he got up to the top he was drowned. And nobody was allowed to go there, but everybody did. It was beautiful clear water, crystal-clear water, and Burroughs Wellcome was using it and throwing the chemicals back into it which made it better still. It cleared the water. They used to swim in it: all Burroughs Wellcome's workers swam in there. And my mother forbade me to do that. But then I had an uncle, my mother's brother, and he was a big six-footer, and a young bloke, he died at 18 with peritonitis, but a very, very good swimmer and he could get anything off my mother, she loved him. He said I'm going to take him over to teach him to swim, he just threw me in. So that was it, I learned how to swim very quickly. MICK GREEN

—

On the Camellia Grove hotel wall they used to play a lot of handball there. That's on the corner of Alexandria Street and Henderson Road. It used to be a big event especially on a Saturday and Sunday. At Alexandria Railway they had a bridge right across the railway lines, down on the workshop side, on the Darlington side, and we used to delight in going up there to wait for a steam train to come along, and then the drivers used to see us and they'd put extra puff on, and they used to blow the smoke and steam all over us. We thought it was great fun.
ROBERT HAMMOND

—

There was a big shed out the back, and we'd sit up the back and play on the railway line which runs right at the back and we'd always get a belting. Everyone got a belting. You'd get a belting every couple of days because you were up on the railway line when the train's were running through. We'd

throw rocks over to the other side of Watkin Street in Newtown because it was real exciting. We never had any close calls with trains. We wouldn't'a been able to afford to bury ourselves anyway. Kids'd run across the railway line, we used to dare to run across, but we were always pretty smart, I mean, gee, you wouldn't take a risk. I never did anyway. TERRY MURPHY
—

In the late 1930s cars were becoming sufficiently common to be noted as a hazard on the streets, but they were not so numerous as to prohibit street play. With the onset of the war, unemployment disappeared and, despite the constraints of the war, a degree of affluence, previously almost unknown to the majority of South Sydney's residents, began to emerge.

Eventually I got one of those little pedal cars and a little pedal truck, and a three-wheeled tricycle. But it was quite a privilege to have those things. I used to get into trouble for riding it out on the road in amongst all the traffic, but if there was any traffic coming they'd just go around you. BOB SLATER
—

I played in the air-raid shelters in Calder Road and Shepherd Street, Darlington, and the trenches over in the park. They were there a few years after the war before they pulled them down. We played 'Knock Down Ginger'; a few times we got caught by the ladies that had the shop. They'd come running 'round to catch us to see who was doing it, once we were hiding in a little lane and she pulled us all out saying, 'Get out of here, Eadie Moon, Gad and get out of here Laurie Vernon, and get out here, you Beverly Smythe. I know you're in there, you little trouble-maker you!' We used to play hopscotch and skippings. We used to get the bones out of the meat and wash and scrub them to use to catch on our knuckles. BEVERLY HUNTER
—

The big event of my early years was being given a scooter for Christmas, a nice red scooter. And I took it out the front here at the top of Ann Street to show off and some clown pushed me, and I didn't know

Boys from Forbes Street, Darlinghurst, in a 1950 billycart derby in Phillip Park, Woolloomooloo. (ACP)

how to handle the thing, and I just remember yelling as I was going down the hill not knowing how to stop; all the way down the bottom of Ann Street, straight across Riley Street — fortunately no cars of any sort coming — and I ended up right down the bottom in the gutter. Tops were a very important thing: we used to develop games. People would start their top spinning and it was up to someone with another top to try and knock as many out as they could. The idea of games of tops was that those you knocked out after so many times you got to keep, as you did with marbles. There were different games of marbles you could play, with a huge ring of marbles, with a bunch in the centre. TERRY GLEBE

We would play games in the street, especially in summer, probably four nights out of the seven. We would play 'What's the time, Mr Wolf?' You would never know when he was going to swing round and chase and run after you. You'd all scream with fear and delight, plus it was dark. At the playground you could play tennis, basketball, every kind of game that was invented. Snakes and ladders, drafts, painting; of course they had swings and monkey bars. Just hours and hours of fun. BETH THORPE

In Paddington there was very strong family groups and kids would play constantly. Like cricket used to be every afternoon in the streets. The streets weren't all cluttered up with cars, because people didn't own cars in Paddington. You'd have the whole street, like we used to bowl up Brown Lane and hit into Glenview Street, occasionally a car would come along but it didn't worry us. We used to play marbles for money, we'd play football down at Rushcutters Bay. I was fortunate having a dad who would make things for me, and he made me a little trolley which I could put behind my bike and ride off to a park with all my stumps and cricket gear. He would come over with me and bowl me out all the time, and teach me always to go forward to a spinner. And we had Centennial Park. I used to, again the generosity of my dear old Mum, we wouldn't have much money, but if I wanted to go horse riding, I could go and hire a horse in Centennial Park, which I did about every Saturday. CLIFF FOGARTY

By the 1950s toys like Meccano became perennial and hula hoops, bride dolls and yoyos were recurring fads. Kids continued to play in parks, the street and vacant allotments.

Freddy Hartop was a great friend of mine; he lived just round in the back street, and we spent a lot of time playing in the backyard, that's all I can remember; endless hours playing in the backyard in Newtown. I had this wind-up train set for example, and we'd set up the tracks in the backyard, so you could have little hills and you could have it going through water and you'd sort of make up a whole city railway system in your backyard, that's one thing we did. I s'pose being boys, a lot of our games revolved around toy cars and little wind-up motors and things. And I had a Meccano set, that was a big thing my father gave me. Well, gradually over the years he built up a huge Meccano set which was in this big box, and sometimes he would help me make things. So, you could make structures out, you know, buildings and cars and things. It was like Lego; it was very popular. BRENDAN DOYLE

On Sundays the playground didn't open until two o'clock. Okay, while we were waiting for the playground we played 'Hares and Hounds' and we'd go all the way through the Botanical Gardens and past the Art Gallery, the Australian Museum, all the way through town. The boys would give you a fifteen-minute start and you'd mark an arrow on the footpath or on walls or whatever and then you'd send a couple of girls off to lead a false trail — it was the first one back to the playground, you had to beat them back. We had the Domain pool around the corner and I used to do swimming there. It was open all year round then because it was just netted off in the Harbour. When they made it the concrete pool, I think there was quite a few who were quite sad. I mean, it was nice to start off with but then it wasn't the same as the old Domain Baths. We'd go there and swim winter comps and then we'd play table tennis upstairs there. CHERYL LINDO

While cars were becoming more of a hazard for street play, in areas like Redfern and Surry Hills vacant lots and building sites provided adventure for wandering children.

Redfern was great; there were lots of kids, we all played together, we played in the lane; I mean, cars used the lane, but it wasn't a problem, there were piles of kids. I can remember twenty or thirty kids and we'd play outside till it got dark, and then all drift off home, it was great, I loved it. And we had the park at the end of the road, Redfern Park's at the end of Great Buckingham Street. And then, when I got a little bit bigger, we used to go to Prince Alfred Park and go to Coronation Playground, which was great, I really loved Coro, you know. And we'd also go there on weekends, when it was actually closed, but we'd sort of climb the fence and we'd go and play basketball and play on the swings and stuff like that. My friend, Janice and I liked wandering through empty buildings, buildings under construction or deserted houses. All those flats that are now on Elizabeth Street just before Redfern, that was all sandhills when I was a kid, so all that construction was going on. I mean, we'd get yelled at on construction sites,

A Coronation Park Girls Basketball Team made up of Redfern girls, including Bev Wood (later Karonidis) standing second from right, c.1948.
(Courtesy of Bev Karonidis)

by workers, and told to get off. But there just seemed to be lots of empty houses, and we always had stories to tell about empty houses; they were always haunted and we'd frighten ourselves and fall down the stairs running away. Cathi Joseph

The big fads were bride dolls for girls, skipping ropes, hula hoops, jacks and netball. I wanted a netball so bad, but I couldn't get one, I was really upset with that. And hair things, you know, like the plastic headbands; and I remember when I was about five I had plastic high heels and I loved them, with a little net skirt, and I thought I was beautiful. And prams; I always liked footballs too, I always wanted

to play with my brother's footballs. My brother had a Meccano set and a farmyard with animals, I loved that. Oh, the tricks we did was with yoyos and the hula hoops, all those tricks, I loved them! And ball tricks and handstands and staying up the longest and catherine wheels and splits and all that. Jill Edwards

I was one of the fortunate ones. I was never really short of anything. Like, my three friends across the road, they'd get a bike, for instance at Christmas, the three of them would have to share it. I remember Dad buying me a nice little pushbike and I had a great time with it. We used to build our own billycarts as well. Where I lived, in Forbes Street, there was a hill; we'd go up to William Street and sit on our billycarts and race each other down Forbes Street. There used to be a Holden factory there and mum's brother was a mechanic and he used to give us all the ball bearings that they didn't use any more and we used them as our wheels. And I can recall flying down Forbes Street on a billycart with a mate of mine and a car was coming out of the Holden factory and we ran bang into the side of the thing and virtually got stuck under the car. So we had some pretty close shaves with those. But I think everybody down there got to know that there was always kids flying down that street so they'd always be careful not to run them over. ANDREW LAZARIS

■

We used to go down to the university and there's a building that you could use, the fire escape was always opened, and we used to get into that and just play up there. Or we'd just play football in the university. The Seymour Centre wasn't there then. We didn't really have any parks or anything to play in, so that was really one of the only places we could go. It was mainly on the weekends, so there weren't many people around ... We used to play brandings, and hand-ball on the university wall. In summer, the focal point for the kids was probably the Victoria Park pool. We had to cross City Road to get there, but it wasn't as busy as it is now. Not by half.
SUSAN ALLOWAY

For kids in Surry Hills, Woolloomooloo, Darlington, Redfern and Waterloo, the 1970s seems to have offered less scope for community interaction and free play. There were fewer children in the area than in the 1930s; and the redevelopment of housing for the Eastern Suburbs Railway, the expansion of Sydney University, and construction of large high-rise flats in Surry Hills, Redfern and Waterloo had destroyed much of the older communities.

The only toy I remember having was a robot, I can't remember if it ran on batteries or if I wound it, and it used to shoot bullets out. We'd make our own games, you'd get cardboard or masonite or some sort of thing that you'd find, and make things. A lot of the time we'd go round and throw rocks at people, 'cause there wasn't anything to do, that sort of stuff. If you had money you'd go into the city and go to the movies, it was only a dollar twenty-five or something in those days, probably even cheaper. But we didn't have the money, or if the family did, we didn't see it, so we made our own fun. A lot of it was mischief, but didn't really hurt anyone. Most of the kids around there were mischievous, because we were all sort of bored. We'd wander around; we used to wander up and down Oxford Street, we'd go up to Centennial Park, 'cause they had this great big rocket, and we used to climb that. And there was a great big hill, we used to get cardboard and slide down that. There was a place down at Moore Park, we used to do roller-skating and play basketball, volleyball; you'd pay twenty cents for your skates and we'd buy lock-jaw toffees. Kinselas was a funeral parlour. It was all blacked in and there used to be scratches in the glass, and we used to try and peer through at the bodies. I think if we ever saw someone we would have just died on the spot. SHANE CAMPBELL

■

We didn't really go out anywhere, we didn't do anything. I have a memory of my father taking us for walks around the block and stuff and throwing a note into the gutter and when we came back saying, 'What's that there?' and we'd all scramble for it. But as for going on outings or to the movies or anything like that, there was none of that. We didn't have a car for a long time, so there were no picnics. We used to go up to the Boulevarde Hotel, me and Suzie Spoon and Cassie and say that our aunt was staying in the hotel, but pressed the button that takes you up to the indoor pool, and we used to swim there. A couple of times, we got chased out of the pool, but not very often, I think they just sort of let us go because we were young and weren't doing any harm. It didn't matter how far we were allowed to roam, we used to roam everywhere, anyway. More towards Kings Cross and down the back towards Woolloomooloo. There's a park down near the new Police Centre, we used to go down there where there's a playground sort of thing. We used to go and play in the school a lot, too. Because we lived right next to Oxford Street, there weren't many parks. We weren't the type of kids to go and play on swings, we were more wandery, into-mischief sort of kids. ZOWIE CAMPBELL

■

But you know, we, with the local kids, and my cousin who is just about six months older than me — she lived with us when she was six months until she was about ten — so we'd all go and play in the University grounds. Living in sort of inner-city Chippendale, there is not a lot of park area, so, the university was like this huge playground for us, it was wonderful. It was great to go in there, and have adventures and play pirates and things like that. We spent a lot of time in the area that is around the back of the Seymour Centre, and over towards the Engineering Department. They used to have native rosemary shrubs everywhere, and so we would go into those, and it would be like travelling around in an old English hedge maze, so we had sort of little cubby houses here and there. They set up these large metallic sculptures out the front of the Seymour Centre, and they were just great to climb on, you know, being a ten-year-old kid. There's one part at the back of the Seymour Centre where you can go in and look in to one of the rehearsal rooms, and sometimes there would be forty people in there, with a variety of instruments and everyone rehearsing, it

was fantastic. It was great to see these huge sets sort of rolling past the door and wondering what was going on in there. We also spent a lot of our time up at Victoria Park swimming pool, we would come home every afternoon during summer, and I would be straight up to the pool, and we would be up there until it closed. So my happiest memories are of being at the swimming pool, because everybody would be there. COLIN BELL

■

Games. Oh God. Elastics, Poison Ball. Then there'd be hand ball. In our area at the Waterloo Flats there was a sand park, so you had the flying fox, at that time it was new; there was a swing that went all the way around, just forever going, and you had mazes and you would have a little game area where you'd just rollerskate, and a little park where you could sit down and talk, but everything was on a scale for us, the kids. We spent a lot of time outside, rollerskating everywhere, all over Waterloo and Redfern and probably even Surry Hills, and bike riding everywhere; we'd go riding down to Centennial Park. We used to do the City, Redfern, Surry Hills, Chippendale, we knew the whole area. ESOSA EQUAIBOR

■

Living in Raglan Street, there used to be an after- school care centre just directly across the road from my place, and I used to go there after school and in holidays; they had the holiday activities and stuff. It was good, they would have different things, like, one day they'd go to the movies, the next day they'd go to the beach or they'd stay in. So each day of the week you'd do something different. That was probably the main thing that we'd do during the school holidays up until I was around about twelve. And where I lived, there were about four or five neighbours who were my mates, and I can remember just hanging around with them in the paddock next door to our place making cubby houses, stupid little things like that. Catching grasshoppers too, that was one thing I used to love doin'. DEAN INGRAM

" If you ever got barred from a playground, that was heartbreaking."

A notable feature of inner-city life for most of the century has been the various services which organised play, arts and craft or sporting activities and arranged outings for children. Ann Ramsay, who was born in Redfern in 1914, recalls attending the Young Eureka Lodge at Waterloo Town Hall in the 1920s. While numerous social and cultural organisations have existed, the most often and warmly commented on are the series of Council-run supervised playgrounds.[3]

From eight years old I belonged to Young Eureka Lodge, and it was held up in the Waterloo Town Hall.[4] It was a friendly society, we used to have picnics, we'd go out to La Perouse, and then there was the big picnic we'd have at Balmoral about once a year, and that was absolutely fabulous, there would be hundreds and hundreds of kids from all the different lodges around, and they'd hire the big ferry. They'd make sandwiches and lemonade — water with lemon floated over it! ANN RAMSAY

—

The Settlement was a big club run by Sydney University for the people in the area to have social activities. They had Boy Scouts, the Girl Guides, and they used to teach you how to play badminton; some of them were Australian champions. And they had bowls; they had the old people's club in the day time and they had the ladies', mothers' club of a Wednesday night, which went for seventeen years. People from the university used to come down and give us talks on their trips overseas and they would teach us acting, singing, cooking and craft. I started going there from about eleven or twelve. It was very popular. We also used to go out of a night time and sit under the lights in the gutter, and then a man from the mission, called Mr Fluker used to have a concertina, and he used to come around. Us kids used to sing the choruses, and some of us would get

up and dance and he used to tell us stories; he was a missionary. JANE LANYON

—

The first Police Youth Club opened in Woolloomooloo in '36 and that was a great asset because a lot of the children used to learn boxing and physical culture, and they'd take them away camping. NELL LEONARD

—

The Catholic Youth Organisation was the social thing for young people in Darlinghurst. We'd maybe go to the pictures, go to the fights down at The Stadium or the wrestling. People would go to housie, like bingo. Our church or school used to have it every Friday night and I used to go up and sell tickets there, and that used to get crowded. PAT WRIGHT

—

When we lived in Goulburn Street my father and mother decided to send us to the Sydney City Mission Sunday school at the bottom of Campbell Street. I took two of my sisters, and they gave me directions, but I got lost and I went to the wrong church; to the Church of Christ and it was small, there were only one or two families running it, and it was a very nice atmosphere, and that provided most of our social life for the next few years. They had Sunday School in the morning and church in the afternoon, and Sunday School anniversaries and concerts and picnics, so that provided quite a lot of our social life. At the back of Crown Street school there was a 'Golden Fleece' kindergarten. The teachers there ran a day drop-in centre for the primary children in the afternoon, and they had a nice little library, and we'd go there and read books and make pot holders from bits of felt and do crafty sorts of things. That was run by the Children's Craft Movement which was very good. They were lovely

---

3   See also T. Taylor, 'Inner-City Backyards: A History of Sydney's Supervised playgrounds, 1932–1990', MA Thesis, 1991, Macquarie University.

4   The Young Eureka Lodge was a juvenile lodge of the Manchester Unity Friendly Society. It should not be confused with the Eureka Youth League of the Communist Party which developed much later.

The playgrounds offered art, craft and sporting activities and are reputed to have saved many children from a life of crime. (SSCC)

teachers, and there was another family of girls there whose father was Greek and their mother was Australian, and they took both families to see a pantomime down in Loftus Street near the Quay. It was 'The Boy with the Golden Goose', and that was one of the highlights of my childhood. PORTIA FITZSIMMONS

—

There's Phillip Park Library and Craft, more or less across the road from St Mary's Cathedral. And they had lots of crafts for children after school and during the holidays, and of course it had a library and I was allowed to take out the encyclopaedias one at a time. Not everybody was allowed to do that. They had a stage and we'd put on plays, and we

were allowed to paint the walls and we did pottery, and oh, it was wonderful. It was free and I went there from the time I was four, until I was sixteen, until I left school. You could make puppets and I met Edith Murray there who started the Puppetry Guild, and I used to paint back drops and help her with puppet shows at the Town Hall, and birthday parties. That's when I saw how the other half lived. Of course they were rich houses, and I think I used to stand there like a country bumpkin with my mouth open. JUDY CHAMBERS

—

At Coronation playground they always had what we call a 'miss' and a 'sir', and if you wanted to play anything you were given balls or whatever and we did weaving and when I got older, I played basketball for them. My girlfriend came from a very large family so she had to take her brothers and sisters, and we would go down there for the day, and just play in the school holidays. Nobody was allowed in except the children. BEV KARONIDIS

—

Mr Rossbrook would have been the father of recreation in Australia. Moore Park playground was the first fully supervised recreation area in Australia, and he was the first man there. He was a terrific bloke and he did more for the kids in Surry Hills and Paddington than any man. He was very strict, he had sets of rules and if you didn't stick by them, you finished up outside. It wasn't like school, you weren't regimented into going there, you went there because you wanted to, and if you got put out, it broke your heart.[5] One time, we didn't have a push bike but a fella across the road gave us an old bike frame and we bummed a couple of wheels and we built our own bike. I got on and raced over to Moore Park to show Mr Rossbrook, and I rode into the playground on the bike and said, 'Sir, sir look at me bike!' And he said, 'You're out for a week for riding in the playground', and I thought, 'You lousy bugger'. But he was a beautiful man. Something like thirty-five kids from Moore Park represented Australia in different sports, all because of Rossi. One of them, Herby Barker, ended up the sports master at Newington College. If it hadn't been for Rossi he would have been in jail, he was a bugger of a kid when he was younger. He was in and out of boys' homes. Rossi just got him and made him get involved in sport and he represented Australia in three sports: athletics, basketball and Rugby Union. There's not too many people done that. KEVIN RYAN

The playground saved us from a lot of the crime, because we were pretty rough and ready, but Miss Straughan taught us to play sports, swim, and we've always had a lot of respect for Miss Straughan. No name calling. Miss Straughan wouldn't put up with that. She was a sergeant major in the army, used to kick us up the backside, pull us by the ear. And we had the Police Boys Club, and my God! That's where you got rid of your frustrations up at the Police Boys Club, you just put everyone in the ring. We were all into sport, paddle tennis, swimming, basket ball, and we got a lot of champs from football, we all played for the Fitzroys [The Fitzroy Hotel Team]. We used to go barefoot. We'd swim down the Domain swimming pool and they had a big gym down there, and we used to play hand ball and every Sunday they used to throw a duck in there, and anyone that caught the duck, kept it. SAM DONATO

—

I was probably about nine when I first started physical culture; and that involved going to the playground once a week, of a night time. Miss Straughan used to hold the classes, probably from about eight years of age up. It was the Bjelke Peterson Physical Culture: you did the same exercise week after week, to get it really perfect for a competition that was held once a year, and then you got medals for who came first, second and third. We'd also give demonstrations during Health Week, which was held some time in October. This was either held at the Sydney Town Hall or in Martin Place during lunch hours or of a Saturday morning. Physical Culture was for girls only and they loved it, loved it. BETH THORPE

—

Oh, I think I was lucky. I think the playgrounds helped a lot because everyone used to go there and you'd want to get there, and they taught me a lot. There were several playgrounds; there was Moore Park, Maybanke, Camperdown, Pine Street. There was Coronation, Woolloomooloo, Joseph Sergeant and a few, and they used to have inter-sports on the Saturday. And that's where you'd get to see everyone because you'd see them all year and you'd just become mates with one another and you'd go and play basketball with them, and when they had State championships on, all the playgrounds used to combine and put one team in, and 99% of the time we were State champions. We used to have swimming carnivals, athletic carnivals, we'd have football days, cricket days, all sports games, I think — no matter what, you name a sport and I think I've played it and I've learnt, not only me, there's probably hundreds of thousands of boys and girls my age, and younger and older that learnt all these sports at the playgrounds. And if you ever got barred from a playground, that was heartbreaking. They had standards, you weren't allowed to swear. If you ever got caught smoking you were banned, probably for a week, and I'll tell you a week felt like a lifetime. Of course you could wait outside the fence there and you'd see everyone playing. 'Please Sir, let me in!' 'Nope!' WHACKER [WARREN] RICHARDSON

—

Oh, I'd go to Coronation Park after school every day. And one day a week the library would be there, so that was my first experience of a library. And it was Miss Brolly, who became Mrs Walters, and was still running the City of Sydney Library when I actually worked for them in 1970, so it was just sort of this bizarre long association. It was great, I loved Coro, it was a home away from home. CATHI JOSEPH

—

We'd go to the City Mission Hall on the corner of Redfern Street and Walker Street, which is now the Nursing Home. Oh, it was all just for girls, doing tunnel ball, captain ball, sewing, girls' club, it was wonderful, cost you nothing. JILL EDWARDS

—

Even the kids that you'd classify as the wild kids also learnt a lot through the playgrounds with the Council supervisors teaching us a lot of discipline. There was this bond there and even after we left Woolloomooloo, after the railway went through our homes, we went back down there and still played basketball for Woolloomooloo. ANDREW LAZARIS

The Settlement was like a youth centre in Edward Street, Chippendale. Some of the top ones from university ran it. It was very good. We used to play basketball and the Brownies and the Girl Guides were in there; I was in both those. We used to go on trips and we used to have little meetings, you know, they never really meant anything. The 'Do Be Good' meetings. SUSAN ALLOWAY

—

Mr Ryan and Miss Straughan were in charge of the Play Centre. They were fantastic, the pair of them. They always seemed to have either chocolate crackles or cornflake-type biscuits, honey jumbles. And they were very encouraging with sport and with just the interaction. They were there for everyone. There was another Play Centre around near the Police Boys Club, and we also used to go to the Police Boys Club and do gymnastics there, that was good. JACKIE GRATTON-WILSON

—

After I was twelve, sort of thirteen and fourteen, I was basically just allowed to do what I wanted sort of thing. Basically, I'd come here to the Police, the Youth Club. It was good, they used to have a trampoline in the main hall, and all these gymnasium bars and things like that. They used to be open until, I think about nine o'clock, so that was the latest I was allowed out 'til. DEAN INGRAM

---

5 Mr Ray Rossbrook is mentioned in *The People,* 'Playground/Supervisor: A Moulder of Citizens', June 1953.

"If you didn't have a red and a green eye, you wasn't from Redfern!"

An incredibly diverse range of sporting activities have featured across the century, including fencing, roller hockey, tennis, baseball, cycling, cricket, vigoro, swimming and all the football codes — with a passion for the Rabbitohs Rugby League team being a dominant theme.

Because of the particular people in Alexandria being mostly of Irish extraction, you always had an affinity and you played with each other. There would be situations where every one of us participated in sport, and that's why I was never very good at school; I only wanted to play sport. You could play any of the three grades of football — Rugby League, Soccer, Australian Rules — and everybody would play cricket, one street would play another street, and sometimes if the team that batted in the morning didn't turn up in the afternoon you'd have a punch up. CLIFF NOBLE

—

I played all the sport I could. You name the sport, I played it. Before I was seventeen I won the State fencing title, you know, sword fighting, and I held that for thirteen years. My brother fenced and he taught me. After he finished his Bachelor of Arts in Sydney, he went to Italy, he's an artist, and got his Diploma of Arts in Rome and Florence, and he learnt to fence there, and then he brought it back and he insisted on teaching me. I got my University Blue in fencing as well. It must have been the old warrior blood, because I used to like to get behind a piece of steel, with one man in front of me, him and me, with these two bits of steel. It was a gentleman's sport. So I played football, A-Two tennis, first at football; I played cricket, first in cricket at school and so on, inter-faculty, I played all those sports; golf, I played them all. Tennis, I used to play with my sister, up at Bellevue Hill courts, she had a friend up there at Bellevue Hill. DARIO LO SCHIAVO

There was skating at The Glaciarium down at Central Railway. There was also push-bike riding as a competitive sport. They had a velodrome up in Surry Hills and there was a lot of competition. I was skating and rollerskating from about twelve onwards, you weren't encouraged to do a lot of things before that. Well, there wasn't much money to get to things either, but it was relatively cheap. Once there was some sort of a gala and a billycart competition and I won it, but my mother put decorations all over it, which I considered stupid. LEO HANNAN

—

My dad was a great friend of one of the Eastern suburbs players; a chap named Chimpy Bush, who was the first Australian Rugby League player to go to England under a contract, and he got the huge sum of five pounds in England for a win; three for a draw; and two for a loss. FRED FOREMAN

—

Rollerskating was my sport. My sister played tennis, and in later years I played tennis; we used to play at courts around here at Rosebery. But I got up into an A reserve grade around there as a young boy. The big events of the year were South Sydney football, for a start. I went to every game I could get to. And they used to play right opposite where we lived. If you didn't have a red and a green eye, you wasn't from Redfern! My mother wouldn't let me play football because she reckoned it was too rough. I could play tennis quite well. If the war hadn't interrupted when it did in 1939, I'd have been a rollerskating speed-skating champion, because I was very, very good at it, even at a young age. In Prince Alfred Park at that time was the Exhibition Building.[6] It was a huge old building, and they used to have a museum in there, they had aeroplanes and some of Kingsford Smith's aeroplanes, and when they got rid of the museum they opened it up as a rollerskating rink, and I went there many, many times and I played roller hockey with the South Sydney roller hockey team. TED McDERMOTT

I knew nearly everybody around on the side that we lived, Alexandria was a big place. The friend that I had, Maisie Roberts, I used to play vigoro with her of a Saturday morning. I was a sporty person and I was in the ladies' cricket when I got up to about seventeen. The Spinning Mills that I used to work for also had a ladies cricket team and the Alexandria Kio-oras were their Vigoro team. They were very well known, Mrs Healey used to run that. But I didn't play with them, they were all professionals there. Betty Moulds

I played football for many years with the local junior football, the Carringtons. In the twelve- and thirteen-year age group, if we were playing a team on a Saturday, we'd go there on a Friday and fight them so as they'd know what they were going to run into on the Saturday. The South Sydney Junior Football Club was Kensington, Mascot, Botany, Zetland, Redfern All Blacks, teams like that. Maybe 30 or 40 teams. We were about the wildest, this Carrington football club was forever being told they'd have to get out of the competition and go and play somewhere else. Mick Green

We were all mad South supporters. South's, we just loved all the South's players in those days and there was a women's New South Wales football team in the 1930s, Eileen Matter was the hooker and Kitty Cohen was on the wing, both from Redfern.

Sir Nicholas Shehadie

We'd go down and play locally at Rushcutters Bay and play football down there. I was fortunate in as much as always being a fairly good sportsman, I got into representative teams from school very early on. And, if I wasn't playing, I'd get myself organised. For example, I used to play in the East Sydney Australian Rules team, that meant I'd practise twice a week and play on Saturday morning. So if I wasn't playing for the school, I'd be organised into local competition, or I'd be playing organised tennis. So that tended to be my life. I couldn't stand going down and mucking around,

playing scrap football. If I was going to play a game of football, it was going to be a game of football. I wanted an atmosphere for cricket, I wanted people in their whites, I wanted a pitch that had a mat on it at least, and a new ball; and if I was playing tennis, I wanted the tennis court to be nicely rolled and watered and an atmosphere and someone scoring. I had a great sense of competition, and when I was in a boxing ring, it was going to be never walk back, never walk back, no matter what happens. So I had a strong competitive spirit, probably undesirably so, but it kept me occupied. Cliff Fogarty

The Botany Harriers was a running club and they'd always run around at the local football at Redfern Oval when the juniors were playing. And then they'd hold a gala day, and anyone could go and run against them, so all us kids'd go over there and run against them and we'd take all the prizes, and they'd get really cranky because we were all good runners; we could run like greyhounds 'cause we had to run to take the messages for our mother. And I just think that's so strange; it was a real big event and we used to win everything. Jill Edwards

Sunday morning, you'd wake up and the football was on, you'd hear it from Redfern Oval and everyone had to go to the football, whether you liked it or not. I didn't like football at all, wasn't into it, but my brothers played it. In that area a lot of people played football or cricket on Saturday morning, so you'd go down to Waterloo Oval and you'd watch them play football. Esosa Equaibor

6 The Commonwealth Government leased the Exhibition Building in Prince Alfred Park from Sydney City Council for ten years from 1925 for the display of World War I memorial exhibits. References and resolutions appeared in the Proceedings of the Municipal Council of the City of Sydney for 1924 (p. 508); 1927 (p. 434) and 1934 (p. 389). Relevant City Council Archives are: CRS34: TC 4694/23; 2063/23; 2714/27; 2509/34.

NOBODY WAS ALLOWED TO GO THERE, BUT EVERYBODY DID

My father lost his job

Reuben's Monte de Piete Loan Co. in Botany Road, Alexandria, in 1926 — the poor man's banker in hard times. (SLNSW)

Unemployment levels amongst unskilled workers rose to eleven per cent between 1925 and 1928 but were never, even in the early 1920s, below five per cent. From late in 1926 jobs in the manufacturing sector, where many South Sydney residents were employed, declined markedly. This meant that working people had scarce reserves when, after the October 1929 Wall Street stock-market crash, all sectors of the economy declined and Australian credit dried up. Unemployment rose to almost one in three by June 1932. With initial government efforts focussed on meeting interest payments on British loans, it was a particularly tough three years, in a very tough decade.[1]

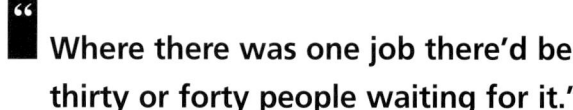

Where there was one job there'd be thirty or forty people waiting for it."

The Depression started in '29. There were a lot of young blokes in Woolloomooloo, the first job they ever got was when the Second World War started, when they became a soldier, 1939, first job they ever had. From the 'twenties up until 1932 it was impossible to get a job, impossible. I had to leave home when I was sixteen in '28 because if your father was working you couldn't get the dole, so I went bush, oh hundreds of us went bush. Billy Pascoe

It was just over ten years after the war that the whole of Sydney, particularly all the western suburbs of this area, were battered by the Depression. I know

"WE NEVER HAD A HOTBED OF CRIME"

for a while my father did have a florist shop in Enmore. In the 'thirties he did caretaking and a bit of cleaning around the RSL, in Petersham, and my mother used to go up there to help him. During the Depression there was the misery of the men wandering the streets and knocking on your door trying to sell something, knowing that those people had been really good in businesses. JEAN HENDY

Dad put himself through what was called 'Working Man's College' in Melbourne, and he was a qualified industrial chemist. My father having come back from Britain after the war, with the other chemists who worked on the war effort there, would've been pretty much guaranteed a job, but he was not the sort of man who liked work very much, and I think he must have lost his job for being late or falling asleep or something. Having been out of work, of course, when the Depression hit it was impossible to find work. Eventually through some contact that my mother had, he got a job with the Water Board digging ditches. He actually started his own business about 1930, '32. He packed these tiny little packets of antacid powder or something in the back of the shop and went out trying to sell them. He built his business up, it supported him and the family for quite a long time. KATE DUNBAR

In the Depression my father lost his job at McMahon's.* Unfortunately, like everybody else, the Depression hit us, and there was not only people like my father, but everybody else, except those that had a government job, suffered. Dad put a lot of effort into his work, it didn't matter what he did; he took to doing show cards. He'd make cards and he'd walk all over Sydney, the main purpose was to get the money to pay the rent. We used to get old magazines and cut out pictures, and we'd be sitting cutting the pictures out for Mum to stick them on, like tomatoes, 'Please don't squeeze me 'til I'm yours' and 'Do not ask for credit because a refusal often offends.' LORETTO THURGOOD

* McMahon's was a well-known Redfern-based carrying business which had extensive stables on the corner of Redfern and George Streets. Adding to its fame is the association with former Liberal

Prime Minister, Billy McMahon, who reportedly lived there as a boy when his grandparent's owned the operation.

Dad's father lived in Botany Road and they had horses and carts and drays, and my father in his early life was a brick-carter. He'd cart bricks from the brick works, which was only up here in Waterloo, to places like Maroubra and earnt fairly good money. But when the Depression come the building stopped and he just could not get work. I think he was out of work for over five years. Our neighbour was getting on in years then, he was much older than my parents, and he used to give my mother money to do his washing and his ironing and cleaning his house. And in that type of way they would get through. At one stage Dad was working on the tramways here on Botany Road. But it wasn't for long; they'd put them off after a couple of weeks and put somebody else on, then they'd rotate. There was that much unemployment that, where there was one job there'd be thirty or forty people waiting for it. MICK GREEN

Dad got an apprenticeship with Murdoch's, a big men's manufacturing tailors in the city, but when the Depression struck when he was older and entitled to better wages, they sacked him. For most of my childhood we had little corner shops which at least gave them a roof over their heads. Sometimes there wasn't much left over, but it meant they could get their vegetables and groceries wholesale. My mother could run it while he tried to earn a living by selling oranges in baskets door to door or getting fish at the markets, cleaning them and taking them round to the boarding houses, all sorts of odd jobs like that. Families did everything to help one another. Everybody was out of work; people did absolutely anything they could think of; my father was out of work the whole of my childhood. He joined the army in 1940, like many other people; that was the first job

1 To place the South Sydney experience in an Australia-wide context, see *Australians, A Historical Atlas,* Fairfax, Syme & Weldon Associates, 1987, Ch. 12, 'The Great Depression, pp. 239-250.

he'd ever been able to get. And so all my childhood they spent trying to make a living, 'cause the dole in those days was only food vouchers. Towards the end, before we left Surry Hills, before he went in the army, so that's 1939, 1938, he had a big cart with shafts on it, and he collected bottles. That was the last thing Dad did before we moved out and he went in the army. At one stage, he had a suitcase full of books, and he started a little sort of lending library. He called on people and they paid a penny or tuppence to borrow a book, but somebody, in one of their moves, lost the case of books, and that was the end of that. Later on he had a hot-dog stand. He used to go out near Moore Park; near the Cricketers Arms, there was a big tram depot, and he had that as one of his hot-dog stands when the trammies knocked off at night. When I was about six or something, we were living in Ann Street, Surry Hills, he sold ice-cream. He had a sort of a bike with a thing on the side that had the dry ice and the ice-cream in it. And he'd go to where there were a lot of people congregating, like down at the Gardens or the Quay, especially at the weekend; even where people would be coming out of the football ground. He also got the relief work, on roads. He used to have to go down to the Quay to get called up and be sent to where you were going. They used to issue you with big boots made of really hard leather. My mother's cousin and his wife's family all sold fruit from a horse and cart, and so often they might even share the horse. Portia Fitzsimmons

—

You had Metters here with three thousand
working in the early days, just across the road here, and it was all heavy industry; and of course, on the other side of the road here, you had Alexandria Goods Yards, you had all the goods from all the country areas coming in here, unloading. I started up working for the Tigers and Slaves, it was known then as that, ATNSA, and they had their garage in Gibson Street, Camperdown, going back to '30, '36. You'd sit on the sidewalk, and you'd get a couple of hours, you might get half a day or a day's work, casual. And then there was McMahon's, you'd get another day casual there. Then I got in, I worked for him for

twelve months straight, and then I joined the CCC [Commonwealth Civil Constructions], it was part of the Commonwealth war effort. I've got to tell you that they had another name for it, but I'm not gonna mention it. Frank Altoft

—

On Sunday morning, Italian fishermen from
Woolloomooloo would come up the rear lane of Corinthia and one would play the violin, one would sing and the other'd be looking for any donations that would be thrown down. And I used to think their singing was absolutely beautiful. But my mother soon told me, 'Gladys, if they were any good they would be at La Scala, not singing in the street behind us.' Glad Willis

—

My father worked at the brick pits up until the
1940s and during the Depression he was considered employed because he worked one week in three. Fortunately, he was a bit of a gambler and I think we were lucky because of that. He wasn't a bad gambler and that supplemented to a great degree. Terry Murphy

—

He wasn't a bad gambler at all, as Terry's sister, Maureen Oliver said.

My father supplemented our income with things;
like, I'd go over with him to the canals in Alexandria where they used to have the boat races. Men used to race match boxes down the canals and they'd bet on them, and Dad would do that. He also used to sell dog cards on the dogs of a Saturday night; they'd have ten races, so you could pick the ten winners, I think it cost you sixpence. Dad used to get a bloke down in Sydney Street, Erskineville, to print all the cards up, and we'd go and pick them up on the Friday; and then you'd come home and he'd have so many people, like say, one bloke might've sold fifty cards and someone would sell another fifty cards, so they were all done up; and then I'd walk around with that on the Friday night and we'd deliver the cards. If you won, if you got the ten up, you got ten pound, which was an absolute fortune in them days. Dad was a punter too, and I suppose often the mere fact that he

A shop in Forbes Street, Woolloomooloo. (SSCC)

could gamble and maybe win a quid, you know, used to help out a lot in them days. MAUREEN OLIVER

What I remember most vividly about Newtown is the poverty. You never forget the taste of poverty; my father never got constant work. I can even remember eating bread and dripping for tea; Golden Syrup, Cocky's Joy, we ate heaps of that in the 'thirties. I'm talking about a family sitting down to a meal; that was the meal. They used to get occasional work, relief work, they used to call it, and that was because he had a family. If you didn't have a family, you didn't get much at all, in fact you had to hit the road and jump the rattler. You got a dole in the form of food.[2] You'd do anything to get a shilling. My father cleaned bricks, he was digging drains in Centennial Park. Those ponds were dug by people that were out of work. That was very hard work for

very little money. We used to get handouts, but my family was very lucky because my aunt happened to be one of the nun's for the Brown St Joseph's, the Josephites. She was able to supply our family with clothes. LEO HANNAN

Dad tried very hard on making a go with the taxi all through those Depression years, but couldn't earn very much at all. So my mother started taking in boarders and between the boarders and the taxi, we sort of survived until the war started, and they started building the Cronulla railway line. That's when Dad started to branch out. BOB SLATER

2 See T.H. Kewley, *Social Security in Australia,* Sydney University Press, 1965, for a history of the development of social security and health benefits from 1900.

MY FATHER LOST HIS JOB

The women went in and done the male work for female rates of pay."

While women suffered discrimination in the public sector, often being sacked on marriage with their positions given to men, in the private sector the discrimination was reversed. Because under most awards women were only paid some 57 per cent of the male rate, the unemployment rate of female wage-earners, at just over 15 per cent, was almost half that of men.[3]

One of the things that happened in the Depression was the women could get jobs because their wages were so low and the men couldn't. So my mother was working. She was sorting eggs in a big egg depot. And when I lived at Goulburn Street, which was from when I was eight to when I was eleven, Mum had part-time work as a housemaid to rich people in the eastern suburbs, and usually she'd be home by the time we got home from school. When I was eight they wanted her to go down to Bowral with them on their holidays, and she had to do that, so she was away for about two weeks, and I used to have to mind the children after school and sometimes I had to help get them off in the morning too. I was very proud of myself because I was being grown up. Dad was busy because nobody had cars, and so everything you did had to be done

"WE NEVER HAD A HOTBED OF CRIME"

Above: Another view of Woolloomooloo photographed by the Housing Investigation Committee in 1936. By this time the living conditions of the workers in South Sydney were the subject of official scrutiny. Subsequently many residents were rehoused and relocated to Sydney's western suburbs when 'slum clearance' became a political priority. (SLNSW)

Opposite: A Woolloomooloo street which captured the attention of the Housing Investigation Committee in 1936. (SLNSW)

on foot. I don't think actually, that my mother was allowed to work as a housemaid; you weren't allowed to work if you were on the dole. That was illegal when she did that, 'cause I know we were told that if the police came round, not to tell them anything. PORTIA FITZSIMMONS

The IXL Jam and Preserving Company would have seasons, fruit seasons, the canning season and it was very big in December and at Easter time, with all the stone fruits, apricots, and peaches towards the end of the season. I put my age up, I was fifteen or sixteen, to eighteen or nineteen, to get the adult rates of pay. And a friend wrote me a letter and I queued

3 Peter Spearritt, *Sydney Since the Twenties,* Hale & Iremonger, Sydney, 1978, p. 59.

MY FATHER LOST HIS JOB

up and got put on; she worked there all year round and tipped off someone to give me a job. And that was another nasty experience for me, my first factory experience where I saw women push around these big preserving vats on rollers, and all the women working there were doing male work, because the male rates of pay was about £3 a week, and the full adult female rate's pay was £1.12.6 a week. And the men were all queued up outside, right down Forbes Street, but they had women in there doing the men's work, and their men would be home minding the kids and doing the washing and housework; they talk about house parents, the men done it during the Depression! GRACE SCHWEBEL

—

When she was fifteen, my sister, Faith, went to business college, which was really a disaster, because by the time she came out of business college, she was too old to take a junior's job, and she had no experience, so you couldn't get work. Faith was out of work for a long time. She used to knit beautiful lacy jumpers for seven and six; she worked like a slave. She had plenty of go in her, even though she was only sixteen. She probably took a couple of weeks to finish a jumper, but see, she wasn't doing anything else, it was better than nothing. PAT NICKS

We lost all our properties."

While South Sydney residents who derived their income from shares, property or manufacturing were better prepared than the majority of 'workers', having some financial reserves , they also suffered in the climate of economic uncertainty and general depression. For some their situation was a painful 'disgrace'; for others it meant hawking goods from door to door, after previously being engaged in manufacturing; others lost their capital and the chance of establishing their own business. The Moratorium Act, 1930 *and the* Interest Reduction Act, 1931 *aimed at providing relief to mortgagors and tenants and restricting evictions. Nevertheless, evictions and foreclosures, as debts accumulated to an unserviceable level, occurred.[4]*

The Depression must have been affecting my mother when I was fourteen, in 1934. My sister and I went for a walk around all the poorest places around St Vincent's Hospital, and there were men there who were staggering who were drunk and had bloody bandages and men with no legs, from the war. And Ingrid said to me, 'This is where we'll have to live when we lose our money.' And I said to her, 'Are we going to lose our money?' And she said, 'Oh yes, I think so'. And I came home with this terrible headache. Then we hung on without a lot of money. I think an aunt helped in the Depression, but my friends were rather amazed when sometimes I had to say, 'No, I can't afford to go to the pictures'. It really was a disgrace to be poor, so my mother must have really felt it, because most of my relations were very well off, and it was a disgrace to be a single parent in those days. PAT ROSE

—

We lost all our properties; Dad bought four properties, big bunches of flats, but Jack Lang broke in with the *Moratorium Act,* which meant they didn't have to pay their rents, so Dad couldn't keep up the payments and lost the lot. DARIO LO SCHIAVO

4 See Stuart McIntyre, 'Winners and Losers', Ch. 12, *The Oxford History of Australia*, Vol. 4, Oxford University Press, Melbourne, pp. 275-296.

*William Roberts, an original Anzac, and family
evicted from their Redfern home into the street
in 1934. (SLNSW)*

My mother never got over the Depression, she always regarded it as pure terror, the idea of being unemployed. Coming over here from New Zealand she'd invested their savings into running a boarding house, and it just collapsed, the clientele couldn't pay their rent and she had debts and eventually had to walk away from it, they were horrified. PAUL HERLINGER

In 1932/33 they stopped the parking outside Morrison's Cake Shop at Kings Cross and we lost all the business trade. We struggled on for a year because we were on a ten-year lease, so we couldn't just get out, and it was about £15 a week which was an enormous rent. I think we sold it eventually to Sargent's, thank goodness. It was around about the time when the Government's Saving Bank closed, when Jack Lang closed the banks because we had trouble getting our money out of the bank to live.[5] They had it that you had to pick up the money on a Thursday, say at 2 o'clock. Well, anybody in a job couldn't get to the bank for Thursday, and according to how much money you had the maximum you were allowed to draw out was £2.10.0 a week. I remember a girl at school being very upset because they'd lost all their money, and it was £7. GLAD WILLIS

Dad originally had a manufacturing company, *Wah Ying,* but the Depression set in, and he went hawking, 'cos if you weren't an Australian citizen you couldn't get any Social Security. The company made dresses, it was on the corner of Campbell and Foster Street, Surry Hills. In about 1932 when Lang brought in a moratorium act and the people didn't have to repay their debts, that got him into trouble. My father couldn't collect, people owed him money and also the banks closed. He hawked clothing, men's and women's, all over the metropolitan area. He just used shank's pony and carried the goods in a suitcase, that was quite professional. People had to buy a certain amount of essential clothing, and they used the time payment/lay-by system. For my father, going from door to door was a matter of survival. FRANK W.

 You'd have to go down to 7 Circular Quay, pick up thirteen loaves of bread, and it had to last you the two weeks."

Unemployment relief was a State, rather than a Commonwealth, responsibility. Initially the 'dole' provided little more than rations, also known as 'the susso' or sustenance, but, after pressure from the unemployed, from the beginning of 1932 men were transferred from the dole to 'relief' works.[6]

My father's family lived down in George Street, Erskineville, and his father took off to the country to try and make a living because there was no money or jobs here. So men would go through the country, picking up whatever they could, and they had to keep moving to be able to pick up their dole and their food supplies, and yet my father was still here. Women were the major people of authority of that period if you go back to 1938, they were the bosses. Vera Roach, Lillian Fowler, all those women were really very, very, strong women, because the husbands from the time of the Depression, were often out walking looking for jobs, and some of them just used to travelling the route because you could pick up food in various places and you could be fed. You didn't have to worry about them, they kept alive, they just kept travelling. But sometimes they never came back to their families. TERRY MURPHY

In the country when you went on the dole it was worse. You had to be in one town today, then you had to be in the next town next dole day, then you had to be in the next town, roughly it would be about twenty-five miles something like that. And you walked, you'd walk to that town and then you'd walk to another town. It got very, very cold up there, that's what drove you back to Sydney. When I was eighteen, after coming back from the bush I got a room for eight shillings a week, with a bloke who was an ex-digger, he'd come back with one leg off.

A mass rally of Eveleigh workers listening to an election speech from Jack Lang at Redfern in 1934. (SLNSW)

I'd only been there for about a week, went everywhere and couldn't get a job; he said, 'Listen, I might be able to get you a job.' He come back about a week after, 'Look,' he said, 'I've got a job for you,' he said, 'I'll put you in as my son.' And he got me this job; instead of getting the dole, you had to work two weeks in seven. The first job was out at Botany, you had to dig a trench six foot deep, two foot wide, and twenty-three foot long. You could have a smoke if you rolled your cigarettes before you went, but you weren't allowed to roll a cigarette in the trench. You dug two yards of trench a day, you were flat out. They gave you a trial run and after you were there about an hour he'd come and have a look at you, if he thought you wasn't strong enough or wasn't doing your bit he'd say, 'Come up snow' and he'd throw you two bob and you were finished. I done that for about eighteen months. We went to another job up at Como where they blasted these great big rocks up, ten foot high, might be forty tonne, and you smashed them up into little pieces to put in the drays and I did that for another eighteen months, so I was getting roughly about a pound a week in one of the poorest parts of the Depression. BILLY PASCOE

5 This reference is to the Government Savings Bank of NSW which closed in May 1931, but was absorbed into the Commonwealth Bank in December. Whatever the 'excesses' of Lang's Moratorium and Interest Reduction legislation, debts were still legally binding, but many simply weren't or could not be paid.

6 Kewley, op. cit., p. 155. See also Nadia Wheatley, *The Unemployed Who Kicked*, MA Thesis, Macquarie University, 1976.

MY FATHER LOST HIS JOB

There were quite a lot of people on the dole;
sometimes you got two weeks' relief work, and you had to go out to Concord where they had the swamps out there, and you dug, made the walls to stop the swamp from coming in.[7] My stepfather got the dole, and then he used to get three weeks on and two weeks off relief work. But on the two weeks you was off, you couldn't get the dole. The three weeks you worked had to do you until you started up again. But, they'd get odd jobs if they could, window cleaning, anything at all. In fact I used to make lamps, you see them in town today, they're worth anything up to fifty or sixty dollars. You used to get these boards, and they'd get a frosted glass, and cut a moon shape, put it in, and then just put a globe behind them and a statue in the front.

Me grandmother had a pension which was twelve and six. But you've got to remember that you could get half a sheep for two and six. Although you didn't have money, your food was fairly cheap, the vegetables were cheap. What happened was that you got your dole, which was seven and six a week, and you'd get thirteen loaves of bread for the fortnight. You'd have to go down to 7 Circular Quay, pick up thirteen loaves of bread, and it had to last you the two weeks. And then you'd go to the Benevolent Society in Thomas Street, and you'd get bacon bones, and get the dole coupons at St George's dance hall, which is just down in King Street, Newtown. See you were allowed so much, it all depends on what income came into your family, or how many was in the family. Your biggest problem in those days was your rent. Gas was very cheap, it was all the penny in the slot in them days and of course it went for a good while, you could get about three or four hours, you could cook a dinner easy, for the penny in the slot. FRANK ALTOFT

—

Up towards Cleveland Street, my father used to
go to the milk depot in Balfour Street, Redfern. When he wasn't working, he'd wash it all out and they'd give him as much milk as he wanted. He was a builder's labourer, but in the Depression they

stopped building and they got put off. You got a food slip which you took to a grocer. Nobody smoked in our family and nobody drank and nobody gambled. And once or twice a year we used to get a dole issue of clothing and shoes. Everybody knew what the shoes were like. The pawn shop was a great place to go in those days, you could pawn anything for a couple a bob, and when you had the money you used to get it out; they used to keep it for three months. I'm afraid my mother was a regular customer at the pawn shops. JANE LANYON

—

The dole comprised flour, sugar, syrup, tea. To
collect it, you had to go to Redfern or even Central. Now my father had a twin brother and they were very close, they decided between the two of them that they'd help through the Labor Party branch. They would go and get it and bring it back and dole it out to the people here. Anyway the government agreed, providing they got the dole slips, and that's how it was. MICK GREEN

—

At one stage we were living on bread with milk
and water poured over it. Another time Dad was furious, he went to pick up this food that they were giving the unemployed and he wouldn't take it because the meat was all covered in maggots.
JEAN HENDY

—

You got your vouchers at the Quay and took the
vouchers to shops. In the beginning they gave you so many loaves of bread, but there would have been a revolution if they hadn't changed it because the bread went stale immediately, and what they were giving out wasn't nice. Once, my mother was ill with bronchitis; people got bronchitis and pneumonia a lot then, and my father wanted to get a nice piece of steak for Mum to tempt her appetite, usually we lived on stews, nourishing but not very appetising, and the butcher wouldn't give it to him; he said people on dole coupons didn't get steak, you weren't allowed to have nice things. Shoes were a big problem, they were the most expensive item to buy. They made very, very cheap shoes, and they were

ONLY ONE REMEDY FO R THIS—SOCIALISATION !

Well, things are brightening up. Last week I only got enough out this for the dog; this week there's enough for me, too !

(National Library)

really cardboard, and you put them on when you went out, but they didn't stand up to wear, my little sister had a pair of those shoes. As well as food vouchers they got given lengths of material for clothes, and my mum made us dresses all out of the same material. We had these princess frocks that buttoned up the front with little lace collars, and everyone used to think they looked lovely, and admire us because there were four of us in the same clothes. The first lot were sort of maroon flannel, and the second lot were a blue material, but that material was from the dole offices, it was quite warm and quite good. PORTIA FITZSIMMONS

—

When I was having treatment for whooping cough at the Quay Street Hospital, it was then part of the Children's Hospital, I was able to see first-hand just what happened in the Depression. Men used to have to go to the Benevolent Society in Quay Street to get one paper signed, and then they had to walk right down George Street to a wharf to have it re-signed, then they came back. And on a Monday you got

groceries, bread and meat, very few vegetables, and if you wanted eggs you could only get eggs on a special form, and that had to do you 'til Thursday. But it wasn't only just people in Erskineville that suffered, it was people all over, you know. A lot of people were evicted from homes because they couldn't pay rent. LORETTO THURGOOD

—

In the Depression we were never, never really destitute, for food, we seemed to always have a meal there. Dad got a bit of relief work on road gangs and relief coupons for food; at least it kept the family fed. The Depression made things a little harder. You'd go down Circular Quay and get fitted out with a pair of pants and a shirt and squeaky boots. You never had the money to buy anything, especially a big family; it would have been the same for most families in the neighbourhood, they'd be all

7 See Grace Schwebel's account of Amelia Pankhurst Walsh's opposition to a strike by workers on the dole scheme at Concord, in Chapter 5, p.109.

MY FATHER LOST HIS JOB

struggling. It was sort of day-to-day living, but we were very shaky at the end of the week. Dad's wage packet went into the house, he might have had a couple of beers but I can't remember any squandering of money. My mother used to be responsible for the budgeting side of things. From what I can ascertain of the families living around us, a lot of women used to do the budgeting and shopping. ROBERT HAMMOND

We survived, by very keen shopping."

With shopping largely occurring on a daily basis, when not at school, children did what was called 'the messages', entailing a visit to the butcher, baker, greengrocers and general grocer, picking up what was necessary for the evening meal. They were also good at scrounging, a skill in which many of the children of South Sydney took great pride, though at times, in Leo Hannan's words, the competition was vicious.

As a child we used to go over to Oxford Street to where they used to auction the meat, at two and six a tray. You'd have to go and pick the best tray that had the most meals. Then you'd go down William Street to the vegetable shops because The Cross shops were too expensive, and you'd get the biggest cabbage for sixpence, that'd do three meals, and you'd save the papers. You'd take the papers up and sell them to the fruit shop for a shilling and you'd take a shilling's worth of potatoes, you'd get eight pounds of potatoes for a shilling. That's how we survived, by very keen shopping. GLAD WILLIS

Of a Saturday, my father and my sister and I used to wheel a pram down to Paddy's markets, and come four o'clock in the afternoon, when the markets had finished, the vegetable people used to wipe their stalls of the vegetables, and there used to be big heaps of vegetables that would have went to the tip. So we used to go through there and put in the pram what was edible; well, that was something for nothing. One time a chap took pity on us and gave us

a watermelon, and we got as far as the old Empire Theatre in Quay Street, and my father dropped the watermelon. And of course, rather than waste it, we all sat on the steps of the Empire Picture Show, and with our hands we scooped the watermelon out and ate it. So we weren't going to waste a darn good watermelon because my father was careless. My parents just took each day as it came, and accepted what came with it. There was no future for them to look forward to, they just plodded along, like everybody in those days; they weren't the only ones that were doing it tough.

White Wings used to have their flour mill on the corner of Balfour Street and Meagher Street, Chippendale, and we used to pester them to give us bags of flour and cake mixes. We used to go to Blackfriars School, and on our way home, or going to school, we used to call in at the Vita Brit factory in Shepherd Street and they used to give us big bags of broken Vita Brits. And then in Abercrombie Street, near Cleveland Street, they used to give us all the broken frankfurts and the saveloys from a factory there. Aeroplane Jelly was in Cleveland Street, and that was another factory and we used to sit there and eat the jelly crystals when we were about eight, nine, ten. I'm afraid the Allen's Lolly factory also in Shepherd Street got many a visit from kids from the Blackfriars school. They closed Blackfriars school because of the Depression. The warehouses around the school were hostels for men who were out of work, and they thought they would be a danger, so they closed the school and all of us kids went to George Street school, although they kept the kindergarten on. JANE LANYON

Through me aunt, I got on to a place in town, a wholesale butcher's, Sutton's Forrest was the name of it, down at Central Railway where the Her Majesty's Theatre is now. I used to get free meat, like the offcuts, the stuff that the butcher thought wasn't too good. I used to go around to cake shops and we used to get stale buns and the specks from the Italians, from the fruit shop, they'd give you the fruit that was damaged. I was always an opportunist. I did that from six or seven. That was a bad time because there was no safety net to catch the people. After school I'd get me barrow and race Tibby Handshaw and Whopper Westle to the wood yard of Stuart Brothers who were building contractors.[8] I'd race down where they used to throw the offcuts; people were competing with each other, underneath it was vicious. There was a cake shop down the road where they used to make wholesale cakes, you'd get cakes there, stale cakes. When they'd dropped a cake or something was squashed you'd get them; it was stuff they couldn't sell. Down in Camperdown opposite the school in Parramatta Road was a big biscuit factory. You could go and get a bag of broken biscuits for nothing. One place after school I used to go for wood was Wood Coffill's Funerals and they used to make coffins. I used to go into the factory, off Missenden Road and you'd see them doing the upholstery in the coffins. This is very intriguing when you are about nine. LEO HANNAN

—

In the Depression, to get the big money that we did have, my brothers used to go and get the fruit from the markets and we used to pick the best of it and put it on a plank out the front of our house in Belmont Street and sell it to the people in the street for thruppence or sixpence, to get enough money for all of us to go to the pictures. And what fruit we had left over went in the bowl for food for our mother, to keep us going. Horace Stubbs used to take my oldest brother down there with him of a morning and he'd go around collecting all the fruit. It was just bruised and what had been shoved aside, which they didn't think they could sell. He'd pick them up and bring them home in a sugar bag. And there used to be a fish shop in Belmont Street, Mrs Guerney, and we used to go down there and get our fish and scallops reasonably cheap, of a Friday night for tea, we always used to say, 'Have you got any scraps, Mrs Guerney?' and she used to give them to us. All the batter from the fish that was on the top, and you'd often get a couple of good chips in amongst them. BETTY MOULDS

We had enough food, we were fortunate that way. The main meal of the day would have been rice, meat, fish. You'd see a lot of children without shoes. And they were picking up bottles for the bottle-oh who used to come around. We didn't have to do that. All we had to do was to get fire wood for the copper from the factories and the fruit boxes from shops. And the whole Chinese population, or the majority, were former migrants or immigrants classified as aliens so they had to do the best they could. A lot of them worked down in Haymarket, and they helped in local stores and had their meals there. My father saw a lot of people who were worse off. FRANK W.

—

I can't remember ever starving. I always had a good meal. Mum'd go down to Paddy's markets on a Saturday morning and get whatever she could, practically for nothing. She was a trooper, she'd come back with a sugar bag over her arm, walk all the way. And she'd take the little dog with her or, if she didn't, he'd follow her. She'd make sure we were fed. And I never had to eat fried bread and dripping; we always had a good meal. But there was people near us that didn't have much because they had big families. Mum would see that you had Irish stew or something like that, or roast steak, or soup. I know a lot of people down here did go hungry. They were given food coupons, not money but food coupons; she'd go and get it and that'd buy meat. Meat was very cheap and you paid tuppence for a loaf of bread. The Depression put a lot of pressure on Mum to do extra work to get money. She had her money and then she'd have to wait to see what my father gave her. NELL LEONARD

—

Things were so cheap too, a rabbit was thruppence. Watermelons, they'd almost give them to you. My mother insisted that we eat fruit, no matter what, fruit

---

8 Stuart Brothers were the contractors responsible for building Luna Park which was under construction at this time. See 'Luna Park Heritage Study', prepared for the NSW Department of Planning, Godden Mackay Pty Ltd, in association with Sue Rosen, Robert Irving, Chris Pratten, Colin Crisp, February 1991.

MY FATHER LOST HIS JOB

had to be there. And there was a man just up the street who was a friend of ours, and he was a fruiterer. He'd always see that everybody along the street got it as cheap as he possibly could. So somehow or other they survived. I didn't feel the Depression nearly as much as the adults would've felt it, I never felt hunger as a desire. Yet I know there were times when there was very little to eat. MICK GREEN

There was no money around, good, honest people, just had nowhere to sleep."

Raiding the gas meters, 'midnight flits' and people living in the streets and parks are some of the images that people have retained from the Depression years. Most people recall making do in a society where, generally, frugality rather than starvation was the order of the day. But resourcefulness and a dedicated daily concentration on survival predominated in what was definitely not the 'throw away' society that existed in economic downturns later in the century.

Because there was no money around, good, honest people, just had nowhere to sleep, and they'd go and get an armful of newspapers, every tree you'd see there'd be three or four people underneath; probably two to three hundred people slept in the Domain, every night, and I don't know how they done it in the winter. I never had a pair of shoes, we didn't wear shoes, I was about thirteen or fourteen before I had a pair of boots. BILLY PASCOE

And of course in the real bad times of the Depression, you had gas meters, a penny in the slot or a shilling in the slot, and if people saw people going out and they thought there was an opportunity, they'd get a tin opener and knock the money off. They didn't call it crime, circumstances forced people to do things that they normally wouldn't do. CLIFF NOBLE

Around about '28 or '29, in the Depression, Dad

got out of work and then we went up to Ryde and we took on a shop, up in Church Street. It was half mixed business and half library. But unfortunately there were too many people on the books who didn't pay and after Mum died — she died more through worry than anything else about the way the business was going — Dad lost interest and got rid of it and came back down here. Aunt Lil was Mum's sister and she took Gordon and Irene for a couple of years until Gordon got old enough to work. HENRY BROWN

I lived in Chippendale 'til I was about six and then the Depression was on and we did what they called a 'midnight flitter'; in the darkness of the night we moved to a two-storey house at 19 Vine Street, Redfern. And then we did another flitter to 22 Hugo Street, where we were able to pay the rent; from there we moved to 75 Abercrombie Street. By that time my father had a builder's labourer's job and I was working as an apprentice in a tailoring factory and I was bringing in seven shillings and sixpence. When the Depression was on, if you couldn't pay your rent, the landlords would send a bailiff and he would sit in the house and sell whatever you had until he got the rent that was owing. And that's why a lot of people did the midnight flit; took their few possessions to the next house. There were a lot of empty houses around at that time. You paid rent, but you could only pay rent for so long, because there was no money coming in. But after a while my father got a job building Hurstville School. JANE LANYON

When I came home on Thursdays after school at four o'clock, there was an old man standing outside our house with his hat for money, playing a violin. It was that song about 'When the Nights are Lonely,' it was such a sad song. I used to go in and put my arms around my dog and weep on his neck, I was so sorry for that man, it was terrible. It was after the Depression started to hit. It went: 'Just a song of twilight when the lights are low,/when the flickering shadows softly come and go/though the days be lonely, and the nights be sad,/still that song at twilight, softly comes and goes.' PAT ROSE

Shoeless boys in the Moore Park playground in 1936. (SCCA CRS 57/1363)

During the Depression he was able to keep his job, but it was restricted, they worked three weeks on and one week off. I guess quite a few families would probably have been out of work, although I don't recall a lot of hardship, but we were never what you would call well off. My dad was always on labourer's money, which was the minimum wage. He was a good handyman, able to mend our shoes and any odd jobs around the place. The Depression made people aware of the fact that they had nothing, and if you had a job you still weren't on clover. People were really worried where their next shilling was coming from, and the threat was always there of how long those who had a job would keep them. FRED FOREMAN

 I mean, everybody helped everybody."

A repeated theme that emerges at some time in any lengthy review of people's Depression experiences is that while the poverty was oppressive, because 'everyone' was in the same situation, for many children there was not a personal feeling of deprivation and alienation. Sharing the experience with others, being aware of the constant search for work, concerns about accommodation and food achieved a kind of normality. Of course, for parents, who knew of a better life and bore the responsibility of making ends meet, the matter was entirely different. Whatever the reality, there are also many memories of community support, both organised and semi-official, and family-oriented and personal.

Auntie Maude and Uncle Si run the Sunshine Club in Hatties Arcade a few years there in the Depression time. People gathered together to socialise and help one another, they run raffles and they run little concerts and everything, to get money for people that was being ejected from their houses because they couldn't pay the rent or something like that. One of the great people in Newtown was a woman, a Mayoress of Newtown, Lilian Fowler, and she did a terrific amount of work around the district, for people that were being evicted. See people couldn't afford to pay, you didn't have the money. FRANK ALTOFT

Mrs Papps was the most *marvellous* woman that ever lived. She'd help anybody. She had about eleven or twelve in the family. When the Depression was on people used to wander in and she'd make them sandwiches and give them a couple of pennies, on their way. I mean, it was dreadful, you got food coupons but you had no money for rent.[9] The only way they could get any money was to sell their coupons, which, if they were desperate, they did, and went without food. To make ends meet, you just went out, we went out and scrubbed somebody's floor. You went to the kindergarten and all those people who worked for those kind of unions, that lived out at Vaucluse and all those places, they were honorary, anything going for the kindergarten in those days, was honorary. And of course you'd go up and clean the kindergarten and you'd meet these people, and then if they thought things were tough they'd go, 'Well come out one day and do some work round the house and we'll pay you'. I mean, everybody helped everybody. During the Depression our landlords were very good to all the tenants. They took whatever they had, if they didn't have it, bad luck. If someone was sick, they'd go round and get Mrs Papps, and she'd go round and help you. JOYCE HIGGINS

▬

People that were having problems from the Woolloomooloo area used to come up for food and Mum'd give them a bag of stale scones, and some people would be so very grateful. We couldn't afford to give away the cakes, even I didn't get them because Mum said you don't eat the profits. My sisters used to get me one every now and then, but I could always have stale scones. There were a couple of men that came up from 'the Loo' and when they found that they'd got stale scones went out the door and threw them in the gutter. So Mum retrieved them straight away. Because in the Depression, a lot of them didn't have any money or anything, till food coupons came. GLAD WILLIS

▬

In the Depression we shared food. We had two bakeries in Redfern; there was Jones's Bakery in Walker Street, and there was Lovely's in Morehead Street. On the other side of Redfern Street, in Walker Street, half way down the hill there was an open

block, and people used to assemble down there, and as young kids we used to help distribute the bread down at the paddock to the people who'd line up. That is what I remember mainly about the Depression: handing out bread from a back of a cart, free to a lot of people. SIR NICHOLAS SHEHADIE

▬

Dad was a fisherman. People used to laugh at your prawns, squid, mussels, they wouldn't eat it. We couldn't give them away, tuppence a pound of prawns. People had no money, but Dad fed everyone in Woolloomooloo, there was a parcel for everyone. They called it bartering. Mrs Tarantala up the road had a coal shed, she used to give us coal. That's how they got through the Depression. SAM DONATO

▬

My mother's brother lived up at Sylvania, and because my uncle did not work at all he qualified for dole benefits. So every week or every fortnight he'd come down and bring Mum down a big brown bag full of potatoes, pumpkins, onions, all those kind of things. MAUREEN OLIVER

▬

The Sydney City Mission used to be in Meagher Street, and they used to have what they call a soup kitchen, and all of us kids used to go up there to get a bowl of soup with two slices of bread. And then after school, if we took our billy-cans there, any soup that was left over, we could take home to our people. Things were tough; you wouldn't do it now, but in the Depression, well it was necessary. And then Saint Barnabas, the big church in Broadway, had a shoe day once a month. Everybody used to sit around the hall and they used to bring in these chaff bags of shoes, tip 'em in the centre of the hall, and that was a bun's rush; everyone used to go and try and pair a pair of shoes up. JANE LANYON

▬

The Depression affected everybody in some way, my father was out of work. Nobody had much, no-one had more than the other fella. But people socialised a lot, and if someone in the street got something that you didn't have, well you got part of it. If someone was lucky enough to find something

Children at the opening of Camperdown Park in 1935. The Bonds building, where generations of residents worked, is in the background. (SCCA CRS 57/1219)

that fell off the back of a truck, he shared it with his neighbour. Lots of things fell off the back of trucks in those days, they were very bumpy roads. People had to get by. They were desperate times for some people, some families had nothing. I had two pair of sandshoes, one for school, and one for weekend, if you couldn't afford a pair of sandshoes you just barefooted. SYD FENNELL

" My mother had the same frock for ten years."

Portia Fitzsimmons' account of the personal affect of the Depression on her parents and family indicates the long-term repercussions on the Australian psyche. Some people never lost their 'Depression mentality': their fear of the banks, of credit, of joblessness and homelessness, their abhorrence of waste. The Depression formed the outlook of an entire generation.

The daily search for work took away all their youth and all their young lives. I mean, it didn't affect us much because at the schools we went to everybody was poor, so we didn't feel any different to anyone else. It certainly affected my parents' lives, it made them old before their time. And there was no fun at all. They were anxious all the time, you know, they lived from day to day and it was depressing for them. I can't remember them laughing a lot. They were young, but it took every ounce of their energy to keep us all; we were a big family to have to keep in the Depression. And I've got a photo of them when they were only young in Centennial Park and the most striking thing is the look of weariness on their faces. My mother had the same frock for ten years, one good dress. The worst thing about the Depression was the way ordinary people were treated without any respect at all. You waited for hours whenever you went to hospital or in any government department, but also, anybody who had jobs thought they were better than you, and people who had jobs or had shops were not always nice to ordinary people. The Depression ruined their lives. PORTIA FITZSIMMONS

---

9 See Judy MacKinolty, 'Woman's Place ...' in Judy MacKinolty (ed), *The Wasted Years? Australia's Great Depression,* George Allen & Unwin, Sydney, 1981, pp. 105-110.

The Japanese could have come straight in

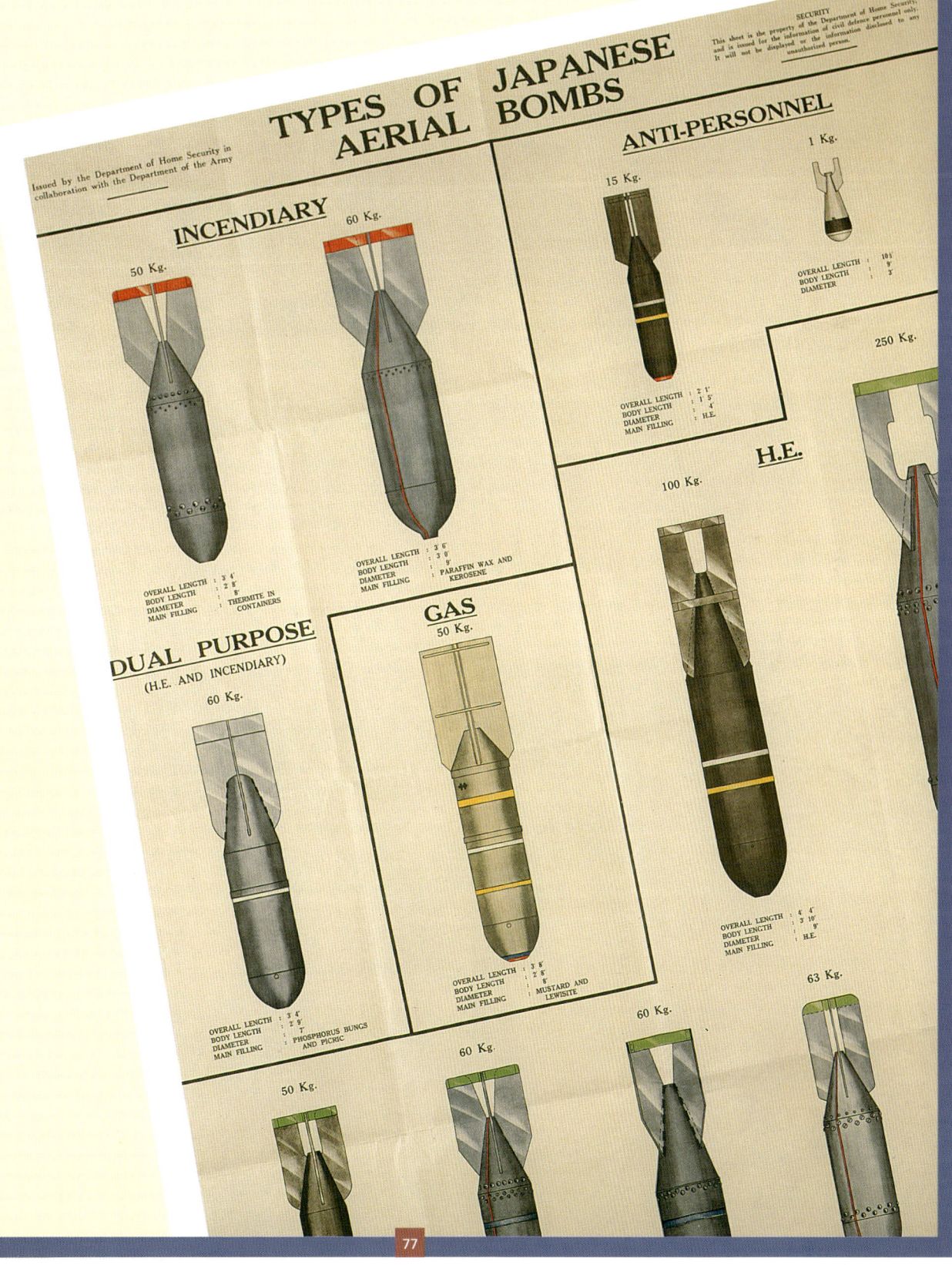

While economic conditions improved in the second half of the 1930s, conditions for workers barely altered. Many men remained unemployed. People were aware of the increasing tensions in Europe, particularly immigrants and 'reffos'. But it was the outbreak of the war that brought a sudden change to people's circumstances. Men enlisted to obtain their first permanent job in a decade, others were conscripted to work in industry. Excitement and dread, consorted uneasily among the residents of South Sydney.

" We still felt a part of history."

A fantastic thing happened in 1939, in the picture show down here at St Peters, there was a picture on about something that was supposed to have happened in the time of Queen Victoria and halfway through the picture they played 'God Save the King' and everybody stood up while it was played on the screen and then they sat down and the film continued uninterrupted. It was a fantastic thing, they rose as a body, you'd have to experience it to really realise the feeling as everybody stood up while it was played. The War hadn't started then, there was tension. At that time we still felt that we were part of history, not so much part of the Empire, but part of history. We believed that what we did was important, and therefore we, our country, was central to the playing of 'The King', we automatically associated that this was something that was important to us, not something that was remote from us, it was part of our living, a part of our life. LES CROSS

I can remember that silly fool Chamberlain coming back from Munich with this piece of paper 'Peace in our time'.[1] I believe that Hitler just turned around to some aide, and said, 'He was such a nice old gentleman, I thought I'd give him my autograph for a souvenir'. And then the war started, and it was a terrible thing. We were all worried. MERVYN JORDON

The Prime Minister come on the radio and announced that we were at war. It was a terrible, terrible feeling when we heard that war was breaking out, because Dad looked like being called up, and our home would more or less be disturbed and broken up for that period, and women weren't very happy about it. Sons looked like going to war. No good. SYD FENNELL

"Some of the neighbours kindly informed the authorities that my father was a German sympathiser."

In the late 1930s as tensions increased in Europe, with the rise of fascism in Spain, Germany and Italy, there was an increase in immigration, particularly Jews. Paul Herlinger's Austrian-Jewish father and Irish-Catholic mother had moved to The Cross and managed a residential establishment there.

My father was very interested in what was happening in Spain. We knew something of what was happening in the US. Dad had one tenant who used to give him the *Chicago Tribune* and we'd go through that pretty well with a fine-tooth comb every week. We were aware of things happening in Europe. I don't s'pose as kids we knew what fascism was ourselves, but certainly Dad was aware of it. And we were certainly pro-loyalist, and anti-Franco, in Spain. Round about 1938, '39 we were starting to get immigrants, we called them 'reffos' at the time, or refugees. They were generally the better-off people because they had the funds to get out. I remember him writing to his sister, she lived in what is now Croatia, part of the old Austro-Hungarian Empire, and she wrote back something like, 'We are two old women, no-one will ever touch us', and of course, the only information you had after the war was they were shipped into Poland. When the war came some of the neighbours very kindly informed the authorities that my father was a German sympathiser. We had a visit from the Security Police. They were totally cleared, exonerated. They just scrubbed the whole thing. But you had that sort of person about. PAUL HERLINGER

Fascism in Australia had been on the rise amongst Anglo-Australians during the Depression and with organisations like the New Guard developing at that time, Italians, as well as Germans came under suspicion. In fact, anyone with an accent, including refugees from fascist countries, was treated with some wariness.

Every street had to have an air-raid warden, and they came to Dad and said, 'Sir, you'll have to be the air-raid warden'. He said, 'I can't be the air-raid warden, I'm in the Air Force'. 'Oh but sir you'll have to be, you're the only Australian in the street.' They must have been all the Jewish migrants you see, that's all I can put it down to. BRENDA HUMBLE

My parents kept well out of the war. As far as Dad was concerned, he served in the First World War, and Dad was British and that was it, he was not interested in that. Some of the *paesani* you can call them, the people who come from the poor part of Sicily, sort of thought that Mussolini was wonderful, and he was doing a tremendous job for them. And so they joined the fascist party, well, they were immediately interned. They asked us all the time, my brother and myself to join, but we never would. I know of one case of one cousin of mine, who although he was a British subject, was interned, and his three sons were in the army. My brother was a brilliant artist.[2] He graduated in Italy, cum laude,

---

1   British Prime Minister, Neville Chamberlain, attempted to limit Hitler's aggression in Europe by negotiation and a policy of appeasement. In September 1938 he agreed in Munich to the cession of the Czech Sudeten territories to Germany, averting the outbreak of war. He returned to England a popular hero for having achieved 'peace in our time'.

2   Virgil Joseph Lo Schiavo, 1909–1971. Born Salina, Aeolian Islands. Emigrated to Sydney 1912. Graduated from Sydney University and from Rome and Florence art academies. Won Sulman Prize in 1945 for 'Tribute to Shakespeare', which had been painted in 1944 for Eastern Gallery of the Holme Building Refectory at Sydney University. 'Tribute to Dickens' in Western Gallery completed in 1952. Refectory mural, 'Mankind', completed in 1971.

THE JAPANESE COULD HAVE COME STRAIGHT IN

which is, you know, about as high as you can get. He did quite a lot of murals. I remember the feeling when Italy joined the war; he'd done a huge mural for a chap called 'Christmas' and this fellow whitewashed the whole mural. So that's what the feeling was like in some areas. In those days there was an anti-Italian sort of beef, the ocker type of Aussie, only that type, very few of them, but enough to make it awkward. So much so that when Italy declared war in 1941, they broke every window of every fruit shop, even the ones that were owned by Greeks and Maltese. There were two young boys killed in Woolloomooloo who were not even Italian, they were Maltese, but they thought they were Italian, they were killed. So it was a definite anti-Italian feeling, everybody was saying I was a fascist. Two big detectives came around and said, 'We've come to arrest your son', and Mum said, 'For what?', He said, 'He's been fencing down at the Italian club', and she said, 'What's wrong with that?', and then she said, 'As a matter of fact he has been in the army for two years, he is in uniform, what are two big men like you doing out of uniform, why aren't you fighting for your country, get out of my house', and they went, she kicked them out. I enlisted under-age and they caught me after about three or four months and discharged me, because I didn't have leave to join from the University, or permission from my mother, so I went back down to Melbourne and re-enlisted down there. Pig-headed.
DARIO LO SCHIAVO

"We seen thousands go to the war."

For many, the outbreak of the war brought the prospect of adventure and excitement, with some going to great lengths to enlist.

The showground was one of the first places you had to go to when you were called up. That was like the distribution centre. Where Moore Park Golf Course is now there was an army station there, barracks; Randwick Race Course, Americans there. And we used to get these tanks and cars coming down Mitchell Road, Alexandria, down past our street to go onto the trains, sending them up north, Darwin, Brisbane, those places. ROBERT HAMMOND

My youngest brother was born at the time of the war. My father waited till he became 12 months old and then volunteered and went in the Medical Corps. Apparently he said, 'I don't know anything about it', and they said: 'That's good, the less you know the better!' MERVYN JORDAN

When I was about five my father joined the Air Force and then, because of the war years, especially after they had the bombing, we went and stayed with friends that were out of the city. My father ended up being a postman in the war in Papua in New Guinea. He enjoyed it, he used to send us food parcels: Lifesavers, Violet Crumble Bars, all these lovely lollies that we couldn't get, because it was rationing, you see. JUDY CHAMBERS

My father loved the war really, actually he put his age down to go, he really enjoyed his time in New Guinea, he looked on it as an adventure. He was very popular with all the soldiers, and they'd get rations and things from the Red Cross, fruit cake in tins, and he used to send that home to us. And they'd get drink rations too, and he wasn't a great drinker, he used to give them to the other soldiers, so he was extremely popular. He was just a private, I never heard of him actually in a fight, he was always in a supportive role, although he got some sort of bayonet

(National Library)

wound, I think he might've fallen on it, they used to do a lot of night marches, and that injury came back on him in later life. GERALDINE OHLSSON

—

I had to falsify my age and I could not enlist because I was in a protected industry making war parts. So, I read where the records in Folkestone in Kent had been bombed and there was no records of births, deaths and marriages; it was all gone, the Post Office had gone, so I cheated, I said I was born there, in England. And the recruiting sargeant told me I was the blackest Pom he'd ever seen, because I was burnt from swimming. He said however, 'That doesn't worry us, as long as you can pass this physical, and written examination, that's all we want'. The RAAF was the only service that would take you out of a protected industry. MICK GREEN

—

We seen thousands go to the war, and Americans too. Everybody around Erskineville used to make cakes and stuff and they'd always be running over to beat the trains which used to stop there, and they would take the letters off the blokes and do things and give them things, because they were all going to the war. They were going for embarkation. TERRY MURPHY

Everyone got employment."

While many men enlisted, at home people were mobilised to assist the war effort by raising money, acting as air-raid wardens and 'spotters' or working in industries essential to the war effort. The Commonwealth Manpower organisation, headed by Nugget Coombs, had extensive powers to conscript people for industry.

Early in the war Dad was employed by the Federal Government to sell Victory Bonds and he'd have to go to various factories and make speeches and encourage them to invest in the war effort by purchasing a Victory Bond for five pound or two pounds or something like that. MICK GREEN

—

My grandfather was conscripted to go away, but was brought back because he was in a protected industry. They converted from making heels for ladies shoes, into making rifle buts, and baseball bats, and crosses to go away for soldiers' graves, and they worked for a mob called Pioneer Heel, which used to be down in McEvoy Street, and was part of Slazenger's actually. So, my grandfather didn't go to war, Dad was too young to go. Dad spent most of his time during the war as a messenger boy for the National Emergency Service, and pop was the assistant warden in the area, up here at the local school. STEPHEN FENNELL

—

Everyone got employment then, the Manpower was in, if you went to work you had to stop there, you just couldn't go and say, oh I don't like this job, because they just put you into Manpower and they'd be on you like a ton of bricks, you were in trouble, my word you were. And it come under the *Defence Act* too. ROBERT HAMMOND

—

My father didn't go to the war, because he was in an essential industry, but he was a Warden, and we had on the front door, a sign with 'Warden' written on it. He had a tin hat and a gas mask, we used to have practice runs, a siren would go off and he'd go out, which didn't thrill my mother because she'd rather of had him home. They used to go along the street to check that you couldn't see any lights. Under the stairs we kept some food and we'd all go out and sit under the stairs, until the sirens went off. They had bandage glued on the windows in crosses and we had to have blinds. When we used to go across to Manly by boat the lights used to go out crossing The Heads, so nobody from out at sea could see the boats and there were search lights always around. But the war didn't touch us very much, didn't worry us particularly. I don't think we really knew much here and we never worried much. BEV KARONIDIS

—

Mum was involved in lots of things during World War II: trying mainly to make people politically aware of what was going on; pointing out the difference of this Second World War and the First World War. The First World War was about money and the control of one nation over another. The Second World War was totally different, in as much as it was one nation who felt that they were far superior, and would just wipe out other nations because they were inferior, whether it was religion or race or colour. During the war she worked with ammunitions. BETH THORPE

—

In 1940 or 1941, I suppose, when the Americans got involved, Dad was told he couldn't join up, he was in a protected industry, working at Cockatoo Island as the crane driver there right throughout the war. It was very much a repair yard for mostly American ships and some Australian ships that got involved with the Japanese up in the Solomons and all that area up around the South West Pacific. One particular night, after the battle of the Coral Sea, an American ship was in for repairs, and they were doing some blasting over near Gore Bay and no-one had told them about it and he said, 'You never saw guns manned so fast in all your life,' because there was always the possibility of the Japanese attacking here. But Dad seemed to enjoy the war years to a large extent. TERRY GLEBE

" You'd always see the smoke stacks belting out."

They were conscripting everybody, even sixteen-year-old girls. They sent me to work for some fellow that had these factories and he was making up all these shampoos for ladies and I always had a feeling he was dealing with other things which was not so nice. I stayed with him for a week and I walked off. If you didn't join up, the army or the navy, then you had to work in these factories. But my father got me to go into the Tech College, and I had all these tests and they put me into doing draughtsmanship. But I was there for a short time and a girl that I was studying with came in one day and she'd got a job with the navy over in Cremorne doing chart work. So I thought well if you can get it, I'll try and I got the job. So I was with them for the rest of the war. JEAN HENDY

—

You'd always see the smoke stacks belting out, from Eveleigh Workshops, it was there all the time, virtually twenty-four hours a day. And there'd be factories opposite spewing out. Everything was coal-fired or wood-fired. And I think there was Metters down Mitchell Road, and Hadfields, they used to be in the war effort too, because they were very big engineering firms. Around the Alexandria area there was heaps and heaps of engineering places. God, I can name hundreds of them. It would've been a very big target. ROBERT HAMMOND

—

They used to have aluminium drives and rubber drives to be melted down for the aeroplanes and for the war fund. The scouts would go around. Rubber tyres and rubber balls and everything. And everyone in Paddo used to look at their cups and saucers and if it was 'Made in Japan', they'd smash them. It was incredible. KEVIN RYAN

—

All the schools went into raising money for the war effort, and so we had days when your mother would make toffees or chocolate crackles. And that went on for the whole six years of the war. People were scared and we all started knitting socks; they issued us with wool at school and we had to knit in our sewing class. We had to knit a plain scarf five foot long for the soldiers, and if we knitted that we were allowed to knit socks after that. And we did that at high school too, we knitted socks all the way through for the army, and I knitted them for my father too at home. PORTIA FITZSIMMONS

Opposite: 'May Day 1942' (National Library)

It seemed to be so far away."

Australian propaganda and government control of the media ensured that the general population were kept ignorant of the real situation in terms of Australian vulnerability to invasion by the Japanese.

We were concerned, because we didn't know what was going to happen, and more so when the Japanese came in 'cause they were on the way to invade us. In the newspapers in those days when they had the maps of the battle places, it seemed to be so far away. When you actually saw the atlases after the war, you realised how close they were. Maybe that was done so people wouldn't worry too much. But you never seemed to think they were close to you. Although it all seemed very remote, we were concerned at the success of the Nazis, going through the other countries, because we were losing the war at the time. People were going away, men and many teenagers, going away to war. One of my uncles was a prisoner of war in Borneo. He just died, of malnutrition and mistreatment. I remember the telegram coming, and all crying. Very upset. He was in the Medical Corps as well. MERVYN JORDAN

I suppose deep down people were worried, but I didn't hear them talking about it much because I think the war wasn't on their doorstep, it was over in the Middle East. They knew our blokes wouldn't fail, that was the atmosphere that came across to me. That our boys were going to clean them up, don't worry about it. ROBERT HAMMOND

People took it seriously alright, particularly when they advanced so quickly. Property values in the Eastern suburbs plummeted, you could of got any sort of flat you liked, right on the harbour for something like a pound a week, the cognoscenti took to the hills, they went like mad to properties up in Bowral. So, there was quite a deal of panic when that happened, but we stayed on through it. PAUL HERLINGER

"WE NEVER HAD A HOTBED OF CRIME"

MAY-DAY
1942

MORE PLANES TANKS. GUNS...

To defeat FASCISM

DEMONSTRATE FOR VICTORY SYDNEY DOMAIN SUN. MAY 3rd, 1942

ISSUED BY N.S.W. TRADES AND LABOR COUNCIL, TRADES HALL, SYDNEY

The Worker Trustees, 238 Castlereagh-st., Sydney. 40-Hour Week.

Dad used to be a Squadron Leader! But he basically used to choose the pilots. We knew a lot because of Dad's stories, the Air Force didn't have any guns, the men had pieces of wood made to look like guns, and I think Dad had a pistol. Everybody was over in the Middle East, that was the disgusting part, and the Japanese, if they had of known, they could have come straight in and there would have been no opposition because we didn't have anything. We had two flying boats, that used to go up North to New Guinea and back on twenty-four-hour continual flying, to make the Japs think we had a lot more than we had, we only had two flying boats in the country. BRENDA HUMBLE

—

People think Darwin got bombed a few times, it wasn't, it was bombed sixty-eight times, I was there through most of them. I remember seeing Darwin a sea of flame, the city itself, a sea of flame, and the harbour all on fire, because it all caught fire, and about a dozen ships (American's) on their sides, sunk, you know. But as far as they go, the Americans were resented, the civilian population thought they didn't need them. I'd say the general civilian population didn't know how dangerous it was. See, when we got hit in Darwin, the news read 29 killed, there were 2500 killed in the first raids. They kept us quiet because there would have been a panic, right? In the city, we knew 'cause we buried them, I was in a hospital up there, we had to bury them. If you go up and see the hospital, the cemetery up there, you'd be surprised how many graves were there. We were hit hard. That's where I got hurt. It was about the third or fourth or fifth week of the raids. A retaliatory measure from the Japanese, because one of their hospitals were bombed, they bombed us, and they dropped a 500-pounder, and the concussion picked me up and blew me through the wall of the X-ray room; it was only fibro-cement, but it broke my back. I was working in X-ray then, I was a qualified radiographer, staff sergeant. I couldn't move my legs for three weeks, but I had to keep working, because I was the only radiographer within two hundred miles. So I worked in my wheelchair. I got a chap to position the patients, and I just lived on APC's, sixteen to eighteen a day to keep going. The worst part was when my legs started to come back, they said, 'Oh, you're going to get pins and needles,' this is like pins and needles ten times over, but they do come back. But still, you know, the damage was permanent. None of us got hurt apart from me. They used 'daisy cutters', they are bombs that hit the ground and explode sideways, sending out shrapnel, so if you are near them, your legs get cut off. Luckily, my tent was shredded, if I had been in my tent I would have been killed. DARIO LO SCHIAVO

I am sure I heard 'Ashdown' crumble."

The shelling of Sydney by the Japanese brought the reality of the war a little too close to home for many residents. Reactions ranged from panic and excitement to 'roll over and go back to sleep'. Some believed that invasion was imminent and were prepared to kill their families and themselves rather than surrender, not surprisingly, that particular recollection imbued more horror than the actual prospect of invasion.

When the Japanese came into the harbour, we spent the night under the stairs at 'Kelburn Hall', Elizabeth Bay, wondering what was happening. There was one hell of a racket, we knew something was going on. I don't think we were really terrified, more uneasy. But one old lady in the flats said something that rather shook us a bit, 'I am sure I heard "Ashdown" crumble.' I remember that phrase quite well; 'Ashdown' was a fairly new block of flats up there, and I thought, 'God if that's crumbled the rest of us won't be long behind it,' but 'Ashdown' is still there as far as I know. The following day we heard what had actually happened, and a training boat with a hundred odd sailors had been sunk by the Japanese, and many of the sailors had been killed. The two subs had been stopped, and the crew killed; apparently they were aiming at a ship, a US ship

Damage from the Japanese submarine attack on Sydney. (ACP)

called the *Chicago* which was loaded to the gunnels with high explosives, perhaps if they'd got that things could've been a lot worse. PAUL HERLINGER

—

I was coming home from Newtown one night and of course it was dark, the blackouts were on. I was walking down Henderson Road and right in front of me I could see all these bright lights, and everything going up and I thought someone had fireworks on, and I thought to myself 'That can't be fireworks'. I just looked at it in amazement, to see how the white and blue and the little red between it. I didn't think any more of it until the next day when there was a hell of a scatter on with the Japs bombing Coogee and Bondi. And of course we were very close to Alexandria Goods Yards where there was a lot of activity with the army using the railways and trains. And over at Moore Park they had the barracks there,

the showgrounds, all along there. ROBERT HAMMOND

—

I was called up as a messenger boy for the National Emergency Services, because I had a push bike. When the Japanese came into the harbour the sirens went, the blackout was on, and we all had to make our way up to the school. I had to deliver a message at Beaconsfield to one of the wardens out there, and the brown-out was on, all the trams were still running, but they were all browned out. We heard the explosion, we thought the Japanese were really coming, everyone was unnerved, they began to realise that Australia was really at war. SYD FENNELL

—

The day of the famous air-raid when the subs come into Sydney Harbour all my older brothers were at the war; my sisters were spotters up on the buildings looking for aeroplanes; and Dad was an

THE JAPANESE COULD HAVE COME STRAIGHT IN

air-raid warden, and he had to take off, like in 'Dad's Army', tin hat, gas mask and the big sign on here 'R.A.P'. My sister, Nelly, organised everyone; we all went to get a peg in our mouths and get underneath the table and lay there, and her and me brother Norman, who was two years older than me, filled up bottles with water in case a water main burst. There was guns going off like mad, a real row, and the next morning when I got up to go and get the papers, I was real disappointed because there was no bomb craters around. There was only one injury, a German bloke out at Double Bay, the shells knocked him out of bed and he broke his leg. He was interned, he wasn't supposed to be out here. But fifteen young naval cadets were killed on the harbour. Evidently when it happened an American ship in the harbour panicked and put all their lights on, and one of the subs fired a torpedo at them and hit the training ship, the *Kuttabul* and it sunk. KEVIN RYAN

—

When the Japanese sank the ferry I heard loud bangs and my mother was getting very upset about it, and said to my father, 'What should we do?' He said, 'Just roll over and go back to sleep, forget it'. Out the backyard he'd dug an air-raid shelter; I guess it would've been roughly about 1941, '42. It turned out to be a bit of a disaster because it's all clay around here, and when it rained it just filled with water. The shelf that he'd put in there, with candles and matches, was almost submerged by all this water. We had a peach tree in the yard, it was against the fence, and when he had dug out all the area for the air-raid shelter, he had almost covered this peach tree, and it always bore fruit every year because it was almost totally submerged by clay. But I guess they were pretty worried. People were selling off their places at Bondi very cheaply because they expected invasion. TERRY GLEBE

—

I remember the night the Japanese submarine came into the harbour. We were taken to a shelter. It was packed full of people, and the panic, and hysteria! I remember the conversation that went on between my mum and dad and it petrified me. It was

that 'the Japanese won't take my little girl I'll shoot you all first', and my father had a revolver, and was going to shoot us all before the Japanese if they came. It was sort of a thing in the district, a policy, the men would go and have a drink or two; they'd come home and they'd all talk that if the yellow man (that was said in those days) ever took over our country, they would shoot their family first. You sort of depended on that happening, that you were going to be shot, before the Japanese came. You shot the children, and your wife, and then yourself rather than let the Japanese make slaves of their women, and take their children. And that was quite horrific, trying to get to sleep with that on your mind. I saw the revolver a few times. My father had it hidden in the house. My uncle brought it back from the war. It was hidden in my bedroom of all places. JOSIE FOSTER

—

Opposite: 'Types of Japanese Aerial Bombs' (National Library)

TYPES OF JAPANESE AERIAL BOMBS

Issued by the Department of Home Security in collaboration with the Department of the Army

INCENDIARY

50 Kg.

OVERALL LENGTH : 3' 4"
BODY LENGTH : 2' 8"
DIAMETER : 8"
MAIN FILLING : THERMITE IN CONTAINERS

60 Kg.

OVERALL LENGTH : 3' 6"
BODY LENGTH : 3' 0"
DIAMETER : 9"
MAIN FILLING : PARAFFIN WAX AND KEROSENE

ANTI-PERSONNEL

15 Kg.

OVERALL LENGTH : 2' 1"
BODY LENGTH : 1' 5"
DIAMETER : 4"
MAIN FILLING : H.E.

1 Kg.

OVERALL LENGTH : 10½"
BODY LENGTH : 9"
DIAMETER : 2"

DUAL PURPOSE
(H.E. AND INCENDIARY)

60 Kg.

OVERALL LENGTH : 3' 4"
BODY LENGTH : 2' 9"
DIAMETER : 7"
MAIN FILLING : PHOSPHORUS BUNGS AND PICRIC

GAS

50 Kg.

OVERALL LENGTH : 3' 8"
BODY LENGTH : 2' 8"
DIAMETER : 9"
MAIN FILLING : MUSTARD AND LEWISITE

H.E.

100 Kg.

OVERALL LENGTH : 4' 4"
BODY LENGTH : 3' 10"
DIAMETER : 9"
MAIN FILLING : H.E.

250 Kg.

OVERALL LENGTH : 6' 0"
BODY LENGTH : 4' 10"
DIAMETER : 12"
MAIN FILLING : H.E.

50 Kg.

OVERALL LENGTH : 3' 4"
BODY LENGTH : 2' 11"
DIAMETER : 7"
MAIN FILLING : H.E.

60 Kg.

OVERALL LENGTH : 3' 4"
BODY LENGTH : 2' 8"
DIAMETER : 8"
MAIN FILLING : H.E.

60 Kg.

OVERALL LENGTH : 3' 6"
BODY LENGTH : 2' 11"
DIAMETER : 8"
MAIN FILLING : H.E.

63 Kg.

OVERALL LENGTH : 3' 4"
BODY LENGTH : 2' 8"
DIAMETER : 8"
MAIN FILLING : H.E.

63 Kg.

OVERALL LENGTH : 3' 8"
BODY LENGTH : 2' 8"
DIAMETER : 9"
MAIN FILLING : H.E.

A house damaged in the Japanese attack of June 1943. (AWM)

" Death and tragedy."

The first thing that everybody did was get the papers and look up the casualty list, to see if any of your relatives or neighbours had been killed. Every second day there'd be somebody from Paddo lost. And I can remember the day, oh jeez, I'll never forget it, it was the seventeenth of December, we were just getting ready for Christmas and Mum had got all the black market tins of fruit 'cause one of me brothers was coming home for Christmas from the war. And my sister come racing up and I wondered what was wrong and she went in the house and my brother's wife had got a telegram to say that he was killed on the fourth, it was 1943. There was that many families that that happened to, a lot of my mates had brothers and fathers that died. KEVIN RYAN

I associate the war with the loss of the favourite son of the family, my Uncle Laurence, who was just a gentle man that everyone loved. And he went away to the war as an ambulance driver, and came back, whether as a result of the war or not, with tremendous pain, with a very virulent form of cancer. He slowly died in Uralla. That was a tremendous impact on the family because he was the youngest of a large family, and he was the type of guy that would never speak ill of anyone, he was, apparently a charmer. And he was the one that was loved by grandmother, who had a big influence on me. The loss of Laurence on her was quite profound, so I associated the war with death, and tragedy. CLIFF FOGARTY

The Kuttabul *on which fourteen sailors died during the attack. (AWM)*

I had an uncle in the air force, two uncles in the army, and they all came back from overseas. One was in Changi* and when he came back I remember him coming off the ship, he was about three and half, four stone, he was reduced to this little, skeleton of a man. He couldn't sit. It took him some time to sit down at a table and eat. He used to sit with his legs up haunched eating, like Chinese style. He was just ribs, and he was very, very sick. For many years after the war he was addicted to dormalin, he committed suicide. He never ever got right. He had war neurosis and was an alcoholic and he never, ever got well. Josie Foster

* *Changi Island, off the tip of Singapore Island, was a prisoner of war camp. Many prisoners were transferred from there to the even more infamous Burma Railroad.*

My father came back from the war when I was ten, but he did come back on leave before that, and then he got sick in New Guinea, and they sent him out to the hospital at Concord. I never thought about my father being killed during the war, and there was no one that I knew well, who died in the war. I don't remember that my mother was concerned because he was in a fairly safe place, I mean they did get bombed and strafed, but it wasn't like going into the war, he was really fairly safe. He did suffer trauma to a certain extent, and he started to smoke in the war, which he hadn't done before, he became a heavy smoker, and got sort of tropical things, like tinea, and malaria. He came home on leave once and he got malaria, and I can remember him lying on the lounge with coats and blankets, piled really high, and he was still shivering, and the next minute he'd be boiling hot. Judy Chambers

THE JAPANESE COULD HAVE COME STRAIGHT IN

The Midget submarine being brought to the surface after the Japanese attack on the Kuttabul. *(National Library)*

There were a number of people who were in the services around here, and I think all of them survived. I remember seeing some of them in uniform, elder brothers of friends my age, one guy lived two houses down. My friend Kevin and I were coming back from the shop and his oldest brother bought us an ice-cream. The brother had been up in New Guinea, and as we were walking to the corner, suddenly he flattened himself against the wall, and we just sort of looked, and he sort of peeked around the corner, and I learnt later that he was just used to being in the jungle and you didn't just walk around the corner, a blind spot, it was too dangerous. I s'pose that would be one of the few experiences I ever had of what war was like for people, although I didn't really understand it at the time. TERRY GLEBE

I was born at the end of '44, the war was almost over, but I had my two eldest brothers Ray and Allan, they went to New Guinea, Kakoda Trail. I remember one story about Ray, he was a signal man, and they used to have a rope, him and his mate, and they used to climb ridges, used to take it in turns to go up, you know, and report back. Ray was lucky this one time: it was his mate's turn to go up, and when he got up the top of the ridge he fell back down on Ray with a bullet between his eyes. They don't talk, and Ray refused to collect all his medals afterwards. That's the only thing I've ever known him talk about, he lost his mate in the war, apart from that he never talked about it. WARREN RICHARDSON

"WE NEVER HAD A HOTBED OF CRIME"

The shelling of Sydney in June 1942 caused a rush on brown paper which was pasted across windows in the war years. (ACP)

" They built air-raid shelters in all the schools."

On the domestic scene, brownouts, air-raid wardens, bomb shelters and air-raid practice drills became a way of life. Food was rationed and public buildings were taken over for military purposes, factories were converted to supply materials for the war effort.

The war was quite exciting, we'd have blackouts and the windows were all taped up. We had an Aladdin lamp which was a great excitement, lighting this beautiful Aladdin lamp every night. It was really cosy in the flat. GERALDINE OHLSSON

—

They built air-raid shelters in all the schools, every school had the air-raid shelter, and we had a terrific old bloke around Paddo, Jackie McMahon. He was the skipper from the scouts, and he used to take all the kids and we'd go into people's houses and build air-raid shelters for them under the floors and all that sort of thing. And at school, everyone at school had to take a bag with a peg and cotton wool. You used to have an air-raid drill, and they'd blow a whistle and everyone would have to walk out in order and then put the peg in their mouths and bite on it, 'cause they reckoned that stopped you from getting concussion if a bomb went off. You had to lay down with your hand over your head, it was frightening. KEVIN RYAN

Once the war started the schools didn't do physical culture or folk-dancing or that sort of thing much because they always thought they were going to be bombed; once the Japanese came into the war they didn't have mass gatherings. In fact, we didn't have a proper Speech Day the whole time I was at high school because people weren't supposed to congregate in big numbers for fear of people being hurt. PORTIA FITZSIMMONS

I was five when it started, right, so as soon as it started they used to send out air-raid warnings for air-raid alerts, so we'd know what to do, and there were air-raid shelters built. The alert would go off and we all had to stand up and file out very quietly in sedate lines, and go and sit down on these benches in these air-raid shelters, which were just like round sort of tunnels, not underground. Once the all clear went, we all used to race through the tunnels going 'Oooohhhhhh' at the top of our voices so it would echo, and our bubblers were in there, so we were never short of water. And they had sticky brown masking tape stuck all over the windows in criss-crosses at school. Actually, Woolloomooloo School was right on the wharves, so we were quite near Garden Island and they had all the ships along there and along the finger wharves. JUDY CHAMBERS

On a couple of occasions we went over to the airport. Of course when the war broke out it was a taboo place, you couldn't get within cooee of it. But there was a railway line that run pretty close along there and we could go up the bank and stand on the railway line because it was only a goods track and we could see all over the Mascot Airport. We used to watch the planes coming in, the fighters and the bombers and it was very busy. ROBERT HAMMOND

You had practice drill. Maybe every second day, every third day. Both the school children and the

adults. I don't remember much what the adults did. But I know that you had black paper on the windows at night and you couldn't have your lights on after a certain time, and the air-raid wardens used to go round in tin hats. And they'd knock on your door if you were making a bit of a noise or had a light showing even a candle glimmer because of the enemy. So everything was in darkness, the street lights were out. Couldn't have a radio or anything like that. You had your dinner. You had a bath. And you just sat in darkness until you went to bed. And you didn't make any noise. I can remember the air-raid siren was on the 'Rose of Australia' hotel. The sound came from there and it was scary and eerie. There was an air-raid shelter in the school, and one on the corner of John Street where we lived in Erskineville Road, adjoining Charles Street, which we went to drill in. Sometimes after rain it would be so full of water and rats. And you would have to get in to your uniform, school uniform, and you'd come up to your waist in mud and water. If they sounded the siren which they sounded off just as drill, you went straight to your own shelter where you were nominated. You were taught to go there. I used to be so scared of going to these shelters. Not scared, the war never worried me but the rats did. You saw all kinds of things in the shelters floating around, like rubbish, and tin cans, and all sorts of rubbish people threw in there. People used to drink in there and go in there. They weren't pleasant memories. My father did a bit of SP bookmaking — I can say it now! Coupons were exchanged and we always had plenty of butter, plenty of sugar, plenty of tea, and black marketing was in. And you could buy alcohol, and you could buy tobacco, you could buy petrol, we knew where to get it all you know. JOSIE FOSTER

And there was sly grog all over the place, but grog was very hard to get, my cousins and uncles were always complaining that they weren't getting enough. It was rationed and for some time after the war too. There was a lot of prostitution during the war, the main area was around Woolloomooloo, it was very bad, there was a real lot there, but there was a lot

Girls of eight different nationalities from Crown Street School, Surry Hills, knitting soldiers' socks. (ACP)

around Double Bay and Darlinghurst. When you saw the soldiers standing in a row, you knew what was going on. But we used to sling off. Sometimes a soldier might ask if you'd like to join in the row, but you'd run as fast as you could. Up at Kings Cross and around Darlinghurst there were gambling places, Thommo's two-up was active in the war years because the soldiers used to really like it. Bob Slater

—

We had coupons; my mother wanted a watch, and she went down to buy a watch, and she had a choice of two; a white face or a black face. There was only so many sold a day. You had to be there when they opened. And I can remember my mother buying me a doll, and there wasn't much choice. We didn't have much trouble with food because they found out my grandmother had a spot on the lung and she was a diabetic so she was given extra coupons. She lost her

sugar coupons, but we got extra butter and milk. I had an uncle and friends in the merchant navy and they used to bring my father American cigarettes, he'd take my father on the boat, and bring them home under their coats. They thought it was a great thing to get American cigarettes. Bev Karonidis

—

We really suffered during the war years, we were denied pink icing for a start, and had to do without Santa Clauses in the shops at Christmas time and that was a real problem. But in actual fact we were rationed, you were only allowed so much meat, but it was a marvellous ration compared to what they had in Britain and elsewhere; we were rationed in butter, we were rationed in tea. Paul Herlinger

" Have you got any gum, Yank?"

The arrival of American servicemen in Sydney brought a glimpse of an affluent lifestyle rarely seen by most children. Women also took the opportunity for romance with men who had both a foreign charm and money. The Americans were renowned for their generosity.

I **thought it was great when the Americans** come here. Kids used to get around the town where the Yanks were and they'd get cigarettes off them, and they used to get chewing gum or a chocolate bar, it was good, and something different, so many different Americans, like army, navy and marines. We eventually got a radio and you'd always hear Vera Lynn, Gracie Fields, Bing Crosby and the Andrew Sisters, a lot of the war songs because there used to be a lot of war talk. My father listened to the seven o'clock news and it would be all bad, it wouldn't be any good news with the World War going on. I loved going to Luna Park, especially when the Yanks were over there. The Americans were very generous. Very generous. ROBERT HAMMOND

The American sailors used to come down here on R&R leave. They were nice and they were kind, and they liked children. They'd give us chewing gum, we'd always say 'Have you got any gum, Yank?', and they'd say, 'Sure kid'. They had their pockets full of it. I really enjoyed the Americans. They probably missed their own kids at home. My mother invited a few home for meals too, they often used to get invited into families, just as a family friend. And if ever they came, you knew they always had pockets full of stuff, so we thought they were wonderful. And they'd come down with mum sometimes and pick us up from school, and they'd be inundated by kids, because they knew wherever they went that what we wanted was chewing gum, because they had different chewing gum, they had long sticks, we'd never seen that before. We could get very few sweets because we were rationed with sugar, tea, clothing. JUDY CHAMBERS

I can remember the clean-cut American soldiers moving around at The Cross in wartime as being charming people. They were so friendly when you'd meet them. One memory that comes to my mind: I was with my mother, we were out at Manly, and I got a ride on a dodgem car. And as I came in, full of the exuberance of being in this dodgem car, my mother had another ticket there for me. It turned out that an American soldier had been there, and he gave money to my mother, just asking her would she mind, can you give your boy another ride, because I am getting so much pleasure out of just watching him, because his own lad probably would've been back home, and he was associating me with his own kid. So I remember that friendliness and I had no fear of the Americans. They were generous and charming, the type of people that I met, they were the good guys in my youth. The American army police all seemed like giants to me, but I never saw them roughing anyone up. CLIFF FOGARTY

The showground was a staging area and was pretty busy during the war. There were always Americans in this house, it was always busy, and lots of parties going on, lots of sing-a-longs, especially with my father being Canadian, and having lived in the States. Dad was working at Cockatoo Island and lots of American ships were in, lots of American sailors. And my mother worked at the American Club in Pitt Street. The Americans were very popular in the house here, and with people around the place because they always had chocolates, they always had lollies, they always had clothing, they had everything. I heard occasionally, when the Americans weren't around, that perhaps they weren't too popular with the Australian servicemen, there was that attitude that they always had too much, more than what the Australians had. My experience of the Americans is essentially that they were just a great mob of guys having a good time. TERRY GLEBE

"WE NEVER HAD A HOTBED OF CRIME"

96

'Fond Farewells' as the USS Lowry *prepares
to leave Sydney. (ACP)*

Sid Constable and Bill Wilkins of Surry Hills collecting coins thrown by Americans into the Archibald Fountain. (ACP)

Then there were the Americans. Black marketeering became more prevalent, when they came. They could sell local foods and so on at a dearer rate to the Yanks than the locals could afford. Certainly the Australian soldiers didn't like the Yanks there for fairly obvious reasons. They took over a house in Macleay Street as an American club, the place was called 'Maramanah'. It was an Italian-style building, it had very elaborate ceilings and murals throughout, and they quickly plastered those over and put Donald Duck and Popeye on. It was a centre for the soldiers, sailors, their girlfriends, but I don't think we liked the idea at all. Paul Herlinger

There were some very, very beautiful old houses in Macleay Street and there was the Cairo Hotel, it was rather North African in architecture, something like you'd see in the film *Casablanca,* and it had beautiful palm trees out the front, really gracious and had a great big garden. I think a lot of American servicemen used to stay there in the war. In the 'forties you used to see American serviceman up at Kings Cross walking along in rows, with Australian girls. They walked in pairs one behind the other, and the women would have the most fantastic clothes on, a lot of them seemed to wear those long slacks with flared bottoms, and the big platform-sole sandals. Geraldine Ohlsson

"WE NEVER HAD A HOTBED OF CRIME"

Woolloomooloo children demanding autographs from US sailors. (ACP)

THE JAPANESE COULD HAVE COME STRAIGHT IN

Now while the war was bad, the American soldiers and sailors brought in a whole new lifestyle for teenage girls growing up, all of a sudden we had men to go out with. And when a ship would berth they'd walk up towards Kings Cross and they would pass the flat in which we used to live. Well they hardly ever got past the flat, either my mother would have them in or I would have them in or my sister, although my sister was married, but her husband was away half the time, he was in the merchant navy. It was wonderful, here was all these men, like after the great Depression, here's now all these men with flowers, manners, cigarettes for Mum, chewing gum, chocolates, taking you out to restaurants, we couldn't believe all this. The soldier was here for a month, and then when you went to look for your soldier, they'd be gone, they'd be shipped out and gone. That didn't matter, you got a new boyfriend the next day or the day afterwards. And they were very courteous, so then started the life of going out, dancing, wow, found out about jitterbugs, music, and all the things that came along, which unfortunately came through the war, but it was another lifestyle altogether. So actually as teenage girls and for women here, the war made things better.

When some of the American ships left harbour there would be a small ferry boat, and once, a lot of the girls went out on the ferry boat, *Rodney,* to wave goodbye and all the girls went to one side, and the ferry capsized. Now some of the American sailors were jumping overboard trying to save them. There were quite a few ladies, quite a few young girls drowned on that ferry. There was one ship that was stationed in Woolloomooloo during World War II, an American ship, the USS *Dobbin,* it was used as a base ship, so eventually they called it the USS *VD* because everyone on it had venereal disease.
JEAN JURD

It was a lot of fun with the soldiers, the stories they would tell, which I have no doubt were totally exaggerated. I had no sense of fear at all about it. Some of the radio serials like the adventures of Biggles, were high adventure stories, and a lot of the serials were set in war-time situations, and it was just one great pack of fun. TERRY GLEBE

Women were moved into many traditionally male occupations. The Women's Land Army undertook a great deal of agricultural work, whereas others conscripted under the Manpower organisation worked in armaments factories or in other industrial settings. Thus, the myth of the helpless, hopeless female was irrevocably debunked. (ACP)

The war broke up their marriage."

The war changed life irrevocably. While not everyone suffered tragedy, the social changes that had come from an economy that had been artificially restructured to meet the crisis had wide-ranging social implications. The immediate feeling when the war ended, however, was one of relief and joy with sadness and regret for those who had not survived.

One of my happiest memories was the day my brother came home from the war. We knew he was coming home and he'd been away for a damn long time, and we were sittin' on the footpath outside and right up the end of the street we see this, looked like a black fellow walk around the corner in an army uniform. He had his gun and his haversack and dilly bag over his shoulder, and we took off and we all run flat out and we all jumped on him, and he walked down the street with me and two brothers all hanging on him, you know. Yeah, I'll never forget that. KEVIN RYAN

I actually can remember being in Kings Cross when the war ended and being lifted up by the people around me. There was a sense, this tremendous relief and joy. I can visualise the place. I suppose I heard through word of mouth, as a kid I picked up that this dreadful war was over and you would be able to buy cars, and footballs, those things which we couldn't have and Coca-Cola and fountain pens, which you know we could never have, and biros. CLIFF FOGARTY

But I remember the big warships coming in and the soldiers coming off and waiting for a loved one to come, and the excitement, but with the sadness in those whose loved ones didn't come back. So my early memories are of being happy and sad. Happy and sad and frightened. JOSIE FOSTER

When it stopped, it became more exciting. Well, the lights came back on, you see, there was more to do, you could go out at night, you didn't have to have blackout curtains up. You didn't have to be so careful about everything. My dad came home, the only thing I remember about that is I put up on our verandah 'Welcome home to all the soldiers, sailors and airmen', and I spelt 'soldiers' incorrectly, and he went crook at me about that, 'You are ten, you should know how to spell soldiers'. I spelt it 'soldgers'. But I suppose when the Americans went it probably did seem quieter. I learnt to read at the beginning of the war, and I would read the newspapers as I got older. And when the war ended when I was ten, I remember saying, 'We won't have newspapers anymore, will we?' and my mum said, 'Why?' And I said, 'Well, they won't have anything to write about'. JUDY CHAMBERS

The war broke up their marriage because he was away for five years. Dad wasn't sent overseas because he had all these children and he was old, but they became different people, they were apart all that time, and my mother had to run everything, and she became very capable, she changed altogether. She practically built the house, she had to do a lot of the labouring work. Mum was used to doing things on her own. Like when the war was on, nobody had cars, and if any of us got sick she had to carry us up to the tram shed and take us on the tram to hospital, and that happened several times. There was a thing called the National Emergency Service; they made themselves a brown uniform, like a Girl Guide uniform, and she and my friend's mother were in that together. They went to lectures on first aid and made bandages for the soldiers and all that sort of thing. There was a camaraderie, because there were three women whose husbands were all in the army, and they did lots of things together, and they got used to taking the initiative. PORTIA FITZSIMMONS

The four Leedham girls, from right to left,
Portia (later Fitzsimmons), Carlotta, Loretta
and Anne in Centennial Park in September
1936. (Courtesy of Portia Fitzsimmons)

5

My parents talked politics all the time

Saluting the flag at Blackfriars Public School in 1923. Loyalty to the British Empire was instilled from the earliest years of schooling. Saluting the flag and the recitation of 'I honour my God, I serve my King, I salute my Flag' became a compulsory (and controversial) ceremony in the State schools when it was introduced in 1922 to counteract the influence of Bolshevism. (NSW Department of Education and Training)

South Sydney's political history is characterised by a dynamic activism; that's not to say that everyone was politically active, but many were, and passionately so. Oppressive working conditions and long spells of unemployment until the outbreak of World War II united people in an effort to enhance the living and employment situation of working people. The Labor Party was strongly supported, as was the Communist Party, and in the 1930s Jack Lang was a hero. Many politicians from the area, such as Bill McKell who became a Governor–General of Australia, progressed to State or national status, and are still spoken of warmly in the local community.

They killed the Germans for a shilling a day, and killed the Irish for ten bob a day."

For children with Irish heritage, republicanism and anti-British sentiment were an underlying element of their upbringing. But for many there was the contradiction of standing — as a mark of respect — when the national anthem, 'God Save the King/Queen', was played at almost every public function, including the Saturday arvo flicks.

I remember my aunts, Dad's sisters who lived in Erskineville, and on the dining-room wall they had a photo of Parnell, the Irish patriot. Parnell made a great speech, and they had the speech printed under Parnell's photo. And they had the photo of Abe

Connell, the great Irish statesmen. My grandmother (my mother's mother) her famous saying which used to be trotted out on occasion was: 'They killed the Germans for a shilling a day, and killed the Irish for ten bob a day.' I think that was her political comment on the English scene. MAUREEN OLIVER

—

The Easter Uprising in Dublin affected most
Catholic families, it was talked about for years and years later. We were very anti-British, very anti-monarchy, they were always republican. Yet every morning you would sing 'God Save the King', but at North Newtown School, they still also sang 'Advance Australia Fair'. Amelia Pankhurst Walsh was one of the daughters of Emily Pankhurst, the suffragette in England, and the wife of Tom Walsh of the seamen's union, and during the war, he was a bit of a rogue, and played a renegade position 'cause they were English, and during the conscription years and all the rest of it, they supported old Billy Hughes and conscription. GRACE SCHWEBEL

—

My mother grew up in Dublin when they had the
Black and Tans and it was a very frightening period for her, and so she was always very anti-British, my father not so much. But she would always support things like standing up in the movies for the Queen. When the Queen and Prince Phillip were first married and came here in the 'fifties, we went down to The Domain with another friend from school, my mother packed us up and we must've got up at four o'clock in the morning and all trooped down there waiting for the Queen to come. GERALDINE OHLSSON

The working class were very badly treated, especially returned servicemen."

After the sacrifices of World War I and within the memory of the bitterly fought conscription campaign, the high rates of unemployment experienced right through the 'twenties, particularly by ex-servicemen, was considered a disgrace. Working people became increasingly politicised as conditions worsened in the Depression.

Right up until the Depression broke there were still people out of work, the unions weren't really off the ground. And if you were in the building trade and you got a wet weather series there was no work, and you didn't get paid. There was poverty. Another serious thing was consumption, TB, a lot of people had TB and they couldn't work. Social Security was non-existent.

I was conscious right through the early 'thirties, of all the families being tipped out one by one, off Wilson Street [Newtown], that area facing the railway line. And those houses were gutted, nothing was left in them, people would raid them and strip them, the coppers were taken, the leads were taken, the timbers were taken and the floors were ripped up. The evictions of the early 1930s tied people closer together, made them more responsible.[1] Their husbands or their fathers went through World War I, all that terrible loss of life and their contribution to Australia's war effort, and here they were starving, no food, no money. It was disgusting that returned servicemen went away and fought for their country and here they were on the corner selling matches and

---

1 See Nadia Wheatley, 'Meeting them at the door: Radicalism, militancy, and the Sydney anti-eviction campaign of 1931' in Jill, Roe (ed.), *Twentieth Century Sydney: Studies in urban & social history,* Hale & Iremonger in assoc. Sydney History Group, 1980, pp. 208-230. For a work of fiction based on the Union Street eviction see Nadia Wheatley, *The House that was Eureka,* Viking/Kestrel, Ringwood, 1984.

MY PARENTS TALKED POLITICS ALL THE TIME

(National Library)

"WE NEVER HAD A HOTBED OF CRIME"

couldn't get a living, or even a proper pension. Even if they had one arm, or even one leg, they were battling even to get a pension, and even able-bodied men couldn't get work. I think they really had a hard time. Now, the workers were forming these parties and these groups to prevent the evictions.

People were very conscious, and if you were a family of four or five and there was one member of the family working, there was no dole, no one else got a dole, you all had to live on that one person's wage. During the Depression we would follow the dances around, and there were a lot of songs developing, ballads or they would parody the latest song and talk about the basic wage. It was a rising consciousness of the class system, and why they and others were suffering. And while they say all sorts of people at different levels were unemployed and that may be so, I still believe that the working class were very badly treated, especially returned servicemen.

Then during the 'thirties, about '32, '33 the government of the day introduced instead of food coupons you got one week's work in three, and preference went to married men and they started the canal system. The men were expected to work up to their hocks and necks in this slosh and mud, and they went on strike; and that was terrible, that was awful to think the men on the dole wouldn't even work one week in three. Anyway, Amelia Pankhurst Walsh was very involved in the Australia First movement and the New Guard—all that was developing here in Australia at that time. During the Depression, the New Guard would go out and belt up the men on the old stadium site at Newtown and break up these demonstrations where the people were demonstrating for more dole or whatever. Amelia Pankhurst Walsh took some of her friends, they were the Women Against Socialism Party, and the new Australia First Party and she got publicity in the newspapers, jumping into trenches to do this work.[2] So the next thing, she turns up at the IXL Jam Factory, it was three storeys, and had a long stair that was only broken by the landing at each floor. Amelia

Pankhurst Walsh came in to talk to these women, to try to get them to talk to their men; she took it for granted. She was doing the rounds, all around Sydney to talk wherever women congregated, to tell their men to go back to work 'cause they were starving their children. Now this was my first experience of union activity, really one to one, and those women, there were some strong women, they got her and literally threw her and her cronies down the stairs. Anyhow, the men won that strike and they ended up getting big bleacher boots and all the rest of it. GRACE SCHWEBEL

My father's father had been Irish and he was a bit of a Sein Feinna, IRA man, and we were brought up on that rubbish. He'd get maudlin drunk and he'd sing Irish rebel songs and go on. He used to get into all the anti-eviction campaigns. He'd go out and the police would come. They were terrible times. They used to evict families. They'd be given so much time on a court order and if they didn't adhere to that the police'd come down, and they would put all the furniture out in the street. And the people too, they'd physically evict you. There was no beg your pardon about it, no big brother system you know. LEO HANNAN

2 The New Guard was a militant right-wing organisation, opposed to Lang's policies, who physically attacked working-class activists. The organisation became increasingly fascist after a visit to Germany and Italy in 1933 by its New South Wales leader. The Australia First Movement, officially formed in October 1941, was another ultra-nationalist party.

Everybody was for Jack Lang, because he seemed to be for the workers."

During the Depression years, New South Wales premier, Jack Lang,[3] was considered by many to be a hero since he had called for a moratorium on the interest payments on the foreign debt, a reduction of domestic interest rates to 3 per cent, and the abandonment of the gold standard. Lang's decision to pursue these policies resulted in the expulsion of the New South Wales branch from the ALP and the exclusion of East Sydney's Federal member, Eddie Ward, from the Labor Caucus. Local loyalty however, remained firm.[4]

The big issues at the time were unemployment and the foreign debt, the overseas debt. Lang had his ideas of how the place should be working, and there was the New Guard, they were quite a strong group. My old man thought that Lang should've taken it a little more slowly; with a little more discretion he could've worked it through, but by forcing the issue he made himself vulnerable. The money we owed overseas he reckoned was crippling us [so] that we should not pay it for a period until we got back on our feet. Lang wanted to have a moratorium on rents and on all debts that were beyond your capability of paying. The Unemployed Workers Movement and everybody was in favour of it until the bank was closed on us. They closed the State Bank and then everybody got frightened that they might lose all their money, they then changed their vote at the next election, but prior to that they were all behind Lang. It took all the people five hours to walk into The Domain, to hear Lang give a speech just before the election. You could see that there were a lot of people supporting him. LES CROSS

—

The saviour of all this was the great Jack Lang. He was the great saviour who, like Moses, was going to lead them out of the wilderness. And he was fighting what was happening in England and the closure of the banks. And then I can remember very clearly the big rally in Sydney, the people all marched right out to Moore Park. Then they sacked him, they had to call another election, and everywhere you had the New Guard going around breaking up the demonstrations and Labor Party meetings. And those people that were in work were told that if Jack Lang got in, they needn't report for work on the Monday because he was a terrible, terrible person, he was going to introduce socialism in this State. GRACE SCHWEBEL

—

I remember walking with my mother and father, Jack Lang was around at the time, and people used to sing 'Vote vote vote for Mr Lang, he'll throw Stevens out the door, if it wasn't for the law we would sock him on the jaw and there'd be no Stevens any more!' My mother and father were always Labor voters, all their lives. My father was a member of the union. He had one job as a night watchman out at a fertiliser place and they weren't paying him the right wage, and the union came out there and got him the right wage. I remember he got his back money, and it was the first brand-new overcoat I ever had as a kid. I had a red one and my sister had a blue one. JANE LANYON

—

My father also took us to hear Jack Lang talk, and in the Depression a lot of people became involved with the Communist Party, because, you know, they saw Russia; the workers were supposed to be on top. Everybody was for Jack Lang, because he seemed to be for the workers. ROSE CLEMENTS

---

3 See Heather Radi and Peter Spearritt (eds), *Jack Lang*, Hale & Iremonger & Labour History, Sydney, 1977.

4 See Elwyn Spratt, *Eddie Ward, Firebrand of East Sydney*, Rigby Limited, Adelaide, 1965.

Working Class Hero — Jack Lang. (National Library)

When Jack Lang was going to nationalise the
banks I was with my father at a big meeting in
Centennial Park and within the next week was the
elections. Now, Lang was going to nationalise the
banks but the Englishman, Oppenheimer, the
financial ex-wiz and the Governor-General, they
worked a deal. Anyhow Lang was voted out. My
Dad was a rabid leftist and he was convinced that
Jack Lang was going to get in, that the world was
going to change. There was terrific excitement, you
could emotionally feel it. LEO HANNAN

My parents talked about politics all the time. They
believed that it was unbelievably sad what was
happening to the ordinary people that lived around
them. I knew Lang, my father and Lang were friends.
Everybody around here thought Lang was the best
thing. When I was a small boy I'd been down to The
Domain and heard Lang speak on many occasions. He
was a very good orator. Jack Beasley was almost as
good a Labor man. Lang's trouble was that he could
not get on with the New South Wales Labor party
machine, and when he got out he formed the Lang
Labor Party. And this branch went to Lang and so did

most of the local Labor parties in this area. But he was big enough a couple of years later to come back and say, 'There's no sense in staying with me. You go back to the Labor Party'. So they did. And they didn't do it sheep-like, they understood what he was saying. That to help the people of New South Wales there was no way that Lang could further help. MICK GREEN

" Anybody that came to the stadium talking politics other than Labor, would get the rotten egg or the tomato thrown at them."

Political campaigns and intrigue were relished. Politicians were known and causes were personally felt as election campaigns were conducted in the streets, with politicians and their supporters directly addressing the people. Speakers were a source of entertainment in themselves; heckling and the art of a quick riposte were greatly respected. There was an immediacy and personal contact that was lost as the mass media increasingly mediated the message in the post-war period and onwards.

In Erskineville during elections a Labor bloke would stand up on a box and he'd be cheered and cheered and cheered, but a UAP, United Australia Party, he'd get pelted with tomatoes, they wouldn't listen to him. They'd stand on the corner of Charles Street and Erskineville Road, outside Trippies fruit shop. No matter what the Labor would say they'd be cheering him. Used to be fun for us kids in those days watching them. BILL SCHWEBEL

—

At the Domain you could not move on a Sunday, I'd say there'd be at least twenty thousand people up there. Oh yeah, we had a lot of fun up there on a Sunday, there were some real ratbags. Some good speakers too, Donald Grant, he was a great labour bloke; up till '29 he was a commo, one of the great Labor people. Oh yeah there was some good'ens. Everyone was Labor mad, everyone. BILLY PASCOE

My parents voted Labor for the principles involved. But my own cousin who was a Thompson, was a foundation member with Dr Earl Page of the Country Party and that caused some confusion in the family to have this so-called traitor in the house. Anybody that came to the stadium talking politics other than Labor, would get the rotten egg or the tomato thrown at them, and kids used to love watching all the political games going on. One of the most well-known people involved in local government was Lil Fowler, she became the first woman mayor. But that came later in the early 'thirties. Everybody was politically active and very conscious of politics in the area. On that vacant allotment, that we all called the stadium,* there was always political rallies when elections were on, the politicians would get there on soapboxes, on a regular basis because the elections would run for about two months to the campaign. Jack Lang was developing then and coming up as a force on these social issues. There was Joe Gardner, Jock Gardner he was called. Jack Beasley was a bright, brilliant, well-known person, and ended up in the Curtin Government as a minister; but when they were young, they all used to come over and regularly hold these political meetings. They were great spruikers, great talkers. I was always missing, and if they couldn't find me, I was over there listening. I was very conscious of the stadium being used in 1931, '32 when an election was on. GRACE SCHWEBEL

* The stadium was located on the corner of King and Fitzroy streets, Newtown, and was a vacant allotment on which the Sydney Stadium had stood. It was an important social focus for the community.

—

In Springfield Avenue there were considerable political rallies of all sides, particularly just after the war when Menzies was trying to make his comeback. It was not quite a cul-de-sac, but almost so, and quite a reasonable place for a meeting, without stopping the main traffic. There were a lot of little meetings, and of course at that time The Domain was very, very important in its own way. You had all the ratbags about the place there, you know the Flat Earthers and the Communist Party, and every now and again the

(National Library)

Labor Party, particularly at election times. I heard one gentleman spruiking something called Atokism, which apparently meant money without interest, which of course would be of no interest to any bank. Newspapers were used a great deal, the radio was used quite a bit too by the major parties to push their views. But apart from that, the public appearances were the important things. PAUL HERLINGER

Mrs Green used to scream out, we loved her, she'd be frantic, she'd be screaming out about church and religion and everything. There was a lot of talk about politics at The Domain because the Depression was on, and there was a lot of wharf labourers talking about Communism to give people a better life, and about Lang and the unions and people getting together. JEAN JURD

" You voted Labor. That's all there was to it!"

The local affiliation to the Labor Party was strong, and although during the Depression there was an increasing interest in the Communist Party, the local political differences lay mainly in the Labor Party factions.

My parents were both so sympathetic to what was happening around them, with the people. And I think that's what made Dad go into politics and it's what made the people around here form the Australian Labor Party. He started a branch with a man named Tom O'Connor in 1923 and the great majority of the people here turned to the ALP when this trouble was on because there was nobody else to turn to. And they helped in every way that was possible. That little dance up there on a Saturday night: everybody would take up sandwiches and coffee and tea, and the men would bring the beer and some lemonade for the women and that was their night out. For my family, this house was the central place; for the community, it was the ALP. A lot of women were in the ALP. In this branch alone at one stage there was over 280 members which was a third of the population of the area [Beaconsfield]. Chifley and my father were friends, but I only met Chifley on two or three occasions. Very strongly opposed to Lang, and Lang, very strongly opposed to Chifley. But a good man, Ben Chifley, they were there to help the people. As my father said, and as Lang said, the worst Labor party, the worst Labor government in the world was ten times better than the best Liberal party in the world. It still is the Labor party. MICK GREEN

My mother was one of the founders of the Botany branch of the Labor Party, whose meetings were at first held in our kitchen and it wasn't unusual for Bob Heffron or Joe Cahill to be sitting at the kitchen table. She worked for Dan Curtain, and Eddie Ward and a few of the other local Labor people, and she was a great Labor woman. She marched in 1926 banging pots and pans with Jack Lang to the Stein song, through Bondi Junction. She was active in the Alexandria branch, and she's still a member, I think she's the oldest member there. Mum's always been strong, and she still has fun. HARRY BRENNAN

My parents voted Labor and there was talk of politics at home all the time. My dad was involved politically although he didn't have a position in the local branch, he supported someone that did, a chap by the name of Kevin Dwyer, he went on to be an alderman on the City Council. We handed out how-to-votes, put stickers up on telegraph poles. Some funny experiences there. We put stickers up one evening and the opposition come along and pulled them down. The opposition was another Labor branch actually, there were two factions in the area. We were associated with the Right. There were quite a few meetings in my father's place. My parents were Church of England, a lot of people believe the Right were all Catholic, but no. SYD FENNELL

Dad'd always go to Bill McKell who was then Premier, and demand that he help this person or that person. He was a very great friend of Bill McKell, who was our local member. He lived in Dowling

An official portrait of Redfern identities, Lady and Sir William McKell at his swearing in as Governor-General. (National Library)

Street, and I used to run messages for old Bill McKell, who was a legend in Redfern, everyone just loved him. I can remember, on election day, old Stanton Melick used to say to him, 'Billy, how much calico do you want?' so they could put the signs up to vote for Billy McKell. He was a politician everyone adored; he was so warm, and so accessible. Nobody knew if he was Liberal, Labour or what. Bill McKell was just a good man, and Bill never forgot his roots in Redfern, and the Redfern people of those days never forgot Bill. Sir Nicholas Shehadie

My father was an identity in the area, he was originally a plumber on the railway, and when Mr

McKell become the Governor-General about 1945 my father won the seat. My father was McKell's right-hand man, it was always 'Go and see Harry Noble' and Dad would see McKell and McKell'd do what he could. The most interesting thing that come about was, there was some rather dubious sort of people, in a lot of people's minds, and one of their friends was in jail and they wanted McKell to get him into a prison farm, where it would be a lot easier for him, and McKell did nothing. So they got one of the local Irishmen, put a new suit on him, took him up to church every Sunday morning, and he cut McKell's margin nearly in half. So McKell panicked, and he rang my father and said, 'Can you see them?' so Dad

MY PARENTS TALKED POLITICS ALL THE TIME

went and seen them. Any rate, McKell did what they wanted, and of course they come on side, and when McKell went, most of these people supported Dad. You only had to win the pre-selection ballot and you were in, and when the ballot was taken the returning officer, for some inexplicable reason says that in the event of a dead heat the candidate with the most primary votes would be the winner. Dad and Fred Green run a dead heat. CLIFF NOBLE

Dad was the State member for Redfern for 18 years, from 1950 to 1968. His name was Fred Green. He was the Government whip, but never a Minister. The sitting Labor member was William McKell. Then there was another man named Harry Noble that beat my father in a pre-selection ballot, and he was a member for about eighteen months after McKell went into the Governor–Generalship, and then he passed away. Then they had a pre-selection ballot with the usual ALP dog fight, and he won. MICK GREEN

I think I was a bit like me mother, because she had a lot of go in her. She was very political. She loved it, loved it. She was a Labor person, she never twisted. She worked on different election days and she used to work for the candidate of this area.* When there was politics on, in those days they had to stand on a box on a corner, and a local member'd speak to the people. In my time Albert Sloss was the State member — he used to stand on a corner just up there in Cathedral Street. He was a *local*. NELL LEONARD

* Nell Leonard who still lives in Woolloomooloo was very active in the resident action campaign to save the 'Loo from redevelopment in the late 1960s and 1970s. Those events deserve a publication in their own right.

Eddie Ward and his wife, if somebody was sick, they'd go and mind their kids for them. He was a minister in government and he'd do things like that. Beautiful bloke. My parents weren't really politically involved, in as much as Dad was very good friends with Maurie O'Sullivan and Eddie Ward because everyone in Paddington were. But he was a real Labor man, although I don't think he knew much

about politics, but if anyone said anything about Eddie Ward, Maurie O'Sullivan or Jack Lang he'd fight them. The family hated Bob Menzies. Everyone in Paddington hated him, 'Pig Iron' Bob because he was selling iron to Japan to kill blokes like my brother. KEVIN RYAN

Menzies was definitely neurotic. I mean, in the 1954 elections he pulled Petrov out of the hat. And it was on the cards that he would have lost those elections, and then there was a resurgence. Once you bring out the bogey man, the Communist. BETH THORPE

And the other thing is the stairs, the big stairs that go down to Woolloomooloo from Victoria Street, that's where Petrov used to leave all his secret papers there, on that seat halfway down, in a box stuck behind the seat and I think that's a scream, I don't know whether it's true, I don't believe it, but, you know, the seat's still there. BRENDA HUMBLE

My Dad was very big on Curtin and Chifley. Ben Chifley was always a popular name in this house. The man most hated was Menzies; he was considered to be the enemy of the worker, and I can remember my father listening to him on the radio and then switching it off, calling him all sorts of names, the meaning of which I would blush to say that I was aware of at such a tender age. TERRY GLEBE

I would say my father was involved in the union 'cause he was always saying, 'That pig, that bastard, that fat "Pig Iron" Bob Menzies!' He used to have a go at him all the time, he did not like old 'Pig Iron' Bob. He used to say a few choice words — especially when he had a few ales in him. WARREN RICHARDSON

Years ago, Dad and my grandfather were both involved in local politics, the Labor Party, and the DLP. At one stage I think my father was the youngest treasurer of the DLP when they first broke away from the Labor Party, when what they call their split was on. Oh, they were hedging their bets, a little bit each way, some of them. You know, the

Local MP Fred Green, Clive Evatt and Mrs Green with schoolchildren at the opening of Green Court, Redfern, in 1953.
(Courtesy of Mick Green)

Premier, at the time of the evening before the split was on, in 1956, was in this kitchen, and he was going to split the next day, and go with the DLP, but the Catholic Church spoke to him and changed his mind for him.[5] Yeah. Catholics got a lot to do with the Labor Party. STEPHEN FENNELL

---

5 See Geoffrey Bolton, *The Oxford History of Australia, The Middle Way, 1942–1988*, Vol. 5, Oxford University Press, Melbourne, 1993, for a discussion of the split that places it in a more generalised context.

There was a recession in '59, '60, and up until then my father was in property, and he was doing well. He had a block of flats at Randwick, he had a dozen houses in Paddington, he owned a couple of others somewhere else, only during the recession he went bankrupt, and he ended up with just enough to get the deposit on the place that we had down in Paddington. That was during Harold Holt's year. So he was a bit unlucky, and he's been very anti-Liberal ever since. GEORGE TOUVAS

MY PARENTS TALKED POLITICS ALL THE TIME

I remember Bob Menzies I s'pose. I didn't have any opinions, I still haven't got many opinions about politicians because it doesn't interest me. I don't understand it, I know a lot of people talk about it. I just vote Labor because I've been told to vote Labor. KATHY INGRAM

—

I remember Pat Hills, 'cause his name was on stickers all over the place, so that's the only reason I remember his name. This is strictly when I was just in Redfern, it was kind of the local theme. It was just kind of a given, you voted Labor, that's all there was to it. CATHI JOSEPH

As a Communist you were made to feel a little bit of an outcast."

Unemployment after World War I, the experience of the ex-servicemen, and then in the late 1920s and 1930s the devastating effects of widespread unemployment all helped to radicalise people. The lack of social services and the contempt with which the unemployed were treated when what little relief there was got doled out led to a rise in activism.[6] Membership of the Communist Party, however, never achieved respectability or mainstream acceptance in the way that membership of the Labor Party had.

My cousins played with Ray and Leon Lewis, and their sister was Freda, she eventually became well-known as Freda Brown, you might've heard of her as a militant communist. We'd all go round there to sing in the Lewis's house. They lived in this beautiful big freestanding house in Erskineville Road and while people were going off to church we would go over there and they'd have these workers' songs. We'd sing the 'Workers of the World Unite', 'Red Flag', the 'International' and all that sort of stuff. GRACE SCHWEBEL

—

As far as I know Labor politics would have been talked about at home, but my father, without him realising it, had Commo ways, yet if you said that to him, he would near kill you. We had a photo of

Stalin framed on the wall. The Communist Party would have socials that we went to. One was held at a place called 'The Button Hole'. You could hire clothes from there for functions, like fancy dress and that, but they were down in Liverpool Street, down from Pitt Street. PAT WRIGHT

—

We were always interested in politics in the household. Certainly we were anti-Lyons. Joe Lyons was of course the UAP, or it was then, the Liberal Party, Prime Minister. He was followed by Menzies, and of course Menzies made such an absolute disaster of the war that he was given the heave-ho, and Curtin came in. We were much more enthusiastic about that. We were always left wing. I remember feeling at school particularly with all those pro-fascist leanings of the school teachers at that time it was as well to keep quiet. PAUL HERLINGER

—

My parents met in the Communist Party. They belonged to the East Sydney Communist Party. They were very politically involved, I suppose because of the Depression. Basically it was an education, that if you were working class you either went Labor or you went Communist. I mean, my mother was a woman raising a family but only getting two-thirds of the male rate of pay, and that's a single man's rate of pay, and yet she was raising a family. So she was interested in equal money for equal work, better working conditions and to make yourself politically aware of your rights. And that's why she basically was involved in the union movement.[7] Probably most of the people who were on the executive of those sort of things, like the Unemployed Workers' Movement, were Communists anyway. They got into organisations

---

6 See Chapter 3, 'My father lost his job'.

7 Jessie Donovan [Beth Thorpe's mother] began living in Woolloomooloo in the early 1930s. As a working single mother, after a divorce, she experienced the injustices of the wage system and became a union activist and very active in the anti-eviction struggles. She fought for a fair go until aged 48 she died from cancer, thought to have been caused by exposure to chemicals in the ammunitions factory where she worked during the war.

Jessie Donovan on May Day 1941. During the war Jessie worked in a munitions factory and developed an appalling skin condition due to exposure to the chemicals. She became active in Miscellaneous Workers' Union after the war but died from cancer in 1958.
(Courtesy of Beth Thorpe)

where they could have an influence to motivate the people and to get them to lobby their parliamentarians, to get things done. It's like 'Sheepskins for Russia', I mean, there was a lot of Communists in that as well.[8]

During the war Mum was the Secretary and Phyllis Johnson was the President of the East Sydney Communist Party. A lot of women were active politically, because they were the women that went out to work; it made them politically active and motivated. She went to university probably in the late '20s, the University of New South Wales, so she probably got some political awareness through better and higher education; that probably started her off questioning certain ideals, certain ways of living. And then when the Depression came, well that made her very aware and she wanted change so it would never come again.

The Communist Party was very strong in the '50s, very strong. I mean we had Jim Healy, who fought for the Waterside Worker's Federation. We also had the Seamen's Union. Menzies took banning the Communist Party to a referendum, and there was another resurgence. They all got together and said, 'Well, it'll be the Communists one day, and it'll be the Labor the next', so that was beaten. As a Communist you were made to feel a little bit of an outcast. I mean, marching on May Day some of the younger people of my age, people you played sport with, and who were your neighbours, would probably call you a 'commo', you know. But if you'd had red hair or freckles you'd probably get called names anyway, so you wore it.

Another issue was the 'Ban the Bomb' campaign and that was the atomic bomb. That was very big. It was probably only a very small group that supported it. I mean, the majority of the population were fed propaganda, via the Federal Government and the newspaper editors, so that the public in general never got a chance to really think about the issues. And, I

8   See Heather Radi (ed.), *Jessie Street Documents and Essays,* Women's Redress Press, Sydney, 1995.

mean, it was only ratbags and commos that thought about banning the bomb. BETH THORPE

—

My father was a communist. Well, he named one brother Karl Maxwell, after Karl Marx, and spelt with a K. And John, his name was John Stalin — he was named after Joseph Stalin. WARREN RICHARDSON

" They weren't going back to that cap-in-hand sort of nonsense."

There was an expectation in the period following World War II that living conditions would improve. Industrial action had ceased during the war, but strikes became a feature of life in the late 1940s as unionists and ex-servicemen fought for improved wages and conditions. Later in the 1970s strikes were for social, political and environmental causes.

During the war years there was always complaints about the wharfies going on strike, and not without cause because the wharfies had the dickens of a job. They had no real facilities for meals, they had no facilities for keeping themselves clean and it was a dirty job. The method of employment for wharfies at that time was pretty terrible, you know before the war it was virtually the one ganger picking his men and perhaps selling the rights to the others. With the advent of war the union came to some sort of agreement. There were other strikes of course, rail strikes, but these were very occasional. Strikes came much more after the war; before the war people couldn't afford to go on strike. PAUL HERLINGER

—

I think the end of the Second World War was when things around here changed. The men that had served overseas were not going back to the dole; they were never going back to letting the bosses get everything and them get nothing. The unions become stronger. They weren't going back to that cap-in-hand sort of nonsense. Jesus! they'd fought the

Beth (later Thorpe) and Jim Donovan, Jessie Donovan's children in Brougham Street, Woolloomooloo, in 1952.
Jim came to hold many senoir positions in the Waterside Workers' and Maritime Workers' Union, retiring in 1999 after a lifetime of work and activism, much like his mother. (Courtesy of Beth Thorpe)

toughest enemy in the world and defeated him everywhere they fought him. MICK GREEN

—

There were power strikes in the late 1940s and I can remember the darkness; that was a very lonely period because you missed out on your serials. And it was spooky and dark and big large shadows on the wall from candlelight, it was awful. There were lots of strikes on the wharf. That was a period when people would go round to pubs and take a collection for the waterside workers. The waterside workers' wives would be on a committee and they would hand out the money that would go towards buying food, and the women would hand out parcels to needy families. That would've been starting from about '49, '50, '51, '52, '53. I was in a few of the marches. My mother dragged me in to a few of them and I was told to take a banner and march in support of the waterside workers.

My mother was very active in the Miscellaneous Workers Union: she was a union rep and she was also an executive of the union from probably the late 'forties right up until she died, in 1958. I think she got a job as a cleaner because she knew she'd be able to get a job as a cleaner and she needed money. And then once she became politically active in the union she loved it. She probably didn't like the work she did, but she loved being in the union. I joined the union when I was 15. I probably did that because I wanted my mother to be proud of me, because it wasn't a workplace where you could be active. We really didn't have a lot of grievances. That was at AWS Huntington, in Mary Street, Surry Hills. I was very much part of the Communist Party. I joined the Union of Australian Women, which is probably an offshoot of the Communist Party, because all of the Executive of the Union of Australian Women were Communists. So I really wanted to carry on the tradition of equality, of involvement and of stimulation. BETH THORPE

—

My parents were very political. My mother was a mad unionist from way back. My brother was a BLF member with Jack Mundy; my father's in the Plumbers Union. We were told, 'You don't let any boss stand over you and your work, you make your conditions alright for you'. The toughest I've seen was my brother out for long periods, because with the BLF he was blackballed for ten years from the building game. That's when Norm Gallagher come up from Melbourne and took over Jack Mundy's BLF and so my brother suffered the hardest with any industrial problems. Anyone that was doing buildings wouldn't employ him because he didn't go over to the BLF with Norm Gallagher and Steve Black. They came to my mum's house, well, we can't prove it was them, but they came there brandishing guns and you know, 'We want your son,' and all this. JILL EDWARDS

" **My mother, I'd describe as being a feminist before her time."**

Feminists had been active in the Depression years and during the war; in the era following World War II, women who had absorbed the propaganda about their capability to perform tasks previously only undertaken by men were not all entirely happy about giving up their jobs and status to men.

My mother got into trouble during World War II because she was a suffragette, right, and she was mad for women's rights. She chained herself to The Domain railings, she was anti-conscription, she refused to do women's work, as they called women's work; she said she'd either drive an ambulance or do nothing.* And she chained herself to the rails, and the crowd got around her, all men, and she was abusing them because she said women are slaves here in Australia and they should not be, and the police had to come and cut her free. DARIO LO SCHIAVO

* During World War II the Manpower organisation, directed people into specified occupations under wartime emergency powers.

I used to say to people that I was a feminist because my mother taught me to be one. When I was young, she gave me a really strong sense that women should have a right to do anything, and that you shouldn't listen to other people's opinions of what you can be and what you can't be. I mean, not that women could do anything, because she was very disempowered by society, but she was very strong. She was a very militant person, very pro-workers ... lots of really good attitudes. CATHI JOSEPH

My mother would never join a party because she said once you joined a party you're answerable to them, you can be a free agent and say what you want and be an independent force. She had that thinking from when she was a young girl; my nanna has told

me my mother was political since she was a young girl. In the book, *The Matriarchs,* she has quoted her teacher at Erskineville School, Miss Woodcock, who went to Russia and came back and told the girls about Russia and my mother said, 'You know, it's not how people tell you.'[9] And she always said that women were strong; my mother always told us girls we can be just as good as the boys or better. My mother's auntie was very, very political, and I think she got it from her aunt, Zennie Mack. My mother's always been pro-abortion too, she was always for women's rights, so she was always involved in the peace marches. My mother and I marched in the Vietnam War march and always in the May Day march. JILL EDWARDS

9 See *The Matriarchs: Twelve Australian women talk about their lives to Susan Mitchell,* Penguin, Ringwood, 1987.

MY PARENTS TALKED POLITICS ALL THE TIME

"The only thing that I can recall was Russia versus America."

The Menzies Years (1949–1966) were known for their stability and affluence, along with a Menzies-fed paranoia concerning reds under the beds. The Vietnam War broke the somnolent spell and, eventually, in 1972, brought to an end 23 years of conservative government.

My parents never discussed politics at home. I mean, if they did we most probably didn't take any notice. The major thing was when Kennedy got shot. Vietnam was a big thing, conscription, which luckily my brother missed out on. I remember Mum being worried sick about that. A couple of friends, boyfriends, went overseas but, I mean, you saw it on telly, the riots and things like that but no, we never really paid that much attention to actual politics. I don't think anybody local went to Vietnam. CHERYL LINDO

The only thing that I can recall was Russia versus America and that type of thing at the time. Oh I can remember John F. Kennedy and I can recall when he got assassinated. I remember Khrushchev from Russia, you know, and I remember Sir Robert Menzies of Australia. That's who I remember the most. ANDREW LAZARIS

I can remember watching on TV all the anti-Vietnam War demos, because I knew a couple of people there. I remember seeing Dr Cairns going for it in a big way, and I must admit, although I was still a bit young to actually go to war, I had a lot of sympathy for them. I couldn't see why we should have to fight over there, against something that clearly wasn't our war.

One of my cousins got shot, accidentally mind you. She was only fourteen or fifteen, and there was some sort of demonstration up in Taylor Square, and she was there with my sisters, and a couple of other male cousins, and she got shot through the leg, she's still got the mark today. Shot by police. He was just shooting in the crowd, and bang, she copped it. I can't remember whether that was about the war, but it was some sort of demonstration, and she was just sitting on a fence minding her own business watching all of this going on, and she had the bullet. GEORGE TOUVAS

Opposite: (National Library)

RALLY FOR VIETNAM

- END U.S. INTERVENTION
- THIEU MUST GO
- RECOGNISE P.R.G.
- SUPPORT VIET AID APPEAL

IN SOLIDARITY

MARCH ON MAY DAY

Saturday MAY 3rd 10·30 a.m.

I think I vaguely remember something about Whitlam, I would've been eight or something at the time of his sacking. They would've been shouting and screaming, mum would've been 'Grrrrrrr, how dare they,' and all that sort of stuff, but that's probably as far as it goes; they would've complained for ages. SHANE CAMPBELL

" They would have quite happily pulled everything old down."

The redevelopment of Woolloomooloo and Victoria Street, Kings Cross, was fiercely resisted by residents, assisted by the BLF. A partial victory was achieved, in terms that a high-rise extension of the city was averted, but in the process the old established community was destroyed. The majority moved out.

The 'seventies was characterised by high-rise development, it was going on everywhere. And there were plans by Londish to make Woolloomooloo into a high-rise sort of suburb, and that's what the fight was all about, to stop this massive development that was unchecked and there didn't seem to be that regard for history, they would have quite happily pulled everything old down.

There was the Residents of Woolloomooloo (RAG), of the five hundred or so residents left in Woolloomooloo they started to fight the developers, initially one group was formed and because they couldn't seem to agree on things, there was a breakaway group called ROW. Basically, again, it's the Eastern Distributor and it was the concept of running an expressway straight through Woolloomooloo and cutting it in half, but it was demolishing so many houses to do it. The initial community meeting was outside the woolshed, and a lot of those residents were sort of diehards, so they worked on the wharves. So I think the split was a pretty natural thing. But the Residents of Woolloomooloo was a group of about five, and they were probably just as active as the thirty or so that formed the other group.

At the time there was demonstrations going on all

A demonstration in Waterloo to protect the housing from demolition.
(Courtesy of Brenda Humble)

"WE NEVER HAD A HOTBED OF CRIME"

Anti-Vietnam War demonstrators in College Street,
Sydney, during American President Johnson's visit.
New South Wales Premier Askin is reputed to have
said to his driver, 'Run over the bastards!'. (National
Library)

over the place, it started with BLF and Kelly's Bush and it was Victoria Street and Ultimo and all over the place, so it was just a general sort of movement of residents against that sort of development. I can only remember going to one demonstration, after that I think Mum thought it was better that we didn't. So the one demonstration that we went to was Ultimo, Fig Street. There's now a distributor for the expressway there, but we were demonstrating against it. I think there was a loss of about thirty or fifty houses. I couldn't get over the brutality of the police; we were sitting down in front of bulldozers, but they just would physically manhandle people, and it was really quite shocking to me. I was in tears.

Mum got arrested down in The Rocks shortly after that one demonstration we went to. She probably kept us out of it at that stage because it did become quite dangerous when Juanita Nielsen disappeared. Apart from running errands and things I actually got to meet Juanita Nielsen shortly before she disappeared. People were disappearing and getting bashed and it wasn't that uncommon. It was definitely the developers that were behind the bashings and then they were backed up by the police for the fact that we were the ones who were doing illegal acts. The fact that Council was approving these hideous 35-storey office towers was beside the point. The original plans for Victoria Street was three huge office towers. There was a feeling of tension at demonstrations definitely.

And then I was quite actively involved in saving the land under the viaducts from becoming car parking spaces, so initially the campaign involved trying to fence the area off with, oh steel bars, bed frames, whatever we could find, and establishing a park there and keeping that going; I think we put in about two hundred trees. And I've got a letter from Tom Uren, I think he called me precocious at that stage; I was about nine. But we saved it, it's a park now. I used to go down in the mornings and stand by our little picket and ask people not to park there. I was physically manhandled out of the way on one

occasion; people couldn't appreciate what we were on about, the car is always king and they thought it was their right. Occasionally people would agree to park elsewhere, but I suppose as a kid that one incident stuck in my mind of this fellow physically moving me. JACKIE GRATTON-WILSON

" I'm not necessarily just a white person."

Aboriginal Australians increasingly resisted the institutionalised racism and inequity that had governed their lives. From the early 1960s when Aboriginal people obtained the franchise they became an increasingly vocal group in the community. Land rights and the provision of community services and facilities became contentious issues amongst Aboriginal and white groups. The issues were integral to the battle to wrest equity and resources from governments with a European heritage and bias.

The Aboriginals were really disadvantaged. There were disadvantaged migrant people as well, but the Aboriginals were really down the bottom of the pile. They were living in appalling conditions and they were really blatantly discriminated against. They couldn't find any jobs as nobody would employ them. When they were trying to find housing, they wouldn't rent them the houses, and also the police were harassing them and picking them up when they were drunk, more so than white people. They used to come to our shop and they used to say that they had no rights in everything. So when I found a job in 1972 as an Aboriginal welfare officer at South Sydney Community Aid which is still in Redfern, the migrants and Aboriginal people worked together for Human Rights, housing and welfare because they were common problems for all the people in the area. VIVI GERMANOS KOUTSOUNADIS

Jackie Gratton-Wilson of Bourke Street, Woolloomooloo, in a park established by residents in 1973 on the site of the proposed car park.
(Courtesy of Brenda Humble)

MY PARENTS TALKED POLITICS ALL THE TIME

My father was not involved at all in politics. Don't know why he never has been. Oh well, I suppose I do know why. I worked with the Aboriginal Land Council in Redfern for a while, and even though I am of Aboriginal background, my skin wasn't black enough for them. So you know, I've copped it from both sides of the fence, and I think that's part of the reason why he won't go into it. Also because, particularly with places like the Land Council, and the Aboriginal Children's Service, and all those sort of places, they are run by the one family, you know, it's like the Aboriginal mafia almost. Unless you are a direct relation to them, they make it incredibly difficult for you when you work there, and, you know, if your skin isn't black enough then they make comments about that, 'Oh you white people, you all look the same to me anyway, so what difference does it make?' And it's like, 'Well, hey, I'm not necessarily just a white person, you know, and I do have that history and that culture behind me as well, and I do understand it, and I do appreciate it, and that is part of my life, it's part of who I am'. So I think that's why Dad didn't really get into it much. He's fairly dark, Dad, but people often will ask, you know is he Greek or Italian, because he doesn't necessarily look Aboriginal, and I think he never wanted to set himself up in that situation where they could say, you know, 'You're not black enough for us.' He held on to the fact of who he was, and where he came from, but I don't think he was into banging his head against a brick wall trying to get things done, you know. COLIN BELL

—

My dad was really into sort of fighting for land rights and things like that. Every year we used to go to the land rights march, I think it might have been during Aboriginal Week. We used to march from Redfern into the city, into the Town Hall there, in the middle part. Everyone used to march there and just have a speaker, and people would get up and talk about land rights and things like that. But then they stopped having them, I don't know if it was about five years ago or more, but I remember every year we used to get ready, and dad would start makin' the badges and headbands and everything else, and get ready to wear flags and whatever.

During the Bicentenary, like there was a lot of focus on that, but I think that there also was a lot of focus on Aboriginals and whatever had happened and stuff like that. But I mean, yeah, we was there, you know, like going to the demonstrations and the events. We went down to Circular Quay on Australia Day and the marches went around, and we went to part of the march. 1988 was sort of like an important year, like, with fighting for land rights and demonstrations and things like that. DEAN INGRAM

*Brenda Humble and a girlfriend walked around Woolloomooloo
with five children and graffitied the area with anti-Askin slogans
during an early '70s election campaign. It was about midday and
they expected to get arrested at any moment, but nobody took the
slightest notice. (Courtesy of Brenda Humble)*

6

I'd work me arse out too!!

"The ordinary person worked in factories."

By the 1880s Sydney's factories and their workers were well established in the City of Sydney and to the south and west of the central city (including areas now part of South Sydney). In 1889, of the 25,000 factory jobs available in the metropolitan area, 15,425 were in Sydney and 2,822 were in Redfern.[1] With the pattern set, in the first half of the twentieth century, most people in Newtown and throughout South Sydney worked locally, or relatively locally.

There was a Panama hat factory up the top of the street, a sheet metal works and the big Alpha House boot factory, it was very busy in the war, they made the soldiers' boots. The IXL jam factory was on the corner of Golden Grove Street and Darlington Road there and down into Forbes Street, a lot of people worked there.[2] You could smell when they were cooking melons or pineapple or what have you. There was a lot of fruit and stuff coming in from the country, you'd see loads and loads of melons and things of that kind. KEITH MULHEARN

I used to love hearing the whistle blow at Eveleigh workshops, no matter what you were doing around five o'clock, you knew when the whistle went, that was the end of the working day, and the men would stream out, come up the street and go onto the trams. GRACE SCHWEBEL

There was a big Bonds hosiery and underwear factory down in Church Street. For years and years, most of the population around worked at Bonds.[3] There were several big stores: Sweet Brothers, opposite the post office was a large sort of department store; another big one, Brennan's, next to the post office. Girls used to get jobs there. ZENA SACHS

Newtown was residential and basically working class. Everywhere you looked there was factories. Down the road from where I lived was Bonds, a huge mill, there was Bradmill, there was little factories like the chocolate manufacturer, mixed among the houses. The main businesses were manufacturing and engineering. A lot of people worked in the factory system whether it was clothing or sweets; girls worked at the biscuit factory. Kirby's used to make the Silent Night refrigerator. It's one of the early type of refrigerators, very early models made in Australia. David Jones had a storehouse down in Camperdown, there was clothing manufacturers, there was Speedo, the big knitting mill. LEO HANNAN

Most of the industries in Erskineville was boot factories. Up the street was Walker's Boot factory, wherever you'd go there was boot factories; Makinnley and Ninnes, another one down in Park Street, used to make the Dally M football boots, there was a saddlery down the bottom of Rochford Street. BILL SCHWEBEL

Housing and industry co-existed, many residents refer to factory neighbours.

One of my very early memories is just up here where these new units are on the other side of Devine Street, Erskineville, originally that was Ross' Glassworks and when I was two or three, that burnt down, it was a very big fire. Then later on they built Spencer's Shoe Factory there. Also on this corner used to be a terrazzo factory, which belonged to old Peter Callander and all the terrazzo steps in the Museum Station and the War Memorial were all made in that factory. I worked at Nally's for about three years, I worked at Bruce and Berg's plastic moulding and I worked at another plastic moulding company down in Eveleigh Street. Later on I worked at the Bradford Cotton Mills, Bonds, and at Alexandria Spinning Mills. Old Friday McCloud, Reggie McCloud's father, worked over here at the Austral brick place, he was the panman. HENRY BROWN

John Hunter's Boot Factory at Redfern in 1912. (SLNSW)

There was Slazenger's [established in 1958] that made the tennis racquets, they were in Alexandria. Most of the industry around was shoe trade and my mother worked in the shoe industry, my grandmother had worked in it, all our family. My father was a tanner at Botany. We rented a little double-storey cottage in John Street, 68 John Street. It was owned by a Mr Poly who makes candles, and I believe he's still got his factory there. His factory was at the back, and he owned the three houses, and he made candles for churches and all that sort of thing. JOSIE FOSTER

We lived right opposite Metters,[4] that used to make the stoves. There was Hadfields engineering and there was shoes factories. The Lion Shoe factory, that was where my brother was taught a trade. My eldest brother worked in the city. Metters used to blow their whistle at twelve o'clock every day and at

four o'clock for them to knock off and that's how we knew the time. Peter's Ice-cream factory was at the back of that. And there was Barnes' Meat Works up in George Street, Waterloo; every time we'd go to my auntie's in Garden Street, Alexandria, you could smell this horrible smell of all of the meat being boiled down, it was shocking, it used to make you sick. BETTY MOULDS

1 Peter Spearritt, *Sydney Since the Twenties,* Hale & Iremonger, Sydney, 1978, p. 116.
2 See Grace Schwebel's account of life at the IXL in Chapter 5, p.109.
3 Dorothy Hewett's *Bobbin Up,* Australasian Book Society, Melbourne, 1959, describes life in the spinning mills of South Sydney.
4 Metters expanded from 18 to about 28 acres c. 1935. Spearritt, op. cit., p. 118.

I'D WORK ME ARSE OUT TOO!!

There was Bradford Kendall's, Austral Bronze, these are just to name two that employed over a thousand men. A great deal of the locals worked for them but when the Depression come they were put off. There was the boiling down in O'Riordan Street where they killed the old horses; skinned them and boiled him down to become glue; that was on for many years. MICK GREEN

—

My dad was a wood machinist, in the boot trade. He worked for the Pioneer Heel Company in McEvoy Street and for the British Last Company up in Redfern, making shoe heels for women's shoes. My mum worked for a period at the pickle factory, up behind Henderson Road, a lot of people in the area worked there. Alexandria was very, very industrialised, and most of the kids' parents worked local, at the glass works, or the steel places, at Frank Spurway's, Metters. Metters were very big in the area, very big. They made baths, sinks, everything like that. SYD FENNELL

—

The amazing thing was of a morning, from six o'clock you would just see one stream of people coming off the trains at MacDonaldtown station, which is at the bottom here. Going up to the hospital, to the factories up this end, or down through Burren Street, down past the public school, over the bridge at the railway, down over Erskineville Park. There would be thousands going to Metters of a morning, and then of an evening they'd all start coming back this way. At the bottom here, they had the cleansing sheds for the railways, they just covered acres, where heaps of women and men used to clean the carriages. My father worked up at Homebush in the State brickyards, a really hard, terrible job. And I can remember Dad getting on a pushbike and riding from Erskineville up to Homebush Bay and then of a night he'd come home, and Mum would have to literally lift him off the bike. Oh, it was a hard existence. A very hard existence. TERRY MURPHY

—

Rosebery was mostly residential, but there were some factories in one part of it, where Sweet Acres

(a factory that made chocolates and lollies) and the Wrigleys factory were, and the Eveready Battery factory was there but a lot of people worked in shops in the city. FRED FOREMAN

—

In Redfern

People were mostly all factory workers. Some may have been fitters and turners, but they were mostly all factory workers. A lot worked at Steelbilt and Wormald, which was around the corner, or the glass works. A lot worked at ACI. There was a lot of industry, there was the engineering works, there was the glass works. Claude Neon's was there; I recall Anthony Hordern's were there. SIR NICHOLAS SHEHADIE

—

Just around in Cleveland Street there are two nice cottages. One of them we used to call 'Spruso House' because they used to make Spruso Hair Oil there. They also used to make a product called 'Peach Creme Beauty', it was a hand lotion, and the chap used to walk a couple of dogs, and we would call him Mr Spruso, and he would give you, sometimes a bottle of the hand cream 'cause you knew them. On the corner of Redfern Street, there was a big barn sort of place, and they kept horses, that pulled wagons belonged to the McMahon family. And they had a place in Pitt Street further down. Our biggest thing was Francis's Chocolates, they're still here, up in Stirling Street, the back of where I used to live, and you used to always know when they were making caramels, you would always smell them. BEV KARONIDIS

—

And at Surry Hills

There was a big factory there, David Jones's factory in Marlborough Street, Surry Hills. There was a cake factory, Adams's Cakes, locals worked there, and then there was Anderson's Hat Factory. They all closed down, you know, and there's nothing much made in Surry Hills now. IRENE WEBBER

Workers at the Australian Glass Works in Waterloo in 1947. (SLNSW)

The whole vicinity was a Chinatown because it was close to Paddy's; all the Chinese that worked in the markets lived in Surry Hills and a lot of people worked in the factories close by. We had Silk Knit, they were mostly in the dressmaking; there was Waite and Bull Printers, they were in Mary Street; Ford Printers in Reservoir Street; the Catholic Press in Commonwealth Street, and Fracks General Engineers Store in Elizabeth Street; Jones Brothers, they made hats. And you had a factory that used to kill rabbits for fur to make hats for Akubra up the street. There was Paramount Pictures, the agents for the film studio. FRANK W.

—

My uncle, who was living with us one time at Surry Hills, was a travelling salesman. He used to sell pictures and smoker stands and things like that for a company called Gay and Chippendale. They would sell these things on time payment for a bob or two a week. FRED FOREMAN

—

We lived in a residential area there in Barcom Avenue, and then down towards Rushcutter's Bay and Boundary Street there was a factory called Lustre Hosiery. There was also Advance Tyres a lot of the people around the area worked in Lustre Hosiery. ROSE CLEMENTS

Residents of Kings Cross and Potts Point, in contrast to those of Redfern, Alexandria and Erskineville, tended not to work in factories.

People at Kings Cross worked mainly in offices. It was more or less professional in those days. The ordinary person worked in factories. There was a class distinction between the factory worker and the office worker and the wealthy. GLAD WILLIS

Very few people seemed to be in trades. I
remember one woman in the building ran a group of restaurants called 'Kookaburra'. In the main you'd have shopkeepers and machinists and office workers. Wives tended not to work. Although in and around our place I s'pose most of them did some sort of work, but in the main they'd be available for the kids. I think one of the advantages Mum felt about managing the block of flats was that she was always there. PAUL HERLINGER

We knew people that had shops, people that
worked in offices in the city. My father for a long time, used to open the Glebe Island and Pyrmont Bridge, he worked for the Department of Main Roads. The fishermen in their fishing trawlers would always throw him up fresh fish. GERALDINE OHLSSON

Mum ran the residential and Dad worked at
Amco, a factory in Zetland for a number of years, he was a machinist and then he started to work for St Vincent's Hospital looking after their cars, and driving the ambulance and then he ended up just driving the nuns all the time. CLIFF FOGARTY

Paddington was all residential and industrial in
those days, it was regarded as fairly low class, fairly cheap. There were a number of farriers around for shoeing horses, lots of nice big grocery shops, a lot of bakeries. One family used to run a movie theatre. Another chap was a postman. BOB SLATER

There was Hardy Rubber Company, Tailor's
Paints, Zips soft drink factory, a furniture factory; there was the quarry down the bottom of Cascade Street, and John McGrath's Motors down the bottom. A hell of a lot of the Paddington people worked locally. A lot of them were wharf labourers, and then the rest of them were Council workers and tram drivers and guards. Everyone in Paddington had their house painted from Taylors Paints, everyone wore Hardy Rubber sandshoes and there was a lot of people at Lustre Hosiery, everyone had stockings to give away. KEVIN RYAN

At Woolloomooloo

A lot of people worked on the wharf, and then there was Mitchells Factory which was a grocery packing store. A lot of them worked at Sargeant's Pies, which was up there in Burton Street. They were mostly working people, the professional people were in Victoria Street. People were poor, there was always a lot of unemployment. The neighbourhood had a few garages, a few mechanical places. They had Dalgety's round there in Dowling Street. And they had car repairs in one section, and in the other section they bottled Johnnie Walker whisky. They used to bring the whisky out in casks. We'd wake up in the morning, 'cause we lived opposite Dalgety's, and we'd say, 'Mmm, they're bottling whisky today'. I mean, you could get drunk on the fumes! JOYCE HIGGINS

Dad was a boilermaker I can't remember too
many who had full-time jobs, he was one of the very few. The Sugar House at Pyrmont, he used to work there quite a bit. My father used to leave home at half past six in the morning and get home at six, half past six, seven o'clock of the night, they worked forty-eight hours [a week] them days. That was half past seven until half past five, and four hours of a Saturday. He'd walk to work — you never had your fare — with his sandwich in his pocket, and a little bit of tea and sugar. There were quite a few wharf labourers locally; if they got thirty bob a week they

An amateur male drag ballet at Hibberd Meters Christmas Party, 71 Bourke Street, Redfern, in 1942. (SLNSW)

thought they were made. 'Cause it was two and five pence an hour I think, and you'd get picked up for two hours, that'd be four and ten pence, that might be the wages for the week. And there was plenty of times when you went two and three weeks and never got a job. Quite a few worked on the wharf stores, that was only seven or eight months' work a year, if you got that you'd done really well. And the rest was just only casual work; delivering ice, the fish market, in McCarthy's, that was a bottle yard, washing bottles. Another one, Butler Normans' was another bottle yard. The Elm Express started down here in the 1920s, it was all horse and carts. BILLY PASCOE

Dad used to take me out fishing when I was about seven. They used to go out when the sun went down until the sun came up. That's the only way you catch prawns. They used to trawl the harbour all their life.

He was there when the *Greycliffe* went down.* And when he was trawling, he saved a lot of people. Dad used to prawn and he'd come up with a couple of bodies, covered in prawns, and so he had to take them to the Water Police at Circular Quay. People were always sending him thank you notes on that anniversary. During the war Dad was the only one allowed to trawl the harbour. His fishing boat was number LFB, number three, *The Maria.* SAM DONATO

* About 4.30 p.m. on 3 November 1927, the ferry, Greycliffe, *en route from Circular Quay to Watson's Bay, was cut in two by the liner* Tahiti. *While some passengers were able to jump overboard many were trapped inside and forty died, including many schoolchildren returning home from city schools.*

I'D WORK ME ARSE OUT TOO!!

In 1944 there were 342 factories in Alexandria employing 22,238 workers, and over half the suburb was occupied by large industrial concerns. At Waterloo there were 17,227 and at Redfern 15,208 people employed in factories.[5]

Chippendale was residential and industrial. There were a lot of factories around, so there was always work for someone. They had Firth's cardboard factory; there was the Allen's Sweets factory; Scanlan's lolly factory; Yardley's perfume factory; a bottle-o place; and there was a tobacco factory. The people who lived there were all working people. BEVERLY HUNTER

▬

Factories were always the go; I can remember Gadsden's factory down the bottom of the hill. They're long gone now, but it was a factory which made tin cans and it was always noisy. We'd watch these cans running through the races all the time, and be told by the bloke, 'Get away, bugger off you kids, don't come in here.' There was another place that made tubeless steel beds and springs. But essentially, it was an industrial area, with houses, which were mainly for people who could get to transport easily to get to work. You know, trams here, just one block away, and five minutes walk to Central Station. TERRY GLEBE

▬

The wharf was like the start of our community, lots of people from all over Sydney would come there to work. There was quite a few factories, there was Kolynos Toothpaste in Brougham Street; quite a few locals worked there. And the men mostly worked on the wharves. One place published comics; we gave them a bit of curry running up on their roof, making a noise on the tin roof, and they'd come out and swear at us and tell us to get down, and we just thought that was a bit of fun anyway. Also, there used to be wool stores and we'd go in on the wool bales and jump all over the wool bales just to get the foreman or somebody to come out to tell us to get to buggery out of it; it was a game. The ice works was right down on the Woolloomooloo waterfront. BETH THORPE

In Surry Hills there used to be a lot worked for the Council and the railways, public transport. I remember often seeing 'em walking up with their navy blue or dark blue shirt and pants on, and their caps, you know, they were either the tram drivers or tram conductors. And there'd be a lot used to work at the railway at Eveleigh, there was always heaps of people there. Opposite was W.C. Penfolds, the printers. And next to that there was a few more factories, there was a printing factory, there was Dux Hot Water Service. This was all in a small area. Fountain's Tomato Sauce, that was a good place. Next to that there used to be a film factory. I don't know if they produced films there or what they did. When you went down into Elizabeth Street there was a little machine shop, like an engineering machine shop. There was a few residential houses, ordinary houses. There used to be a 'Money Lent' place, a couple of restaurants, a butcher's, and there was wine shops everywhere. The *Daily Mirror* was only a stone's throw away. There was a variety of little shops and businesses around. The Boomerang Toy Company used to be down the bottom of Clisdell and Butt Street on the corner. WARREN RICHARDSON

▬

Dad's first jobs were in the aircraft industry; he was an aircraft fitter out at Kingsford Smith Airport and he worked for Butler Airlines, which later became Ansett. And then he got a job at Email, in those days it was called Sydney Cook, so he was a fitter in a factory making nails and wire and stuff and that was at Alexandria. BRENDAN DOYLE

▬

A lot of people worked locally, a lot of men worked in the goods station at Alexandria, the goods yard in Garden Street. That went from Garden Street right down almost to Erskineville, over the railway line. When you left school you could go from job to job, if you didn't like it, just leave it and go to another job. HARRY BRENNAN

---

5 Spearrit, op. cit., p. 117.

David Jones production branch factory in Marlborough Street, Surry Hills, in 1956. (SLNSW)

Redfern used to be the centre point where most of the migrant people came, mainly because of the fact that there was heavy and light industry and manufacturing industry in Botany, Mascot, Alexandria, in all of those areas, whereas now, of course, most of them are big warehouses. A lot of the migrants were unskilled and were brought here so they could develop the country; what I call as 'factory fodder'. Most of them couldn't speak English, so they used to come to the shop and sit there looking worried and sometimes crying because they couldn't communicate, they couldn't find jobs, they couldn't find accommodation. Me and my two brothers who learnt English very quickly, used to take them to the factories to look for jobs. Crown Glass was a very famous place, practically everybody went through there. VIVI GERMANOS KOUTSOUNADIS

A lot of them worked down there on the wharves and they would come in and get lunch and that. The Frisco Hotel had the Frisco Flyer and it was an old bus, you know, poor old thing! It would go down to Garden Island to pick the guys up and bring them back so they could have a couple of drinks and have lunch at the pub. It was a roaring success because then they could have their drink and not get into trouble for getting back to work late. You had your navy stores, your printers and you had your Commonwealth cars; you had the navy trucks, which is now where the school is. You had your tyre factories, the printers were all opposite our place virtually, you know, so it was all mixed. Of course we had Harry de Wheels down there. CHERYL LINDO

In the 1960s

My grandfather used to work at the old Morris factory, or BMC. They used to make the Mini-Minors and the Morris's at Zetland. And when my grandfather first got a job there and somebody else wanted a job, he'd say, 'I'll get you a job there' and before you knew it five guys in the same block of Woolloomooloo are working in the same factory. I can recall my grandfather buying an old Holden station wagon. His work mates would meet him out the front of the house every morning, they'd all get a ride together and at the end of the week they gave him two bob or twenty cents or whatever towards the petrol. ANDREW LAZARIS
—

In the Darlington neighbourhood there were
factories, but they were a bit further down, closer to Broadway. There was a chewing-gum factory, Scanlon's was down there. Dad was a wharfie. Mum was at home with us until we were at school. We had a small corner shop and Mum bought into this, so she worked there and we'd go there after school. But she also had cleaning jobs, at the university for a while. SUSAN ALLOWAY
—

Some Waterloo people worked in the city, and
some probably would have worked at Alexandria, working in shops, on counters, assistants, but I think mainly in the city, or even Botany area, or around the South Sydney area itself. A lot of people would try and do anything, work in a hairdressing salon, or at Coles as a check-out person, at the butcher's, a lot of the men used to work at the butcher's for some reason. A lot of them worked for the Council. A lot of people did cleaning work, a lot of people had second jobs, driving cabs. A lot of people were studying at the time, going to uni; a lot of people were new to the country, so that's the only place they could live, and so they did that. But then people would be living there for generation upon generation, who still do the same thing. My dad finished his degree and was working for a quantities surveyor. At first, it was hard, he was working in a tobacco factory. He had sort of a certificate from Nigeria, which didn't mean anything here, so because he is really, really quick, really, really intelligent, he thought, OK, this is what I want to do, and worked it out, got into Uni. ESOSA EQUAIBOR
—

My father has worked for the last twenty-five years
with Sydney County Council, Electricity. He cleans electrical sub-stations, those sort of green boxes you see everywhere with the transformers and things inside them. It's his job to go in and make sure they are not too dusty and ready to explode and things like that. He has been doing that for the last twenty-five years. I don't know whether he enjoys it or not, but he does it. My father is the type of man that thinks that you get a job and you stay with it. COLIN BELL

The Hasty Tasty at 86 Darlinghurst Road, Kings Cross – the American influence of fast food, hamburgers and coffee had infiltrated the area as early as April 1940. (SLNSW)

❝ They thought it was great to be able to go out and work and be equal to a man."

In Australia prior to World War II only 5 per cent of married women were undertaking paid work. In 1939, some 19 per cent of women workers were domestic workers, but thanks to war industries, the number reduced to 4.4 per cent. The character of work changed as opportunities gradually opened up in industry and commerce.[6]

My mother used to work in a laundry, it was a big Standard Steam Laundry down in Woolloomooloo, and then there was one in Surry Hills, Wilson Steam Laundry, and they used to do all the washing for the boats that came in, the American boats, and the P&O Liners. She left work to have my sister when I was fourteen, see, and she couldn't go to work after that. IRENE WEBBER

Mum was a washer woman and incubator and she used to do a bit of midwifery. There was a Nurse Mirth who lived in Wilson Street, Newtown, and when she wanted a midwife to help her, she used to get Mum, 'cause having nine kids she was experienced. BILL SCHWEBEL

6 Charlie Fox, *Working Australia*, Allen & Unwin, 1991, Sydney, p. 136.

I'D WORK ME ARSE OUT TOO!!

The women seemed to do more work than the
men because most of the women seemed to get jobs doing housework in the flash parts, but very, very poorly paid. My mum was one of the few that didn't, but most did. A terrible lot used to work in picture shows as usherettes, cleaning the picture show out, scrubbing the foyer out the front; that used to make you cry, you'd see a poor old woman out there down on her hands and knees, scrubbing the foyer at six o'clock in the morning, and think, that poor old bugger there, must be sixty. A pin-up job for a girl in them days was out at Raleigh Park if you got a job there, you were made because that was one place they didn't put you off, you were there for life if you got a job at Wills. Some girls started there when they were fifteen and they were still there when they were fifty, yeah, Raleigh Park, that was a job. And a good job for a boy if you ever got one, but you had to be very lucky, you knew someone who knew someone. It was stable and it was permanent.[7] BILLY PASCOE

The only time women worked, was when there
was a wharfies strike. And that must've been, I suppose when I was about ten and then the women started to go out, and take in people's ironing and scrub floors, because the wharfies were on strike for *such* a long time.[8] It was a very big strike. But other than that women didn't work. JOYCE HIGGINS

In the early years before my father's business
started to build up, Mum went to work in town, with Reuben Brash's, cleaning the toilets or the cloak room; there would always be cloak rooms for women in the stores in those days. But then she and Blanche Hanks took a liking to one another, and she went to her privately, as a housekeeper, cleaner and what-have-you. She lived in a beautiful place out at Elizabeth Bay, she was the manager of the Reuben Brash family, they had big stores in Oxford Street. She was a very unique woman as a female manager was very rare. GRACE SCHWEBEL

Mum was a mid-day waitress, she saw us off to
school, and then she was either home when we got home, or soon after. She didn't always have permanent work, but she was always working. Women in those days would do anything. She did a lot of different things, like cleaning. She never, never had any relief whatsoever during the Depression. She would never, never go to St Vincents de Paul for help. But I never remember going hungry. PAT NICKS

My mother had a corner grocer shop at Number
10, Ferndale Street, Newtown, and we lived behind the shop, so she more or less kept us in food and she worked very hard. She used to make pies and she'd cut sandwiches and sell groceries. KATE DUNBAR

Mum was working as a barmaid at the Frisco
Hotel and the Tilbury, she also worked cleaning offices. If you had a husband, then the woman wouldn't go to work, men were then in control; you would not really go and get a job if you had a husband because jobs were needed, so men were given preference. Women were given the secondary jobs if you had to work, like cleaning, scrubbing, unless you had the brains or the money to open some sort of a little business. JEAN JURD

My mother worked at the jam factory and at
Sergeants Meat Pies. They used to have little pie shops around the town, up in Redfern, down in Chippendale; there used to be pie and peas, or pie and potato, and a cup of tea or whatever, and my mother was a waitress, at some of Sergeants, but didn't work there for long after we were born. TED McDERMOTT

---

7 Raleigh Park was the British Tobacco Company (Australia) plant and later W.D. & H.O. Wills. See *Tobacco Manufacture at Raleigh Park, Kensington: A History and Description of the Buildings,* compiled by Don Godden & Associates Pty. Ltd., with Sue Rosen and Robert Irving, 1989.

8 For a full account of the 1928 Waterside Workers strike, see Margot Beasley, *Wharfies: A history of the Waterside Workers Federation of Australia,* Halstead Press in assoc. with the Australian National Maritime Museum, Rushcutters Bay, 1996.

*Women machinists at Sargood's Top Dog
factory for men's hats in Randall Street,
Surry Hills, in March 1941. (SLNSW)*

Most mothers stayed home, and it wasn't until the Second World War started that there was a great shortage of men, and labour, that they started encouraging women to get into the workforce.[9] My mother was a sort of feminist, and with some of her other friends, would always be wanting to get equal rights for women. They thought it was great to be able to go out and work and be equal to a man. It became an attitude afterwards, but you could hear, feel it all the time. Most of my mother's friends felt that way. I think the men felt it would have been better if the women had stayed home. BOB SLATER

My mother went to work basically when my father got sick, which was in 1945, about two years before he died, of heart disease. As well as working in the shoe trade, she worked in the bar. She worked at the Erskineville Hotel for many years. JOSIE FOSTER

My family were pretty much working-class people. My mother worked mainly in factories. At one stage she was working in the IXL factory, and then in my early teens she was working at Royal Prince Alfred Hospital. She was the head chef there. TERRY GLEBE

I come from a working-class family, my mother, Jessie Donovan, worked all her life. She said she went back to work three weeks after my brother was born, and she was able to do that because of the Woolloomooloo Day Care Centre. That was Council run, so, you know, Woolloomooloo had a lot going for it. She was a school teacher before the war, but once her family came she knew that she would have to face more exams to get back into teaching, so she did various jobs. During the war she worked with ammunitions, then as a journalist. She worked for the ABC, on radio when I was very young. And when we started school she had to get a job as a cleaner. That was a split work day, so she could be home in the middle of the day for when we were on holidays. She did four hours in the morning and got home by about half past nine then went back in the evenings. BETH THORPE

Over the years my mother worked at cosmetic factories, at cafeterias, canteens for schools, boarding schools, and at places in town like Coles. My mother worked a lot, and she didn't seem to have very much free time. Her free time, Saturday, was sacrosanct, that was her 'investment' day.* It wasn't common, my mother was an extremely independent lady. But in terms of money it was family money. CLIFF FOGARTY

* I.e. spent listening to the races on radio and betting with the local SP bookmaker.

I think my parents liked their jobs. Mum always went, I think she enjoyed it, she was good at what she did. She worked for Evercraft. They make trousers, and I think they are into making uniforms now. And then a friend of hers went and got into business for himself, so they bought a factory at Hornsby, so Mum used to go to work at Hornsby. KATHY INGRAM

My mother was still quite young, I think she was about forty-two when Dad died and she went off to work to help us along. It was frowned upon in those days for a woman to be a barmaid. She worked in the Boundary Hotel, in Boundary Street, near the Eveleigh workshop, and also worked in a factory through the day, and worked in another hotel at night. Mum liked working in the pub, she was very popular and men had respect for women, and the barmaid ruled the roost; if she wanted someone barred from the hotel, she just said so. She had three jobs, six days a week. I often wondered why she used to sleep so much on Sundays. HARRY BRENNAN

My mother was a bookbinder by trade. She came out from Glasgow at the age of nineteen and learnt bookbinding. She'd done a bit of it before she came out here and she continued to do it for a while. She worked in a bookbinding place in Newtown, but she didn't do it for very long. She also used to occasionally bring home some factory piecework, and us kids used to help her. The only other job I can remember her doing was cleaning. She used to occasionally go and clean in some, ritzy houses around the place, locally, around Newtown. BRENDAN DOYLE

"WE NEVER HAD A HOTBED OF CRIME"

Running a corner store enabled women to at least get food at wholesale prices, make a meagre living and manage a family. This photograph of the store at 302 Riley Street, Surry Hills, was taken in August 1934 when bread prices rose. (SLNSW)

Mum was a cleaner at the school. It was a split shift; she worked from six 'til nine and then from three 'til six. On Saturday she cleaned for an office on Cleveland Street, Hodgson and Leigh, electrical company. I think that was about three hours on a Saturday morning she did that. And then her other job that she did at home was machining; she'd been a machinist for years and years for Joseph Dahdah, who's actually my uncle's brother, and she'd worked for him for years. Cathi Joseph

9 In 1939 Australian women made up 25.3 per cent of the waged workforce. By 1943 this had increased to 33.5 per cent and the number working in factories in Sydney across this period increased by 24 per cent. Fox, op. cit., pp. 134-135.

I'D WORK ME ARSE OUT TOO!!

Women from the Lustre Hosiery factory operating stocking-making machines in the Hall of Industries at the Easter Show. (SLNSW)

My mother always did little jobs here and there to make extra money for us kids. She worked in a sandwich shop for years over in Redfern Street; she worked shift work at Eveready, the battery place; she worked cleaning at the Department of Main Roads; and then she finally worked for the Council as a cleaner; and then she went to be a chef at Meals and Wheels, so she did quite well. I mean she was always in work 'cause Mum was a really top worker and a lovely person, and that's outside of community work that she did for nothing for everyone. JILL EDWARDS

—

Mum went to work, she worked at night so she could get the equivalent of what the men got. 'Cause she was working on the machines in W.D. & H.O. Wills, at Kensington (Raleigh Park); she was a machinist where she'd put all the tobacco in. It was really heavy work, and during the day only the men were allowed to do it, and at night because the men

didn't want to work at night, the women were allowed to do it, and they would get the equivalent of what the men would get during the day. I think she liked her work. It was a social thing for her, a lot of the women that she was working with were as independent as she was. And Dad was sort of a man's man, saying a woman's place was in the home. So I think she had to sort of argue for a long time before he let her work. SHANE CAMPBELL

—

Mum's been working at the hospital on Missenden Road the last eight or nine years as a food service lady, one of the yellow ladies that go around and get the patients their dinner and lunch and things. But when we were growing up in Chippendale, she was a barmaid. She worked in a couple of the local pubs at Chippendale, she worked in the Britannia which is on Cleveland Street for a while. In the 1980s she got a job with Alsco Linen and then at the hospital, so

"WE NEVER HAD A HOTBED OF CRIME"

W.D. & H.O. Wills cigarette manufacturing plant at Raleigh Park was considered to be a choice place to work as it provided a job for life and had many social welfare and benefit schemes for workers. (SLNSW)

they've been fairly lucky with employment. Colin Bell

Me mum worked as a cook at Aristocrat Poker
Machines. She'd make all the lunch-time meals, hot
meals or sandwiches, whatever. But I mean, when I
was younger as well, I know that she used to work
for the local Aboriginal pre-school. It started out as
sort of like a lunch thing, where they used to just
give kids their lunch, to make sure that they had
nutrition and stuff like that, healthy food. Mum used
to work there as the bus driver, and I don't know
what else she used to do. Dean Ingram

Every kid was a paper boy in Woolloomooloo."

*Closely linked with parents' work were children's
attempts to either contribute to the household or to
obtain pocket money. From paper runs to more
imaginative enterprises, kids were sometimes
encouraged to get a job as soon as possible, often
through necessity, but also to learn important lessons
about the value of money and hard work.*

[In the 1920s I] used to sell the *Labor Daily* from
six o'clock in the morning. No newsagent would sell
it, although a little bookshop up in Erskineville Road
did, and I'd get about five shillings a week for that. I
worked in a greengrocer shop up in Erskineville
Road, Danny Bow, Chinese fella, and three sons;
Claude, Ben, and I can't remember the other fella,
and Mrs Bow, I used to weigh up potatoes and
onions. Of a Saturday morning I'd take the delivery
in a big cane basket to various customers and I used
to get five shillings a week for that too. The money
all went to the family. I got a couple of bob back I
s'pose. Bill Schwebel

You got a job anywhere you could to help out. I
got a job up in William Street when I was about
twelve, selling papers. We'd go down the news
office, *The News* and *The Sun;* you'd get thirteen
papers for ninepence. I'd make eightpence a night, I
thought I was made, that was four shillings a week, I
took it home to Mum. It'd take me two hours, half
past three to half past five selling them. At
Showtime, you would get a job leading a bull out the
show; four bob you used to get for that. We used to
do a fair bit of caddying, out Moore Park, you didn't
get that every day either, if you got a job you thought
you were very, very lucky. Billy Pascoe

I had a billycart, I collected wood off the wharves
which I sold. I was familiar with every wharf in
Woolloomooloo. Sometimes I'd run onto some of the
ships and pinch anything I could find, although there

wasn't much. Potatoes and onions that you could manage to get off the wharf, because the storeman would let you in, and he'd help you fill up your billycart. I would sell to the local restaurant and the little houses all around in the street, in Nicholson Street and Bland Street. JEAN JURD

When I was about ten I used to do two milk runs, one in the morning and one in the afternoon. Billy Tye would knock me up about midnight and we'd do the milk run until about half past six, all around Redfern, Waterloo and Alexandria, and then I'd come and have a bit of breakfast and away I'd go to school. And then after school I'd go down to Ben Fury and do the afternoon run with him.[10] The milk was delivered by horse and cart, you used to get the pint or quart measure and women used to have the little frilly milk covers with the beads on them. I started on the midnight milk run when I was eight, in 1935, but my brothers and sisters didn't work at that early age, maybe helped at home, but not manual work. When I finished in the milk carts, my father had leased a wood and coal and ice run off Georgie Squires in Alexandria, and I helped him. My afternoon would be taken up going up to Alexandria Goods Yards and bagging hundredweight bags of coal. I'd get the princely sum of about ten shillings and I'd give that to my mother and she'd give me a shilling back and I'd be able to go to the pictures on Saturday night. So I contributed. ROBERT HAMMOND

After World War II, particularly in the 1950s, the economic situation improved greatly. Many children were encouraged to get a job for pocket money or to teach them responsibility, rather than because of dire economic circumstances in the home.

When I was about twelve to fourteen, we were encouraged to go and get a bit of a job. My father arranged with the local paper shop in Crown Street that before going to

Fishermen repairing and drying nets in Woolloomooloo in the early 1970s. (Courtesy of Nell Leonard)

---

10 Also referred to by Betty Moulds.

school at Cleveland Street I would go up to pick up all the lottery application forms, take them down to Barrack Street, leave them there, go to school, come back in the afternoon, pick up the tickets, take them back to the paper shop. I got a penny a ticket, which was a lot of money in those days. That was my pocket money. Generally speaking, my parents just provided everything for us. We weren't expected to contribute money to the family. TERRY GLEBE

—

However, in large families and those without a father, the need for children to contribute still existed.

Everyone had something to do, everyone. If you didn't do something, you didn't have any money, because your family couldn't give it to you. So if you didn't find something to do to make a few bob, well you did without. I used to sell papers at Eveleigh workshop. There was Eveleigh One and Eveleigh Two, and in those days you could put one hundred papers down, and walk up to the next place, and pick up the money from the other hundred papers, and go back and pick up the money from the others. We used to hop on the tram, and sell papers, going down to St Peter's or down Botany Road. Sometimes we would go into some other paper boy's area, and we would have to settle it. I sold papers for about five years from about eleven years old. We used to put a lay-by on a Chinese meal from the Canton in Botany Road. We used to leave a shilling every day and on Friday night all the paper boys would get together and have a banquet. HARRY BRENNAN

I really hated collecting bottles; it made me feel so ashamed; I was absolutely mortified by it, I couldn't stand it. It was okay at things like the footy, you know; like, at half-time they'd open the gates and everyone could go in, and all the kids were collecting bottles. But we did it in a really systematic way, like the whole family was involved; it wasn't for pocket money, it was for really strong economic reasons. So we would all get up at six o'clock in the morning and go round the streets collecting bottles, and all my friends used to be

really stunned. We had a back shed, when I was really little, we used to have chooks, but then we weren't allowed to keep chooks any more, the Council said we couldn't have chooks, so the chook shed became the bottle shed. And we'd fill the bottle shed and then go round and get the bottle'o, and he'd come round and collect them. My friends could never understand why we had all these bottles when we didn't even drink, and I, of course, was far too embarrassed to say, 'Well, we collect them for money'. CATHI JOSEPH

—

In the 1970s and 1980s the money kids earned was usually their own and the jobs were far more 'respectable' than those of preceding generations.

I inherited a job working in a chemist in Kings Cross for the princely sum of fifty cents an hour, and I think Mrs Monty was her name, she had diamond-encrusted fingers and a paucity of hair, a few grey wisps of hair sort of slicked back over her head, she was quite a character, but we'd get sent around on errands to deliver things. I can remember sitting up in the back shelves up the top eating Limits Diet Biscuits and possibly finding out what Modess packets contained and generally educating myself on chemist-shop procedure. I may have been in Sixth Class or First Form or something along those lines. JACKIE GRATTON-WILSON

—

I suppose it was my father's way of disciplining you, making you go and work, like in McDonald's or wherever, so you knew what the dollar was worth, and things like that. Making us go and work was one thing he did purposely, he wouldn't give us money, so we had to go and work. From about sixteen, I worked at Macca's. Lots of kids used to do the paper runs, and like six o'clock in the morning Dad'd hear the whistle and he would wake up at that time, and he might find the paper and say, 'Well look, that's what you should be doing,' you know, that was at nine and ten. But then my mum said, 'No, they're kids, let them grow up'. ESOSA EQUAIBOR

"If you got two or three shillings worth of bottles you reckoned you were a millionaire."

Paid employment was not the only means of making some extra money. Kids used their initiative to find ways to make a few bob by running messages for relatives or neighbours, collecting bottles and newspapers. Some scams showed impressive, but not strictly legitimate, entrepreneurial skills. Sometimes it was a matter of being in the right place at the right time when someone generous might look in your direction. Opportunities depended on the locality, at Alexandria there was the railway goods yard and at Woolloomooloo there were the wharves and the street girls.

Adults used to race boats in the Alexandria Canal, and depending on the volume of the water, and the width of the stream, you'd have either six or eight boats, and people would bet their pennies and thruppence on them. On the side there'd be a lot of green moss, and the bookmakers used to say to the kids, 'If the favourite's in front, if you fall in the stream, there's thruppence in it for you', and people would lose their money, and we'd get the thruppence, we'd also get a big kick up the pants, or a whack across the ear from the people who backed the boats. My mainstay of sixpence a week was my grandmother, who was very sick for years, she had all holes in her legs, she had dropsy, and they used to drill little holes in her, and it all used to be weeping all the time, so I used to get sixpence a week for running her messages, which was big time, you could get in the pictures and all that sort of thing. The only other money that we ever got as children was to get up in the early hours of the morning, go over the park chasing empty beer bottles, for which we got a halfpenny. If there was only one beer bottle and two kids got there, whoever could fight the best got the bottle. CLIFF NOBLE

Once we got some luminous paint we found over the tip and we went 'round Rose Bay and those areas painting the people's numbers on their doors with luminous paint for sixpence a letter. Another time we got a lot of red paint and we went 'round painting people's letterboxes for a shilling a time. We also got a lot of long sticks and dowel tea chests that used to be plywood and we cut out what we called walking men. We took them up to Newtown Bridge just on Christmas time and painted them up and sold them for one and sixpence each. HENRY BROWN

As I got older I used to stand outside the hotels and sing, and put a hat on the ground and they'd come out and give me their pennies and halfpennies. Oh, I was doing alright you see. I used to buy myself a halfpenny lolly and with the other money I used to get half a pound of butter or something that Mum was short of and take it home. She must of wondered where I was gettin' the money from, but when somebody told her I was outside the Glengarry Hotel singing, oh dear, I'll never forget the beltin' I got. So that ended my first musical career. Another job I got when I was little: I was paid a penny for killin' bugs. They're a little tick, and the old-fashioned beds used to have coils, and they used to live in there. This old lady in Hugo Street used to give me a penny to climb under the bed with a candle and burn these bugs in the coils. JANE LANYON

It was quite common, particularly down the railway sheds off Exhibition Park, off Cleveland Street, for the kids to get up and pinch all the lead flashing and stuff off the roof and go and sell it for scrap metal, and get a few bob. I think they snitched a bit off the Lebanese Church up on the corner of Walker Street.* See, money wasn't a big problem, because there wasn't any around. Everyone had about the same amount: nothing. TED McDERMOTT

* The St George Antioch Orthodox Church where Nick Shehadie's father was the priest.

Where the Beaconsfield Park is now, behind there, there used to be a glass factory. Then they moved the factory from that position to another position further down. And one of the kids around here got the bright idea that he'd gather up the glass. And it was big pieces of glass, pieces of molten glass. And he took it back to the factory and sold it. So when all the kids around here heard about that, everybody was up to selling molten glass, the old glass, back to the factory. MICK GREEN

—

Just at the goods yards there, they used to have
what they call a horse dock, to bring in the race horses. So us kids, about six o'clock we'd know the horse train would be coming in, and if the owners and trainers had had a good day they'd have a handful of pennies to throw out to you. Then we used to go through the train and collect beer bottles. ROBERT HAMMOND

—

As children we used to collect newspapers, and go
to the local butcher shop and sell them for wrapping, and we'd get a penny a bundle. And then I used to take the garbage out twice a week, and I got a penny a week for that. MERVYN JORDAN

—

Nobody in Paddington had money, we'd all go
over to Centennial Park in the school holidays with a bundle of comics, and you'd have those big glass pickle jars with a string tied around it like a handle. We'd get there and we'd sit with our legs in the pond, reading the comics and every now and again you'd pull your leg out, and take all the leeches off and put them in the bottle. And then we'd take them up to Washington Soul Pattinsons, they were chemists up at Paddo, and he'd give you a penny each for the leeches. They use'd them for bruises and black eyes. KEVIN RYAN

—

During World War II

I used to go down to Buckingham's Corner, corner of Riley Street and Oxford Street, and busk for money during the war years: singing songs. In the basement of Buckingham's store they used to have sing-a-longs; people used to go down there and buy things to help the war effort. Another

good place to get money was from the Americans, down at the war memorial pool in Hyde Park South there. You'd simply wade through the water and the Americans would throw coins in and you'd just pick them up. Occasionally the police would come and shift you along, but for the most part you were left alone. I don't remember too many kids being there, but I know myself and three or four mates used to do it quite regularly, and my mother used to sound off a bit at us and then ask, 'How much did you get? That means I don't have to give you sixpence pocket money this week, 'cause you got quite a killing.' So, we soon learnt to keep our mouths shut, and you got the pocket money as well. TERRY GLEBE

—

In the 1950s and 1960s

If you were lucky enough in the school holidays, some of the girls'd give you ten bob to go and buy their lunch or something when they were working. They were the girls down in Chapel Street and that was just further down towards the 'Loo. You get ten bob and you'd go and buy them a cake and a sandwich, whatever they wanted and a bottle of Coke, they only cost sixpence. But sometimes you'd end up with four or five bob change, and the girls would never take it off you, and that was good money. It was only thruppence into the movies then, so you can imagine the fun we used to have with four bob for school holidays. But you'd never tell your mum and dad that you were there 'cause you got into trouble, you know, you weren't allowed there. WARREN RICHARDSON

—

I used to have a cartage firm, with billycarts.
'Brennan Brothers—Haulage here, haulage there, haulage everywhere', we had it embossed across the box, and it used to have a flatboard on the box, you'd take groceries home for people: blocks of ice, not many people had fridges, it was mostly ice chests. We sold bits of scrap metal too. Wherever there was a few bob, there was a few bob. HARRY BRENNAN

Hello, the new boy, when did you start?"

Children left school when they were fourteen, some of them left earlier, not many people went on to greater high school or university, we didn't have the money. And most of the children who left school either became apprentices or worked in a textile factory. ROSE CLEMENTS

First experiences of 'real work' ranged from excitement and relief at being out of school and earning a living, to frustration at low wages and hard conditions.

I first worked in a shirt factory to learn the trade, and then I left there and I went to Reckitt's. They used to make 'Reckitt's Blue' and 'Brasso' and 'Sterodent'. When I first started there, that was when I was fourteen, I only got twelve and six a week at the shirt factory. And then when I went down to Reckitt's, I got £3 when I was only about fourteen to fifteen. IRENE WEBBER

Zena Sachs's experience, and her mother's attitude to girls and education, was an exception.

One thing my mother was always very firm about, she would never let us take jobs in the school holidays when we were at high school. All the girls were getting jobs in David Jones and I wasn't allowed because she felt that if we got the taste for money, we wouldn't want to go back to school. So I helped in our shop, but I never had any money of my own until I went to work, after I left high school. ZENA SACHS

On the first day of my first job at Stedmen Hendersons, I got sent to deliver chocolate to the girls at the chocolate machine. As soon as I got there they said, 'Hello, the new boy, when did you start?', I said, 'Today', she said, 'Oh you haven't been initiated yet'. Well, the next thing me pants is pulled down and I got a great scoop of chocolate, well you know where it all went. I came home of the night time, 'I'm not going back there, I wouldn't work with them girls, I will not go back!', and Mum said, 'Don't be silly it might never happen again.' Oh, heck I was embarrassed. If I was eighteen or nineteen, it would've been really good, but not at just fourteen and two days. I was making minties and chocolates for fifteen bob out there. But unlucky, I got appendicitis and I got put off, and when you got appendicitis you were in hospital for ten days. And when I come back, I thought my job was there, but that was it, finished. Then I got a job at the glass works, until I was about seventeen, when you turn seventeen they say you're too old, believe it or not! Seventeen you were too old, 'cause you'd be getting around the thirty-five bob or two pound mark then, so off you went and they put on a young bloke again, or young girls. BILLY PASCOE

My first job, when I was fourteen in 1934, was at McKeown's, they applied for an apprentice for the boot trade down here on the corner, and there was sixty other kids there, all after one job. Fortunately for me, the local plumber was doing some work there, and asked me what I was doing, so he went inside, seen the proprietor, and they come out and they picked me. Well it was great, the only problem was, I was done up in my best, I had a two and six-penny pair of patent leather shoes that had cardboard soles on them and everywhere that I walked in the place the tacks were going through the soles, and I was jumping all over the place. Of course, being new and being Catholic, I never knew much about language, and they were using filthy language all the time. I used to put my hands over my ears so I wouldn't hear it, and then of course it got to the stage where I said one day, 'If my mother was down here, she would wash your mouth out with soapy water'. Well, you can imagine what they did to me after that, and then they start calling the Pope all sorts of names and I wanted to fight everybody, and I couldn't beat a drum, I was never any good fighting. CLIFF NOBLE

The first job I had was the year I left school, just as I turned fifteen, I got a job over the Christmas rush as a telegraph messenger boy at the Newtown Post Office. It was only supposed to be for a few days but the Post Master decided, after I smashed up about five bikes in about three days, I wasn't cut out for telegraph messenger boy. I worked anywhere. I remember one place I worked at was a box factory that belonged to an old German chap and his daughter, and I still remember that, 33 Fitzroy Street, Marrickville, and they used to get the old butter boxes that had the name branded in the timber. I used to have to use a woodscraper and scrape all the name out and they would sand it, and sell the boxes again. Well I worked there for three-quarters of a day, and to my knowledge I held a record for two or three years, because he used to advertise three days a week in the paper. It'd cost him one and six for the ads and most kids would work there for half a day and then leave without him paying them anything. He'd have a different kid every day, but I insisted on my one and six and he wasn't too happy about that at all. HENRY BROWN

I had to pay board when I went to work. At fourteen I went down to the Department of Labour and Industry; you had to get a permit to start work at fourteen, and they just interviewed you and gave you a stamp. I got a job with Robby Twyman on the ice carts and I used to cart ice from McDonald and Eckland who were in Enmore. On a Saturday morning we'd get up at four o'clock, and two of us used to get on the back of an ice cart and we'd go up and load tons of ice and you had to deliver that by hand, into flats and up stairs. We used to do wood, coal and coke. LEO HANNAN

I started work in a little café, we sold three-course meals for a shilling to the wharf labourers. I worked there every day, that was a forty-eight-hour week, for twelve and six a week. I did the preparing of vegetables, the cooking, the scrubbing, the cleaning, the working in the shop, serving the men, so I got back at her because I used to eat all the sweets. It was also a little shop, it's now called the

Woolloomooloo Gallery.* At thirteen and a half I started work in a Standard Steam Laundry, I had to go on a waiting list to get into it. I was bringing home to my mother thirteen shillings, fourteen shillings a week. Now we worked six days a week, I think five days and maybe till one o'clock Saturday. I was there for quite a few years because I worked there during World War II. JEAN JURD

Later in the 1950s and 1960s Cheryl Lindo's family ran this as a sandwich bar and corner store.

I went to work when I was 13 years and 10 months, at Anthony Hordern's, in the mail order. I loved school; I was at St Patrick's, downtown, and I came home on the Thursday and Mum said, 'You'll be going in the morning to Anthony Hordern's, there's a job advertised'. And I said, 'Oh, I didn't want to go to work!' She said, 'Well, you've got to go, there's a job there, you go in'. So I got the job, and I went to work. MAUREEN OLIVER

I left school when I was 13 years and 10 months and I got a job. The sports master at Gardener's Road School got me the job; they made welding electrodes. But later on I went to a place called Alder Stroud, which was down in Alexandria, and I became apprenticed to a sheet-metal worker. But I was only there a short time, and I wasn't seventeen years of age and I enlisted in the air crew. The pilot navigator, air gunner business. And wasn't there bedlam in this house over that! MICK GREEN

I was just under fifteen when I left school; we didn't have the money to go on. I wasn't much good at school anyhow, it was probably a blessing, actually, I mean, I was bringing some money into the family, which helped. I worked at Fox Movie Tone News for a short time. I was there for two weeks, and it was raining, and I was expected to wash a car, and I was a bit stubborn, and I didn't, so I was sacked! So I got a job at Vetoy Biscuits, and you could eat them too! Vetoy biscuits had a factory just around the corner of Young Street, Redfern, and I was the office boy in there, but you cooked on the

*Workers having a break at the Eveleigh
Railway Yards in 1938. (SLNSW)*

oven, you did all sorts of things. Sir Nicholas Shehadie

As far as employment was concerned if you were a
girl you went into a shop or you did hairdressing or
something of the sort. If you were a boy they'd
probably try and push you into a trade. Very few people
went to University. Very few children went beyond the
intermediate; I would say perhaps no more than ten per
cent did their leaving certificate at that time. I left
school at fourteen and eight months, and first of all I
went to work at a printing establishment. I didn't like
that, so I went to the Taxation Department as a very
junior clerk, and worked there for eighteen months; this
was during the war years. After that I decided I hated
the clerical life, so I was apprenticed to woodworking
machining, at a place called Bray and Holliday's over
in Rushcutters Bay, in McLachlan Avenue, and worked
there for eight years. I got the bullet in 1951 when there
was a recession. Paul Herlinger

The first job I had was at Yardley's perfume
factory. I was in the powder room where they made
talcum powder and it was flying everywhere and
that worried my mum because my father was sick
with TB at that time. From there I went to work at
Allen's Sweets in the factory, scooping boiled lollies
and things into bags. I did that for years and then I
got transferred into the office and was there for a
few years. They wanted to teach me bookkeeping
and all this sort of thing, but I didn't get around to
that, did I? I got married and started to have my
family. Beverly Hunter

I could have went to work in an office, but I
didn't want to, because all me friends worked in the
factory. So I didn't even try to get an office job.
The shoe factory was me first job, just down the
road at Packard Shoes and then I went to a lolly
factory, and then I got to Master Craft Chocolates
and I stayed there, that's where I settled, up until I
got married. Kathy Ingram

When I left school I worked in town in an office,
and then I worked up the Chevron, but then when

Mum died I went into the shop, which was good
because I didn't like the office work anyway. You
just had every one; we had the navy stores, the
printers, Lotus Car Parts and tyre place and
everything else, they all came in the shop. And, you
know, every Christmas when they were having their
Christmas 'do', 'Come on Cheryl, we're going
around the Astor,' so off we'd go round the Astor, or
'We're going over the Frisco'. And the guys always
came and got me and off we went to somewhere or
other, and it was just great. Cheryl Lindo

We worked, we had to pay our board. I went to
work at fourteen. I worked at the local supermarket
because I didn't want to go to school. I was a bit of a
rebel in my teenage years, and I was going to be
expelled from high school because I started wagging
school, and my mother got a letter and found out I
hadn't been at school for a month, so when I came
home with my school bag she said, 'Did you enjoy
school, Jill?', but I think she had an inkling before
that, and I said, 'Yes,' and she just hit me right across
the face and said, 'That's for lying,' and she hit me
on the other side of the face and said, 'That's
because you're not going back to school, you're
going to work, if you're not going to school you're
going to work', and she said, 'Get out and get a job'.
I went the next day and got a job and never had to
stop working, I loved it. Jill Edwards

"There's nothing wrong with British Justice, only the bastards what administrate it!"

My family was a real down working-class family. My father's a hod carrier. He used to carry I s'pose about eighteen bricks in it, and then they'd fill it up with cement and they'd heave it on their shoulder, and take it up, and empty it out. And then if it rained, like if you didn't work you didn't get paid, and there was no sick leave. That was the working conditions of the working class, and that was when the trade unions were starting to come up and stop all that. BILL SCHWEBEL

—

I got a job in Annandale, at seventeen, in a factory what made door hinges, and locks, and did a lot of nickel plating. Once you turned eighteen, they put you off because they had to bring your wages up, so you never told them when your birthday was, you kept being seventeen, I kept being seventeen for about fifteen, sixteen months. The wages were right low. I got me first adult waged job at Austral Bronze, over in Alexandria, and me first weeks wages was three pound five a week. That was a man's wages; I was twenty-one years of age. I became very active in the union movement, going for a lot of claims for more wages and shoes, because you used to burn your shoes out about once every two weeks. For a while I was before the Commissioner [the Arbitration Commission], he was a judge them days, didn't have Commissioners. When lunch hour came, I was having a bit of lunch and the judge was there and he said, 'Of course you can talk freely now, everything is off record', and he turned to me and he said, 'You,' he says, 'What do you think of British Justice?' I said, 'There's nothing wrong with British Justice, only the bastards what administrate it'. FRANK ALTOFT

—

My stepfather worked on the railway and while they were sacking people left, right and centre, returned servicemen got preference. He was still employed. He became an activist in the railway union. And in those days, if you worked in any government work, once you went over twenty-one and you weren't married, you were put off. And so many marriages were rushed into from the time people were twenty, to hold their jobs. GRACE SCHWEBEL

—

All the seniors at McKeown's got sacked at Christmas for six weeks and had to reapply for their job, and during the day if there were no orders, they would be sent home half a day and they would have come down from the outer suburbs like Bankstown and Canterbury. When you're young, you get enthusiastic, and I learnt to work four machines. So I found out they were sending these people home, and putting me on; I wasn't as fast as what they were, but I could do the job adequately. So I used to say to them, take a part out of the machine, because all the machines in those days were on lease from the British United Machinery Company, and they'd come out, and after a couple of times a mechanic would say, 'Where is it?', and I would say, 'What are you talking about?' It was a very, very difficult period. There was a union, but you see, they'd get the unions down, they'd take the officials downstairs, give them a couple of grogs or something, and then they'd come up and everything was okay. I found out what was happening and had an argument with the boss's friend, which was very stupid. I called him an ignorant old B, and the boss wouldn't listen to me, so I called him an ignorant old B too. As a consequence I was a radical, and when I turned twenty-one, they made sure they got rid of me, despite the fact they kept people on who weren't as proficient. I left and got a job on the railway. I was only on the railway a fortnight, and this was during the war period, and they got a very big order for making the air force shoes, and they come up and asked me to go back. Well, I wasn't going back because the railway was infinitely better. CLIFF NOBLE

—

Conditions were pretty bad. I mean, Dad took me to the metal factory, Sydney Cook, in Alexandria, and I was just appalled at the sort of working conditions, you know; incredible noise, and of course

it was impossible to talk, absolutely impossible.
There were huge metal presses going hell for leather
making this incredible din. My father got industrial
deafness out of it. They never wore hearing plugs or
anything in those days, you just put up with noise,
and the heat was incredible, and the dirt. I know
there were a lot of industrial accidents. BRENDAN DOYLE

"You could work a person to death."

My father worked for James McMahon
and Company in Redfern, and did all the
sign-writing and the coach painting on
their trucks. He also did work for Sander Sutton and
Whiteheads, and he painted the first pantechnicon to
come into Australia, which was shown at the Royal
Show. It was unfortunate that a man that had his
talents had to suffer so much, and eventually he went
blind because in those days you didn't buy pre-
mixed paints, the only thing that came pre-mixed
was the gold leaf. LORETTO THURGOOD

My father started working on the wharves in the
late '30s, early '40s. He wasn't involved in the
unions, although he might have been a delegate, on a
particular ship at a particular time, but not involved
with the hierarchy in Sussex Street. It was a very
good union, a communistic union as far as getting
things for men because there's no two ways about it,
the ship owners would've just stood right over you,
would've trampled you into the ground. And they
were wealthy ship owners, I'm talking about the
P&O and Adelaide Steamship Company, Union
Steamship. It was very dangerous work, if you didn't
have your wits about you there you could get into a
hell of a lot of trouble. In what they used to call the
bull days, they used to be rushing and tearing
around, there was a lot of men killed. ROBERT HAMMOND

I was working off my old man's fishing boat, and
I'd work me arse out too. When it was raining, I had
to go and pump the boat out, ohhhh, I hated it. There
was no winches in them days, you had to do
everything by hand. Oh, the ferries'd go straight
across you; one of the coal ferries went straight across
and sunk the neighbour's boat, went straight through.
We didn't have lights in them days—the red and green
lights—half the crew went down. SAM DONATO

There was a lot of families whose father had died
as a result of work, especially on the waterfront; that
was considered a very dangerous job. Falling down

holes, loading wheat which got into their lungs. Things that were packed in hessian bags were very heavy, so they must've got a lot of bad backs out of it and weak hearts. There was a saying that you could work a person to death; well, I'm quite sure that with the loads they did move, they would've been literally worked to death. So a lot of men died in their 40s. BETH THORPE

My stepfather was a printer. He used to work at Sydenham for a long time. Whenever he needed a job, he just had to go to the printer's union, and they found him a job. So he always had a job until he hurt one of his legs, and had an accident, had a couple of accidents, chopped a couple of fingers off, and had something wrong with his leg. KATHY INGRAM

Whitely's Chemicals, they're still there in Chippendale, they're down the other end of Ivy Street; they make a lot of cleaning products, disinfectants and things like that, so there was always this smell of disinfectant in the air. They employed quite a few of the locals, and it wasn't until one of the locals got very sick, one of the men who worked there, and he ended up getting huge compensation payments out of them that they decided, oh, we'll make our workers wear masks and gloves and boots. COLIN BELL

My father was injured a few times at work, on the wharves; he fell. The first one he had, he fell off the ship, into the water, but it was low-tide, so he broke his leg there. And the second time, he fell from a container into the hull of the ship, and then he crushed his leg and he couldn't go back to work after that. I think he had worker's compensation payments, and that was about nine years before he got a proper compensation payment. The second fall ended his working life on the wharves, and his working life anywhere, because that was all Dad knew, and he was too old. He was fifty-two. SUSAN ALLOWAY

" My father had his own business."

It was a draper's shop, called 'London–Paris' and we sold women's clothing, both dresses and underwear and that sort of thing. We were just in between Missenden Road and Newtown Post Office. The shop would have been quite successful, but Dad used to go to the country, and he was not a business man, he liked to be comfortable. When we had our books done, they'd find that most of the money, the profit that should have been made from his going to the country, was spent in travelling expenses. He went by train, then he used to either hire someone to drive him to different places, or hire a horse and sulky to go where they were building dams. The Avon Dam was built first, and people lived there in tents. But they had quite a community life with dances and so on, and the women used to dress up. I was always taking parcels down to Newtown station to be sent down to people when they'd be having a dance. When the Avon Dam was finished, a lot of them moved to where they were building the Nepean Dam. They were very good, they hardly ever had any bad debts. He used to let people pay things off, they were all very fond of him, because some of them used to come up to Sydney, and come to the shop and talk to him. He used to pack these two big suitcases to take to the country. He had these suitcases packed with very expensive dresses and things and he went outside to get a drink and someone just came and took them. They'd obviously been watching. This was awful, we never got any of it back. It was decided to shut down the shop when people that we owed money to put him into liquidation. That would have been in 1930, when it was really right in the depths of the Depression. ZENA SACHS

My father was a herbalist in King Street, Newtown; he had the shop there for so long that when a letter came from India, addressed to Henry Cross, Australia, it came straight to him, there was no problem at all with it. Dad had been trained by his mother as a herbalist. Her mother was also a herbalist, Harte was their name and she married a

Mr Cross, who was the great-grandson of one of the immigrants that come out as a guest of the Government in the First Fleet. In those days you didn't have formal training. Herbalism was frowned on by most medical practitioners, though he had a few that he actually treated. He was accepted everywhere and he had no troubles with the medical profession or the community. Occasionally he had a bit of trouble with the police. He was clairvoyant, but that's beside the point. They tried to say he was fortune-telling and in those days, it was a crime actually. Clairvoyants and things like that was very much de classé; witchcraft, in fact. They came into his shop and they questioned him about various things. He wasn't too worried about it because he knew they were police, even though they came in plain clothes, his description was above their head and he had no trouble with them. My grandmother was a recognised medium, even today a lot of people know her name, Mrs Cross Turner, as one of the clairvoyants of the period. LES CROSS

My father was probably about thirty-nine when he married my mother, and by the time I was born I s'pose he was probably pushing fifty. He had a middle-class background; his family were watchmakers and jewellers and they had a chain of shops right throughout the country areas. But he contracted typhoid fever in Crookwell and had six months' illness, then he contracted it again and this caused the business to decline and he went bankrupt. And bad sight meant that he had to give up his trade as a watchmaker and jeweller entirely. They had to start from scratch, and with his middle-class background he came into Newtown, there was no dole or blind benefit so he started a window-cleaning business. He was practically blind, but he went out and provided, it wasn't known for people to be a window-cleaner, it was a demeaning job, but he couldn't practice his crafts. GRACE SCHWEBEL

Everybody thought that Morrisons owned the shop but we owned the shop; we were agents for Morrison's cakes. My mother and my sister, Jean,

ran it, we had a cook and a waitress. We served light refreshments, pie and mashed potato and sandwiches. Of course we'd get the pies from Morrison's, and we'd have cakes, tea and coffee and milkshakes. We sold chocolates. It really was elegant. We used to take about £100 on a Saturday night for suppers and that, from the fight crowd at the stadium. GLAD WILLIS

Where Dad came from, in Italy, there was very little opportunity, unless you had a lot of money, so he came out here and he worked very hard, and he made quite a lot of money. He had a shop opposite David Jones in Market Street, which had like a milk bar, afternoon teas and confectionery, and also a small selection of out-of-season fruit, which is very expensive. So your clientele mainly came from Double Bay or Dover Heights, because they were the only ones who could afford them, and the fruit was like bananas in the middle of winter, and grapefruit from Cairo, Sunkist oranges from America, all this sort of stuff which he imported. Most of the Italians who came out here were *paesani,* they were people from the earth, from farms and that's all they knew, was how to grow things and how to sell them, market them, that's what they did at home, that's what they did out here. DARIO LO SCHIAVO

Later, my Dad was a scrap-metal merchant. He worked for himself. At the same time, he was a registered bookmaker on the course. And I might add, before he was a registered bookmaker, in the rough old days he was an SP bookmaker up in Walker Street, Waterloo. He worked mainly at trots and dogs meetings, on weekends and at nights. And when my dad passed on, I continued on in that train, and when I retired, my eldest boy continued on. My father did it at Wentworth Park and Harold Park, Harold Park Trots, Harold Park Dogs, Wentworth Park Dogs. But originally, early in the piece, my dad travelled all over the State: Dapto, Bulli, Newcastle, everywhere, he worked approximately five or six nights a week as a bookmaker. TED McDERMOTT

My father was a taxi proprietor, he always had his taxi, and when they were building the Cronulla Railway line, he had a tip truck working on that. Dad left Paddington early in the morning and walked down to Central Railway, because the day before he had sat in the line all day, waiting to get a job. The first car on the rank always got the next job, and so you had to come up from the back and sometimes it would take him two days to get one job. He'd leave his car there so that it wouldn't lose its position. And then sometimes I can remember he would come home and he would say, 'Well I have sat there for two days, and all I got was five shillings' and someone would get in the cab and say they wanted to go a couple of blocks up the road. BOB SLATER

My father was a salesman of crockery, and he used to take the cup, saucer and plate, and cutlery around and try to sell it door to door, and he'd bring home the samples, and they'd eat their dinner off it, and then they'd wash it up for the next day, so he could take it out. JUDY CHAMBERS

My parents lived in Darlinghurst Road, where they had a small lingerie shop opposite the Fire Station. I don't think my parents had a lot of experience in running a shop, but my father's brother lived here before they came and it was his idea that they should establish the lingerie shop. People didn't have much money, but my mother had exquisite taste, and so I think everything in there must've been very nice. People would have gone there to buy luxury garments, because they had some very nice dress shops and in that same area, there was a French milliner that my mother used to get hats from and there were also quite a lot of good food shops, and quite interesting and beautiful little restaurants. Many of them seemed to be run by European people who came out as refugees. GERALDINE OHLSSON

Mum and Dad, once they got married, bought an old café in Goulburn Street in the city and worked there for many, many years. That was called Civic Café, it used to be next door to the Civic Hotel, down near the old Chequers Night Club. Dad's told me stories about that café in the old days, how it was only four shillings for a soup, a main course and a pudding. But because they were mainly all drunks that used to come in from the pub next door, the Civic Hotel, you virtually had to fight them to get your four shillings anyway. But then they upgraded and moved up to George Street, and took over a café there called Lucas Café, and that was a bit fancier, Dad sort of hit the big time then. The café was opposite the old Trocadero Ballroom which is now the Hoyts Cinema complex in George Street. They worked very hard there and during the school holidays and on Saturdays I used to work there. Nearly all the staff was relatives. ANDREW LAZARIS

7

You can pay the coppers, or use your influence

A sergeant and four plain-clothed detectives in the 1930s. (SLNSW)

The police were supreme!"

Police such as 'Long Tack Sam', the 'Conga-Gorilla', and later 'Bumper Farrell' became legendary figures. Memories vary from a fondness for the 'law and order' they maintained, to outrage at their summary execution of 'justice'.

They talk about this being a rough area, Erskineville, Newtown, and Camperdown; sure we had gangs, there was the Forty Thieves in Glebe, always in trouble, always fighting; other gangs and amongst themselves mostly. And then we had two big detectives used to travel here in Newtown, one was known as 'Long Tack Sam', and the other one was known as the 'Conga-Gorilla', that was Jack Eyres. Conga-Gorilla, he was a big man, he'd have been around about eighteen, nineteen stone, and Long Tack Sam was six foot two. When you was on the street at night time, you'd be looking

in the shop window a little after eight o'clock, he'd come and say, 'Hey, about time you got home, and if you're here when I come back you'll get a boot in the tail'. So we used to scoot off. You would, you'd get a boot in the tail, there was no risk about that. But it did more good than it ever did harm. FRANK ALTOFT

If Police Constable Snarble caught you being a vandal he'd kick you and tell you to get the hell out of it! He more or less made his own court, but in those days of course they were permitted to do that sort of thing, and it kept the vandalism down very severely. LES CROSS

We had a very tough, stupid person here come from up at Newtown, his name was Appo, and he used to frequent the billiard parlours and at the age of twelve he got in an argument, and he whacked a bloke on the head with a billiard cue, and that started him off. He become an absolute madman. If you was

A police carnival at the barracks at 749 Bourke Street, Surry Hills. (SLNSW)

up the pub having a drink, he'd think nothing of grabbing you and trying to pick a fight. Street fighting was a manifestation, I suppose, of manhood. Now, we used to have a cop around here by the name of Long Tack Sam, he was a very courageous bloke. Every Saturday afternoon, up there at Erskineville, they'd get drunk, there'd be a fight or something, and most of the police used to walk down and when they saw the fight, they'd turn back, but not Long Tack, he'd go right down and start to clean them up. Well, evidently this Appo was playing up, and my cousin, who was a policeman, was walking with Long Tack Sam and as soon as Appo seen him, he took off, and Long Tack Sam said, 'Keep running Jack, I only want an excuse to shoot you'. He stopped there like a sphinx, you couldn't shift him with a crane. CLIFF NOBLE

My auntie's brother-in-law was Sergeant McClone at Newtown police station, and he would

be drinking with his relatives and friends and he'd put the people in the Black Maria that he'd been drinking with. Policemen were always the bogie men, if you didn't behave yourself the policemen would get you. GRACE SCHWEBEL

Sweet Brothers store was over the other side of the road, and you'd pay things off at a shilling a week. This fella didn't get a receipt and he was carrying a big parcel, it's Friday night, thousands of people there and this Long Tack stood in front of him and he said, 'What's the parcel?', and he said 'Oh blankets for my mother, she's been paying them off on lay by', he said, 'Show me your receipt', well he didn't have a receipt, so he had to open the parcel there and then, everyone was walking by, as soon as he saw they were blankets he said, 'Alright'. And this is the type of thing that went on. Everybody was scared of the cops. I've seen two police walk down Erskineville Road on Friday night or Saturday night, and there were two fellas talking outside the pub, and two coppers walked down, just pushed them aside and belted them in the mouth, and off they went. No reason whatsoever, they weren't drunk, they were just talking. And I saw that with my own eyes. BILL SCHWEBEL

▬

Raymond Blissett[1] was one of our most famous policemen, up around Redfern. He finished up a detective inspector, they used to call him the 'Blizzard' because of his cold bloody nature I suppose. I remember Long Tack Sam; he was a very good runner, so it was no good giving cheek to Long Tack Sam because he'd run you down, and grab you. He always managed to get the boot in the you-know-where. But Long Tack Sam and the Blizzard had things really under control. If you stepped out of line with them, you'd know you were really in trouble. People were scared of the damn police force. ROBERT HAMMOND

▬

There was a policeman called 'Bumper Farrell'. I think he was near Darlinghurst Police Station, and the kids used to hang around the corners of that, and if they did something he didn't like, he'd get them and kick them up the backside and send them home, and say, 'Don't let me see you here again, or you'll get it again'. And that seemed to work with the kids. ROSE CLEMENTS

▬

My parents knew all the D's as they used to call them, because they were always on the streets harassing people and everybody knew who they were. We didn't trust them at all. They were authority, and there were very punitive laws in those days, and mainly they seemed to be picking on poor people, like they've always done. I mean, it was police that put people out in the evictions, and all that sort of thing. Police were no friends to the working class. PORTIA FITZSIMMONS

▬

The policeman up in the police barracks at Redfern used to put on a Christmas party for us every year. I would take the little kids up and get

them put up on the horses, and take them around the police barracks. Oh, the attitude of the police in those years was entirely different to what they are now. They were friends. Yes, if anything happened they were always there for us. I knew a lot of them because they used to come down from their country homes, most of them were country boys, and they resided with friends of mine over in Kepos Street. One of them, Big Jim, won a medal in one of the Olympics for wrestling. We also had a black tracker that used to live down in the other end of Phillip Street, but they gave him a hell of a life. Well, people just looked down on him because he was black. He was living in one of the houses down, just down the road and I remember they used to put notices outside his place, to get rid of him, and yet he was a black tracker. A better man you couldn't of wished to have met. I admired him. Oh, I think he found it very hard. ANN RAMSAY

▬

I can remember one time when we had a little bit of a scam going, I probably shouldn't tell. The scam was that you get a electric light globe, and you take it down and you polish it up, and then you'd go into the street and be firm, and say, 'I've got a globe here it will save you electricity, you can have it for thruppence; we'll take your old globe and we'll sell you this new globe for thruppence'. And then you'd take it, and you'd clean another globe up, and you'd go up the street. They were the little things you did, you know, I s'pose it was dishonest. We used to get the horse and carts from Cohen's in Australia Street, and buy the spec fruit down the markets if we could afford it, and then go and sell them along the streets and then the police used to chase you, 'cause the Italian fruit shops in Newtown used to ring them up and say, 'Get them off the street, they're ruining me business!' And 'course what they'd do, the police would ring you up, and say, 'Righto, be in Newtown at two minutes to twelve, we'll put you in the cell'.

1 See Ray Blissett, interviewed by Stephen Rapley, 2 March 1988, New South Wales Bicentennial Oral History Project, Mitchell Library. MSS5163.

A 1928 police class at Redfern.
(SLNSW)

Two minutes past twelve, one minute past twelve you were out. And 'course, it would be a twenty-four-hour sentence, but no-one ever give 'em the right name, and in fact they didn't want to know the right names to be truthful, they knew you were only battling, you know, we wasn't robbing anyone. Just making a living. FRANK ALTOFT

—

There was a famous policeman after the war, Ronnie Waldon, he was a magic bloke, he was that good that they wouldn't make him Police Commissioner 'cause he was too honest. He was an ex-Rugby Union player and he coached the Australian Rugby Union team. The Paddington Basher Gang was getting around, but they come from Darlinghurst. They hung around Darlinghurst and they bashed people up all the time and robbed them. And they formed this twenty-one division, and it was all policemen that were real sportsmen, and they had them in old cars with sandshoes and old clothes on, and they just raced around the street, and if they saw a mob of these blokes on the corner they would pull up and jump out and bash tripe out of them. Within about three months the whole thing had gone, they settled them down. But Ronnie Waldon was the bloke that started that, and then he was at Paddington for years, a very respected man. When I was a kid there was a policeman at Paddo called 'Smiler', he knew every kid in Paddington, a real great bloke. KEVIN RYAN

—

The place next door was Hardigan's Pub, run by Moira Hardigan and her brother Tommy Hardigan, he used to run that and also have a bookmaking thing, and then she took it over. In most of the pubs, blokes'd go there drinking but in some part of the afternoon, fellows like Tommy Rolly and Phil Murphy used to visit each pub to have a fight and some of the houses used to have palings. All the palings would be off everybody's fences because when the fights started, everything was grabbed. When the police come, you'd see them all run on to the veranda because the theory was, and it was the law, the copper couldn't arrest you on your own property unless he had a warrant, see, or that was the theory. Of course, then the coppers'd came down and they would grab Big Jack and pull him off the veranda, and we'd all be saying, 'You can't do that!' Well, the coppers didn't care. I mean, they were worse than the bloody crims, so he'd end up getting arrested. It was no good pleading, and if you were in the house, they'd go in and just grab you. They didn't worry about habeas corpus or the bloody legal right. But what was funny, the blokes that were fighting, and it'd *be* fighting, each other, would be on the same veranda or in the house or waiting to protect themselves from the coppers coming in, and they then would come out and abuse the coppers to such a degree that if you looked, you'd think, oh well, they're fighting them [the police]. Any rate, that's the way it was.

Talking about policeman and talking about harassment, Tommy Hardigan — the police and he had a blue and the coppers got it in for him and for months and months, they used to walk him right out to the back of Roseberry. Sometimes he used to push their bikes for them while they walked or they'd take him all the way up there and back again and get stuck into him, belt him up. I mean, you never had any trouble with coppers. God, who would have a problem with coppers? I mean, anyone was mad, 'cause you could lose your life. Why wouldn't you lose your life? I was bloody careful. They weren't nice, I mean they'd chuck you in the wagon. They were bloody unbelievable. The police were supreme!

You never had any problem with the police because the police were absolutely kings. You didn't have any problem because they'll soon fix your problem. It was like when they arrested me for street betting. I could of got out of it. There's no problem getting out of it. Now, my father's people, all the local blokes, all paid off. There were no operations in these areas that didn't operate without the police knowing. In my aunty's place she used to have a deep bowl, which was to us kids miraculous, it was full of two bobs, and what would always happen is, she would get

Ladies' Day at Randwick, October 1937.
For those who couldn't attend, the local SP bookmaker made sure they didn't miss out on the action. (SLNSW)

raided. They'd come here and they'd grab them and put them in their pockets, and then you still had to pay to get off the bloody thing anyway because you had to send someone to stand up for you, to face the court. Sometimes, you knew early enough to be able to send someone else and blokes were desperate for money, so they'd get five or two pounds or something just for the privilege of being convicted. So you could have somebody stand in. I coulda' paid the coppers off as one way to prevent going to the court, or I could have used politics. I mean all I had to do was ring the federal or State member, and I wouldn't of had a problem, but because I was pig headed, and because I didn't want to do it, I went to court, and took the fine. But when the coppers picked you up, they'd take the money and they used to put it in, and in theory, you used to be able to collect it, after the event, see, and I had probably thirty-five or forty bob, which was a lot of money. So, I accepted the responsibility, I went up. My mother said to me 'You could do it easy, you could pay the coppers or you can use your influence.' And I was being big time, shooting my mouth off, 'No, No, I'm goin' up, all you people can pay, I'm not gunna do it'. My mother came up with me, and she said, 'This is great, having a son being convicted for starting price. Absolute disgrace!' I always had a feeling the problem was I got caught. I remember getting the fine and as I walked out, I went down to the claims office, and the big sergeant was sitting there, and I said, 'I want the money they took off me, mate!' He said, 'Buzz off,' but he wasn't that polite. So they always kept the money. TERRY MURPHY

I'd say the majority of people took SP booking and two-up as a national pastime, but you had to be careful not to get caught, that's all."

One of the sounds ubiquitous to Saturday arvo in South Sydney was the radio race calls followed with an intense interest by most of the adult population who usually bet with an (illegal) SP (starting price) bookie. Legal gambling was only permitted at the track and so until harnessed by the State government when it established the TAB, for many people a stint as an SP was the means by which they survived, as was having a bet for many of their customers. Indeed like Cliff Fogarty's mother, their accounts were often referred to as their 'investments'.

The two-up school was in among the brick works buildings off Mitchell Road. They'd gather there on a Sunday. There'd be possibly a hundred, a hundred and fifty people, playing two-up. Everybody knew it was on, including the police. Sometimes they were paid off, but by and large they ignored that sort of thing, it wasn't doing any harm and they knew where everybody was; if they wanted to pick somebody up, they knew where to find them. LES CROSS

▬

After she came out of the business Mum was very ill for a couple of years. So she used to bet on the horses, SP booking in Darlinghurst Road. And she was very tinny. I used to have to go up and say, 'A shilling each way' or 'Two shillings each way', and I'd have it in my head so that there'd be no papers, it was all done with my memory. And one day I got there and they'd been raided. It helped us survive, it helped pay the rent. Eventually, we were able to afford to buy a car. GLAD WILLIS

▬

There was a two-up school that ran during the Depression for about four years down the corner here. There used to be a shop on the corner, Mrs Pike's shop and they had an awning round it but they

The brickworks off Mitchell Road, pictured in
1929, was a major two-up venue. (SLNSW)

used to play two-up there, day and night, rain or shine. The police'd come down every now and again and the mob would disappear, but the day that they disappeared the quickest was when a big fellow called Coll had an argument with a local SP bookie, dived in the back of Pike's Shop and came out with an axe and the mob disappeared in about three times as fast as if the police were there! HENRY BROWN

—

Police said Thommo's didn't exist, but we knew it existed; they were in Reservoir Street. All the celebrities went to play two-up; we used to see Jack Davey and Bob Dyer go there. FRANK W.

—

Dad and his brothers and his sister, ran all the SP bookmaking in Erskineville. It was great, and my brothers, Jack and Terry and I, used to run the bets. It was serious, but it was fun. Mum and Dad bought Jack a pumped-up tyre scooter and I used that then to run the bets with. But I mean, Terry got picked up one day by the coppers; he was coming out of the house, and he got caught out on the footpath, which meant he got charged with street betting. Had he been caught inside the house he could've been charged with house betting, and there was a big difference in them days, house betting was the worst. MAUREEN OLIVER

—

There used to be a big two-up school at the brick pit. The Boxer, who ran the game, would kick us kids out. You could get between sixty to eighty people betting on it, two-up was pretty rife. You'd often get the police raiding them. They'd come down in old 1927 Chevrolet cars, and all jump out. They shot them into Black Marias. There was always sly grog after six p.m. from what I can ascertain, because my father used to go around bottling the quarts at the Balaclava Hotel, that was on the corner of Buckland Street and Mitchell Road. And you have a favourite knock on the publican's door and go and get yourself a quart after closing time. I don't think they went without a drink, the ones that could afford it of course. Before the war there was one chap who lived around the next street from us, Snowy Holmes,

he had a little SP bookmaking business going at the local hotel and he always had a motor car, so must've been pretty prosperous, the SP business in them days. Most people wouldn't have had cars. But he was very generous because if he had a winning day, he'd be driving past and see us kids and he'd throw a handful of pennies out. ROBERT HAMMOND

—

When I was about fourteen they used to have a two-up and SP down in Harris Street. The Police Station was up in Jersey Road, and they used to pay the kids two bob to sit on the steps up there, and if they saw a police car coming they'd yell out, to let them know. My brother Jackie got a phone put on at our place, no-one in Paddo had a phone, he was going to try and be an SP bookie, but the coppers come down and pulled the phone out of the wall. He lasted about two days. KEVIN RYAN

—

Dad first got into SP bookmaking when someone who'd been doing it died. We had the right premises for SP bookmaking because beside our home, we had a side lane, and a back window, which my father had bars put across so that no one could lean in and take the money. So you went up the back lane to put your bets on. And you came to the window with the bars, and you passed it through the window. He had a penciller and someone that wrote the bets for him. If the police were going to raid they knew and they got someone they knew to be there and the police would take them and fine them £5, for their first conviction, and let them go. But if they had more than three, I think they went to jail. But my father'd always pay them to come and go for him. Dad made sure he was never the one to be fined! JOSIE FOSTER

—

My dad did SP betting for a while[2], once my mother was standing at the gate calling out to me — I was only standing outside the gate and I couldn't understand why. And then a few years later I

---

2 See also Christopher Keating, *Surry Hills, The City's Backyard*, Hale & Iremonger, Sydney, 1991, pp. 62-64.

An SP bookmaker's premises after a police raid.
Many operators, however, worked out of kitchens
and homes with virtually the whole family involved.
(ACP)

discovered there was a bell at the top of a gate post, a buzzer, and apparently at that time the police were coming around, and she was supposedly calling me to come in, when in actual fact she was pressing the buzzer to let Dad know, to get everything off the table and get all his friends playing cards. My dad was into anything where he could make a quid. He used to go down to Thommo's two-up school at the bottom of Reservoir Street and work there at nights, to make a few extra shillings. If you had a lot of money, you could go and play, or you could play as a small-time player if you wanted to. I heard him and Mum talking, saying that the police were on the take. And he was a cockatoo at times, and I couldn't understand; I used to look at him and wonder, 'What's he look like as a cockatoo? There's no resemblance whatsoever.' It was six o'clock closing, and if you knew the right people, as my father inevitably did, he could always get access to bottles of drink or he could spend time with his mates after the doors had closed, with the publican, who he always seemed to know. TERRY GLEBE

—

My grandmother was Irish and they had the penal mentality, a lot of the penal laws in Ireland, they regarded as English laws which they didn't have to obey. I mean it wasn't any sense of ethics or morality, it was the penal laws, and my mother had that idea about SP bookies. I used to, as a kid, run and take bets down to the local SP bookie. My mother backed with SPs most of her life but she wasn't cheating the government, it was just they were penal laws. CLIFF FOGARTY

"If you had dyed red hair and red fingernails you were a wanton woman."

Like the SPs, who were usually locals and occasionally raided by the police, sex-industry workers were also part of the community. Streets such as Palmer Street and Crown Street were well known for their brothels.[3]

All the brothels were down in Surry Hills, like Palmer Street and Crown Street. The Cross was bohemian: artists and poets and writers. All the girls would be sitting on their verandahs. Because we'd be walking past, and we'd be gaping up: 'Don't look at them, don't look at them!' If we went down Palmer Street and that, the ladies of the night were a sight to us, because they'd be very heavily made up, and dressed differently from the run-of-the-mill people. They always seemed to be very bright colours, very tight. ROSE CLEMENTS

—

I used to play in the back lanes where all the prostitutes used to work. And they were okay to us, maybe give us a penny or something to go and spend. A man would go into the back of the house and the lady would take him upstairs, he would hang his coat on the banister downstairs, while he was upstairs having sex with the lady or whatever they were doing, another lady would come in and steal anything that he had in his pockets, that was a term called 'gingering'. Sometimes, if the police had been after them, the women'd come into the back of our house and ask my mother could they run through to the front door, and my mother would often say, 'Yes, come through', and they'd run through the house and escape through the other way. JEAN JURD

3   See Roberta Perkins, 'Being and Becoming "Working Girls": An Oral History of Prostitutes in Sydney 1935-1985' in John Shields (ed.), *All Our Labours: Oral Histories of Working Life in Twentieth-Century Sydney,* The Sydney History Group, New South Wales University Press, Kensington, 1992.

Mrs T. Parsons (a.k.a. Tilly Devine) in front of her crystal cabinet at her Palmer Street home. (ACP)

YOU CAN PAY THE COPPERS, OR USE YOUR INFLUENCE

The next street was 'the' street where the prostitutes all sat up on their verandahs. All I knew was if you had dyed red hair and red fingernails you were a wanton woman. Woolloomooloo was notorious, Palmer Street in particular. Most of my friends grew up to be prostitutes. And there were razor gangs. My mother knew underworld people, and there was that woman, Tilly Divine, now I met her. She was really nice. She always used to give us a shiny shilling if she saw us. She was a big woman and she had black long hair. JUDY CHAMBERS

—

At one stage the prostitutes used to do it in their cars. They used to have these big cars and they used to park them up behind the playground when the playground was closed. And as kids we used to sneak up to the car to have a look, scare the hell out of them, yell something at them and run. We were brats, but we used to get our kicks out of it. There was a bit of prostitution about at the time, but not so much in Woolloomooloo, it was more towards Darlinghurst, especially Palmer Street. But most of it was up the top of Palmer Street, and also on the other side of William Street, around Stanley Street now, or East Sydney. ANDREW LAZARIS

It was The Rocks that had the bad reputation!"

For most of the century there has been a strong sense of community. Repeatedly residents refer to the neighbouring suburbs as being wilder and tougher than theirs which was always described as safe, but often sullied by the unfair assertions of outsiders who were ignorant of the true dynamics of the place.

Sometimes the Razor Gang would come down, but most of them were above William Street. We didn't actually have them down here [Woolloomooloo]. They used to slash your face, but only people that they had arguments with. Well, there were some of them down here that went up there and annoyed them. And then they'd come down here, to get even. Occasionally we'd see a fight. I knew a boy that was slashed on the face, he'd done something stupid, probably. We never had a hotbed of crime! It was over the other side, the top of William Street, where your hotbed of crime was! Oh, we had sly grog, and we had a pak-a-poo joint; it was a family home, but I think one day a week they sold pak-a-poo tickets. You pick your numbers, a bit like lotto. Woolloomooloo had such a bad name, even though it wasn't bad, because of all the other things that happened, I mean, like all the gangs that were around that weren't really in the heart of Woolloomooloo. I mean, they were on the outskirts, but the whole neighbourhood got blamed. It was as if everybody had razors. But I mean, there wasn't none of that. You wouldn't go near The Rocks, that would be the last place you'd go. Kings Cross didn't worry us, it wasn't like that. We used to go up there to the pictures every Saturday afternoon. We never had any problem. It was The Rocks that had the bad reputation. JOYCE HIGGINS

—

In East Sydney when we were down at Yurong Street, there was a man killed by the razor gang in the lane next to our house. I remember going down and looking at the blood and being hauled back by the scruff of the neck and getting a proper whack on the bottom, for going out there. But it was only criminals killing criminals, not civilians. Dario Lo Schiavo

—

When we got to be about fourteen or sixteen there was a lot of street fights. We used to fight the Surry Hills mob. We'd go up to Darlinghurst and there'd be a fight, and then we'd race like mad and come back. We'd probably stop at William Street, they weren't game to come any further than that. Might be a fortnight after they'd come right down Woolloomooloo and we'd have a bash up down here and chase them back. Every fight was what they call a fair go, there was no kicking, nothing like that, even men when they fought, they wasn't allowed to kick, anyone kicking you were a disgrace. There was no damage done, a few black eyes, no broken legs or broken arms, no bottles, nothing like that. Millers Point, they were the toughies them days, no-one was game to go near Millers Point. They'd bash you, they'd kick you, they'd do anything down there, if you ever got stuck down there, you'd get what they call really bashed up. They were really, really, really, really tough boys of what they call 'The Push' at Millers Point. Yeah, they were vicious. Billy Pascoe

—

But there was always characters around the place that everybody knew, but nobody'd think of robbing a working man, you know? I remember one time they robbed the Bank of New South Wales up here [Newtown], but it was done in a clever way which people never got hurt. There was a holiday weekend coming up and there was an empty shop next door to it, so they took the empty shop, they whitened the windows over so that people couldn't see how they were preparing the shop, and in the weekend they just went straight through the wall into the strong room and got all the money in the strong room and they went away and they were never heard of since. I think that was about 1938, '37. Henry Brown

—

The razor gang[4] was very much in evidence, but they didn't come out of Surry Hills and nobody went down there. I used to peer down the streets with

delight, you know, I'd think, 'Oh, that's very exciting; the razor gang's down there'. But you never saw them round the streets. They were young men, and it was the Depression; they were very wild and against society, and I suppose they robbed each other, and anyone who ventured down there. The ships used to come into Woolloomooloo, and they used to rob the sailors, when they were drunk and there were a few murders. Also, there were the murders in Centennial Park. There was a young girl strangled with a stocking and her body was in the pond. That gave me the horrors. I used to read all these things and got a sort of vicarious excitement about them, you know, and you'd think, 'Oh, isn't that awful'. But you felt secure in your own house, so you know that was just a bit of excitement. Pat Rose

—

I've seen my stepfather put a razor blade into a small stick, and that would've been used to cut somebody up. I don't know if he actually did anything, but he was a part-time gangster, and also a wharf labourer. It was a matter of any sort of crime, like stealing off the wharves, selling anything that you could sell because it brought in money. My stepfather, before he was living with my mother, had been keeping company with a gangster's moll, Dulcie Markham (Pretty Dulcie), who used to hang around King's Cross. Dulcie Markham had shot him in the back, he had snow-white hair, he'd gone white within a week. He survived, but apparently two or three people were shot over love affairs with Dulcie Markham. My mother lived with him for quite some time. His name was Dicky Barker, Dicky Mealing. He had two or three names.

Growing up in Woolloomooloo: a series of parties, gangsters and crooks coming to the house; a lot of drinking. They'd send me in a taxi, and I was very young, to go and get sly grog or to go and put a bet on a greyhound dog or a horse; I'd never seen a book in my young years, the only book I'd ever seen

---

4 See Alfred McCoy, *Drug Traffic, Narcotics and Organised Crime in Australia,* Harper & Row, Sydney, 1980.

was the dog-racing form. There were two brothers, Robinson's, and there was a couple of gangsters. I actually saw one gangster pistol whip another crook who was sitting in a chair at our place at a party. Jackie Hodder was some sort of gangster; Kate Leigh had a sly-grog shop, Kate Leigh and Tilly Divine both had houses where the prostitutes used to work in Palmer Street. They were rivals. They were big time, we were only little, they were big time.

There was a gangster called Frank Green, and we used to go swimming, when I was about fourteen, fifteen with my girlfriend from the laundry, Frances, and with Frank Green's daughter who had paralysis. And I've got to give him credit in that although he was a big-time gangster, if he saw us in the street of a night coming home from the picture show or it was dark or late, he'd always ask us, 'Are you girls okay, do you want me to make sure you get home all right?' They would look after their own kind, although they were gangsters and they'd fight amongst themselves, they didn't do anything to the kids, I s'pose they all understood that we were just struggling kids trying to grow up in a neighbourhood that was pretty rough on us. JEAN JURD

▬

They used to call Darlinghurst 'Razorhurst'. If you did something to a razor gang, they'd use a razor and slash your face. But I never heard once of them attacking the wives and children of the gangsters; they just kept it in amongst themselves. ROSE CLEMENTS

▬

A friend's grandmother lived in the street back from Mitchell Road behind the Park View Hotel, and somebody broke into her place and messed the place up and pinched a few things. Two of the local hard men, Limerick and Nigger Fox, passed the word around that if the stuff wasn't back within a week they hoped their funeral fund was paid up, and all the stuff came back again. Nigger Fox was a bit of a bookie and later on he opened up the door one night and someone blasted him with a shotgun; he was dead in Mitchell Road. Limerick was a very wealthy, prominent man; he used to own nightclubs and things like that. But if anybody in those days,

especially around these districts, hit a woman or a child, well they'd have a good chance of finishing in hospital themselves, because there were a lot of hard cases, but they wouldn't allow anybody to interfere with children or women. HENRY BROWN

▬

There were a few criminals down there. There was Nigger Fox, he used to sell sly grog, which meant they would buy the wine from the hotel and then they'd turn around and sell it for dearer prices in their home of a night time because there was six o'clock closing. We lived four or five doors down from them and people used to come knocking on our door of a night time, or early hours of the morning by mistake. In the end my younger brother used to turn around and sing out, 'Two doors up, two doors up!' BETTY MOULDS

▬

Redfern was a great place to live, it was very central. It was a place where nobody had any more than the next person. It was very safe. I recall when I was first selected to go to England with the football, the people of Redfern gave me a farewell at the Redfern Town Hall. Johnny Wade was the compere, and he had Harry Willis and Glen Marks, who were the group that played and sang at the Prince Edward Theatre. And I can remember Johnny Wade saying, 'This is a fun night, everyone leave the hardware outside'. The guns and the knives were left outside. And they gave me a beautiful rug that I took away, and I've always felt proud of that day. The razor gangs were in Surry Hills. But I think, the only people that were attacked were probably people who did the wrong thing by them, you know. There were guys in the area who had criminal records, but they all respected us as kids, they never interfered with us. We knew who the criminals were. Some of them were mixed up in sly grog, and petty thieving, but not locally. I was a cockatoo for the two-up; we would sit down on the corner and whistle if the police were coming down. SIR NICHOLAS SHEHADIE

▬

There was the gangster element around. We had the Reeves family that was always in trouble, two of

Palmer Street was a well-known 'red light' district, but also a residential neighbourhood as indicated by the number of children and locals inspecting this crashed Studebaker in January 1935. (SLNSW)

the three of them got shot dead, but Teddy Reeves was, oh, a mongrel of a kid. To be tough you had to be able to spit, see, that was a big thing, all the kids used to spit, and I could never spit, every time I spat I used to land it on me shoe. Anyway, we all used to go down to Five Ways Picture Show, and when it was a boring picture, everyone would go down into the toilet and have a mag. And there was a window out into the park, and this day we were all down there, it was school holidays. We're talking and I'm practising my spitting see, and I go over to the window, and I spat out the window, and just as I did, this Teddy Reeves looked through the window and I spat right in his face. I was about twelve, he was about sixteen I s'pose. 'I'll f'ing get you Ryanie,' and he took off and I run out. And when I got up the

stairs into the pictures I see him come in the front, so I got down on me belly, and I'm crawling up under the seats, and he's coming down the aisle into the toilet looking for me. And I run out and I ran home, and I never went out for about three days, and Mum's saying, 'Why don't you go down and have a game of cricket?' and I said, 'No, no I think I'll stay home and paint'. Anyway, thank God, on the Friday this Teddy Reeves had a gun fight with the police, and he was arrested. He got five years' jail and I was happy. Kevin Ryan

—

You heard of things like armed robberies, and things like that, but no-one spoke. You heard things like going down the rail yards at Alexandria and robbing the big rail carriages of whatever goods they

YOU CAN PAY THE COPPERS, OR USE YOUR INFLUENCE

had on, busting into them and taking all the goods out of them. There were a lot of stolen goods sold in Erskineville. Like, you only had to say, 'I want two jumpers' and you got them, and I mean, they were Fletcher Jones, and they were the best. Anything from a mink coat to a diamond ring; a needle to an anchor, they used to say you can go to the pub and buy what you like. It was well known, in the Rose of Australia, you could buy your beans, your peas, your tomatoes, your pumpkin, your vegetables off one guy, and you'd go to a set of scales. If you went to the Erskineville Hotel for a beer, you could buy a suit, a collar and tie, cardigan, whatever you wanted. Some of the people just did their shopping there. JOSIE FOSTER

—

Kate Leigh lived in Bourke Street and she moved up into Devonshire Street.[5] I think she belonged to the underworld. When I went to school she used to be good to the children in the district; every Christmas she'd give out things to the children. And she had one of the biggest funerals from St Peter's. You know, she was recognised for her goodness to charity, to the people around that didn't have much or anything. IRENE WEBBER

—

Tilly Devine was a very well-known personality. In Oxford Street there used to be June Hairdressing. My sister, Jean, went over to get her hair permed and in came Tilly Devine. Tilly Devine was looking over at Jean all the time, and Jean's getting very, very nervous, because Tilly was a well-known criminal. It turned out, she wanted her hair dyed the same colour as my sister's. But I tell you she had some very nasty moments while this woman was eyeing her off. GLAD WILLIS

—

I can remember Katie Leigh, you know, she used to have the sly-grog shops. I can't ever say anything bad about Katie Leigh, I always thought she was a nice lady. Not that I personally knew her, but if I seen her I knew who she was. But I got a gun and pouch off her one Christmas; she used to put parties on for all the kids in Surry Hills. I remember I got a gun and pouch and my sister got a doll out of it one year. She used to look after the kids. I think she was classed the Queen of Surry Hills and I could believe that. Of a Sunday, you know, you'd see people walking around and they'd ask you, 'Do you know where Katie Leigh's is?' And you looked at them and if they had a hat on you knew they were detectives and you'd say nothing. But if they were just dressed normal, you'd just tell them where they were. WARREN RICHARDSON

—

There was one guy come down there and harassed some of the kids, and the kids gave him a bit of cheek though, and he chased them into the playground. Mr Ryan came over and grabbed this guy and virtually threw him out of the playground and said, 'You leave our kids alone', sort of thing. And when he left all the kids said to him, 'Oh sir, he's a gunman', and poor Mr Ryan was afraid for the next couple of months, that this guy is going to come back and get him. But I mean, there were a lot of crims that used to hang around, particularly with the Forbes Club opening up there that Percy Galea used to own. The Forbes Club was one of the first illegal casinos in Sydney and it was renowned for a lot of criminals hanging out there. ANDREW LAZARIS

5 See Keating, op. cit., pp. 65-67 and Judith A. Allen, *Sex and Secrets: Crimes Involving Australian Women since 1880,* Oxford University Press, Melbourne, 1990, pp. 168-174. Ruth Park's character, Delia Stochs, in *Harp in the South,* is reputed to be based on Kate Leigh. Chapter 4 of Park's novel is devoted to her generosity to local children.

"WE NEVER HAD A HOTBED OF CRIME"

THE PICTURE OF THE YEAR

Kate Leigh and Tilly Devine — the two most talked about people involved in prostitution and sly grog in the 1940s and 1950s. Yet their reputations were not all bad, with many residents remembering their generosity to local kids at Christmas. (ACP)

"We're the Surry Hills mob, the Surry Hills mob are we."

With larger families and a more family residential orientation than is evident in the late twentieth century, there were many children and so community identity found expression in their 'gangs'. These were neighbourhood-based with the extent of their 'territory' based on how far they dared to roam. Described as non-violent, yet naughty, there is a 'Ginger Meggs' style aura to their activities.

Iwas part of a gang, the Waratahs Vigoro Club. They run from about fourteen, eighteen, nineteen. You got into fights amongst yourselves, sometimes you got into fights over girls, it was mostly girls that we truly got in fights over. There was no robberies or anything like that. There was a gang in the Newtown area, there was a gang at Enmore, there was one in Erskineville. FRANK ALTOFT

Our territory was Erskineville, Newtown, Waterloo. I was in a little gang when I was eleven, twelve, thirteen, fourteen. They were based on neighbourhoods, if you got into their territory there'd be a rumble on, bit of a fist-fight. Each gang had a good fighter, and if you got into trouble you'd call on him and he would fight their best fighter, no harm come from it. At the time we used to think it was big time, but it was nothing, it's a part of growing up. SYD FENNELL

If you came from Alexandria, you were pretty proud that you were from Alexandria and Erskineville, and we used to fight. Down at the bottom of this street, there was a railway piece of land, a construction thing, and they used to have blue metal, and the young blokes on this side, maybe ten to fifteen years old, had full armies put together, and my brothers were all in it, one was a captain. They actually had shields and swords, and they used to have stuff to carry their heavy blue metal, for throwing. We used to go between this area, up into Newtown, which is Watkin Street, and the top part of Burren Street. But there wasn't any viciousness, even though it sounds like it. TERRY MURPHY

We used to do some terrific things; a mob of the kids, we all used to go down to Woolloomooloo Police Boys Club, and we'd get around in a Woolloomooloo Police Boys football jumper and a pair of shorts and a 'gobs cap', everyone had a gobs cap, and all the gang used to write their names on it. We'd go down the Trumper Park, and the old fellow that run Trumper Park, Paddy Ryan — no relation thank God — was a cranky old bugger. Anyway, we used to get down there and you'd get a cat and you've gotta put his head under your arm and squeeze your arm real hard so his head's caught, holding his front legs and his back legs, put his tail in your mouth, and you'd bite the tail and pump, and we'd line up and play bagpipes, march up and down with the cats going 'eeeeehhhhh'. But the thing was to get rid of them you had to get the back leg, and as you swung it, let his head out and you know, 'ssshhh', and so the weight of it threw him away from you. If you didn't do it right you got scratched to buggery, and you'd come home and your mum would say 'What's happened to you, what have you got the scratches from?' 'Oh playing football.' KEVIN RYAN

The kids'd sort of have their own areas; like the crowd of us, especially the boys, used to go down to East Sydney Police Boys Club in Woolloomooloo. That involved going down along Riley Street, which was considered a relatively safe area, but if any of the Surry Hills mob strayed into the Woolloomooloo mob area, apart from Riley Street, then we would have a fight on our hands. It was just kid stuff more than anything, that they had their territory. It was just a usual sort of fisticuffs thing and 'get back to where you belong'. The Surry Hills kids were considered to be just different. We simply saw ourselves as Surry Hills and they were Woolloomooloo, and that's all there was to it. There was one rhyme we had for Surry Hills: 'We're the Surry Hills mob, the Surry Hill's mob are we, the copper came along, he grabbed us by the collar, he tried to run us in, we kicked him in the shins, because the Surry Hills mob are we.' TERRY GLEBE

━

We didn't mix with the Erskineville mob. The Alexandria mob were different, and the Redfern mob were different again, and the Waterloo mob were different again. I don't know what it was, I don't think there was any struggle or anything like that, I just don't think that they really associated with one another. The Redfern boys were pretty tough, the tougher of the lot, and I believe the Ultimo kids were even tougher than that. HARRY BRENNAN

━

Paddington did have a reputation but to my mind I didn't care, because I was brought up there, so I was just a 'Paddo' boy, that was it. It didn't worry me, what they thought. Actually I thought it was quite romantic, it was a good reputation to come from 'Paddo'; it meant you were tough. You know back in those days, it was a bit like Balmain, if you came from 'Paddo' you were a toughie, because there was a 'Paddo' gang. GEORGE TOURVAS

━

I think with Redfern and Waterloo there is a lot of rivalry. Like with The Block at Redfern, that's Eveleigh Street, Redfern, where all the Koories live. They call it 'The Block' because it's like Eveleigh and Louis Street, and that whole block is Aboriginal, it belongs to the Aboriginal Housing Company. And I mean, that's one place where, when I was heaps younger, I wouldn't go, because it was always like a rough area and I was told not to go. I mean, there was always the odd fights, but never like the real big rivalry. DEAN INGRAM

" So we done all these silly stupid awful things to people."

Anyone who was different copped it from the local kids. Memories of cruelties were universally recounted with regret, if humorously, by interviewees and were generally attributed to childish insensitivity.

We used to go up to grandma's for cracker night, Grandma Ferguson's. They used to buy the crackers and we shared with them — Catherine Wheels — and we'd put a bunger in a tin and make a heck of a noise. There were Tom Thumbs, they'd light one end and some of the kids in Union Street were pretty rough, and we had a Chinese family up the top, the Lum Kings, and they put all the crackers in their place one night, and they all ran out, it was a horrible thing to do, but we thought it was funny at the time, we were just kids. LORETTO THURGOOD

━

They talk about multiculturalism today, it's always been here. The other side of Redfern Oval, probably be what they call Elizabeth Street, was Syrian Town and we used to go down there, and cause all sorts of mayhem by ridiculing them. We used to sing out, 'What are you wearing a dress for?' Sometimes they'd pull out a big knife, and when you seen the knife, away you went for your life. Now the Chinese used to operate most of the market gardens all over the other side of McEvoy Street, because this is where the off spin for Shea's Creek was. The poor old Chinese worked from daylight to dark, and as children we used to really torment them. They had a great big fat draught horse, he could hardly fit in the shafts, and the only thing that he knew was going down to the city markets, and on the way back invariably the poor old Chinese would go to sleep, and we would turn the horse around, and he'd go back to the markets! On one occasion, a poor old Charlie, they called them all 'Charlie' in those days, he got home, the horse was outside the slip rails, so we put down the slip rails, put the horse the other side, and the rails back, and threw little stones at Charlie to wake him up. I don't know what he said but he must've called us everything, because he went berserk, he couldn't make out how the horse got one side of the rails, and the cart was the other. So we done all these silly stupid awful things to people. There was a Joss House and the wealthy ones got buried over here at Botany, and on one occasion a couple of smart alecs was over there, and of course at Chinese funerals they put copious amounts of food on the grave, and a couple of smarties said, 'Hey Charlie, when's your mate coming up to eat the food?' and Charlie said, 'The same time as your mate's coming up to smell the flowers!'

A fellow named Mickey O'Dowd, went down pinching the vegetables from the Chinese, and they had a blunderbuss, and bang! Away it went, and whacked him in the backside, and we sat up there over a bucket of hot water, picking the pellets out with a needle. I suppose I got three good hidings in my life, and one was for going over pinching their vegetables. I brought them home very proudly, and when I put them down, my father said, 'Where did you get them?' I said, 'I pinched them off the Chinks,' and he said, 'Don't you know that those poor fellows work from daylight to dark, and you go over there, and just steal their vegetables, and bring them home? Now I'm going to make an example of you.' And he did. CLIFF NOBLE

—

There were some funny characters around, there was the poor old bugger that lived over the other side of Oxford Street, 'Orrible Herby, because there was a bloke on the radio in those days, Horrible Herby Burgers; he was on the Mo show. This poor bloke was a spastic, and the kids used to give him hell. It was that cruel, this is when we were eleven or twelve, used to yell out 'Horrible Herby' and run and he'd chase us around the street, poor bugger. And someone would sneak up behind him and pull his hat down over his head. The Salvation Army used to come around every Friday night and get under one of the street lights and play their music. I remember my brother Norman and meself got a beltin' for sucking lemons in front of them. When you suck a lemon they can't blow the trumpet, their lips purse and they make all funny noises. And we got down

there with these lemons and Dad gave us a lecture on how good the Salvation Army were. KEVIN RYAN

—

There were lots of little back lanes. There was one where all the poor drunks used to get the methos, they drank methylated spirits and boot polish, that was all they could afford. We used to say to these poor things, 'Look out, here come the coppers!' and they'd get their ragged coats, and they'd run up the lane. JUDY CHAMBERS

—

There was a fellow who we called the mad Scotchman, a name that we just came up with. The guy might've been mad but he used to live in the park there at The Domain, near the Mitchell Library, near the Cahill Expressway and we used to attend Plunkett Street Primary School. He used to wear these bright red and yellow clothes and he was very bright, and he'd like wait for us. Every afternoon we used to go up there and have a rock fight with him and we'd pelt the poor guy with the rocks and run. ANDREW LAZARIS

—

There used to be a guy where Kinselas was, and we used to harass him all the time 'cause I think he had a mental health problem, which is really awful. I know it now, but in those days we didn't know. You used to say to him, 'Bow to the Queen,' and he used to bow, and he'd be there all day if you kept saying, 'Bow to the Queen'. So we'd harass him for twenty minutes or so and then move on. SHANE CAMPBELL

" I was a terrible kid!"

There were many 'terrible kids' in South Sydney. Despite the (undeserved) reputations of most neighbourhoods, children, perhaps because there were so many of them, had a great deal of freedom, and together would find fun in places that were unavailable to children later in the century.

I was an average kid for around the Redfern and Alexandria way. Always in trouble of some description, but not serious trouble. On cracker night they'd blow everybody's letterboxes up. They'd knock on doors and then run round the corner or something and disturb them, anything to disturb somebody. We'd scale trams, the tram would be going past and you jumped on, and then the conductor'd start chasing you and you'd would just jump off. All of that silly nonsense. It was peer pressure. I've seen one boy, I don't know how he could ever do it, but two trams would pass one another, and they'd be fairly packed, and he'd go up scaling the tram, and off onto the other going in the opposite direction. MICK GREEN

I was a terrible kid! We used to go down to the Botanical Gardens and we'd build cubby houses in amongst all these expensive, exotic trees, and get chased out and go and build another one. And they had a bandstand where this band played every Sunday; we'd suck lemons in front of the fellow who played the trombone and throw lolly papers in the tuba and see how many we could throw in before we got chased away. My mum took me to a social worker because she couldn't handle me! JUDY CHAMBERS

I can remember playing tricks on my parents with a group of kids I grew up with: we'd tie a bit of cotton to the knocker, it was one of those metal knockers on the door, and sitting over the other side of the street, we thought we were so clever; you just pull the knocker and then break the cotton. Mother would come out and look around, nobody there: 'You kids see anyone?' 'No,' innocent, 'No'. And we'd do the same thing again and then be told to, 'Get the hell out of here, we know what you're doing!' TERRY GLEBE

The street lighting wasn't as good as what it is now, and you'd get about the average height and you'd tie black cotton across the footpath and watch people walk down into it. Oh, you used to see some funny sights with that! Because they stop, and they'd be feeling and they didn't know what was going on. And oh, that used to scare a few people! And any tin roof, you'd get a lot of rocks and throw the rocks on

the roof and run like buggery. Just little bugger things, not meaning to hurt anyone, but just for the fun of it. WARREN RICHARDSON

We used to fish off the wharves at the time, and a lot of the ships used to come in at Woolloomooloo. We used to love jumping on the forklifts and have races up and down on the wharf. One of my friends was driving along in a forklift and couldn't stop it and was going for the edge and he jumped off the forklift and consequently the forklift hit the edge of the wharf and tipped over into the water. Obviously we ran for our lives, once again praying to God that we don't get caught. The next day we were down there and they were pulling it out of the water, and we're saying, 'God! Wonder how that fell in there!'

While the eastern suburbs railway was being built I can recall one time where one of the boys who lived up the street from me, Donald Puddyfoot, and another friend called Carl Hamilton were walking through the eastern suburbs railway because they were mischievous and they wanted to find out what was in there. They were intrigued I think to see where the tunnel was leading. And quite often kids would have a look around and see if they could find something. They'd maybe pinch a bit of lead, because they could go and cash it in and get a few bob for it, scrap metal or that type of thing. And they were walking through the tunnel and Donald Puddyfoot bumped into a guy that had hung himself. They ran straight back out of the tunnel because they were petrified. But Donald Puddyfoot was such a wild kid and he went back in there, and went through the guy's pockets, in case he might've had some money on him. And he came back and when Mr Ryan fronted him and said, 'What's the story? What happened?' he says, 'I ran into the guy and we ran back out sir, but I went back in to check his pockets, but I felt sorry for the poor bugger because he only had a few bob in his pockets, so I left it there for him.' We thought that's pretty good of him, you know, the poor guy was dead anyway, but he decided to leave the money in the guy's pocket because he didn't have much on him. ANDREW LAZARIS

8

There'd be a bit of a song and dance in the parlour

The Salvation Army Band at Newtown in 1942. (SLNSW)

" My aunt won a black bottom contest at The Hub."

Bands, live theatre and dancing at venues like the Surreyville and the Trocadero were popular and frequent sources of fun and entertainment. Whatever the economic situation, vaudeville shows at theatres like Clay's, where Stiffy and Mo were regular performers, are fondly remembered by many South Sydney residents, particularly those from Erskineville and Newtown, who were within walking distance of numerous venues up until the television era.

Locally there were all the bands;[1] you used to go on Friday or Saturday night. Well, the Salvation Army band was a very big band, it was up in Brown Street, where the Salvation Army Citadel is, and a good band. And then there was another Newtown band used to play in Australia Street, about the Town Hall, and there was one outside Sweet Brothers, and around the city, the rotundas in Hyde Park and Belmore Park, they'd all be playing Sunday afternoons. There was a lot of Highland dancing and Irish dancing. They would perform for big celebrations in the street or come and have a day in the park [Hollis Park, Newtown]. There was a band rotunda; the band would play and there would be all these Highland dancers, oh they were really good, you never see anything like that now. KEITH MULHEARN

"WE NEVER HAD A HOTBED OF CRIME"

We use to go to the vaudeville at Fuller's
Elizabethan Theatre, that used to be Fuller's
Vaudeville Show. Then across Newtown Bridge was
Clay's Vaudeville. Jim Gerald was a great actor, a
great comedian. There was another fella, a local
Newtown bloke, Joe somebody, big fat bloke, and
there was a tall, skinny bloke, Skinny Barland they
called him. Mo Rene had a partner, Stiffy, Stiffy and
Mo, they broke up when they were up at Clay's.
There'd be singing, musical instruments, tap
dancing, chorus girls.

Behind Clay's there was a lane, opposite the
Newtown Police Station, and on that side of the lane
was a stable, and that was their dressing room, and
when we were kids we used to stand there and watch
the actors come out with all their lippy, paint and
powder. I think they were more gay than anything
else, and they know how to paint and powder
themself up. I s'pose I've been inside Clay's about
three times, you'd go up to the bloke on the door say
'There's three of us, we've only got sixpence', so
'Righto, go in'. The policeman Long Tack Sam got
that name from a show at the Elizabethan Theatre.
Long Tack Sam was the magician, supposed to be
Chinese but he's very tall, very slim too, and he was
marvellous, and Long Tack [the policeman] got
called Long Tack Sam after that, and he was about
six foot six, and about six inches broad. BILL SCHWEBEL

—

We used to go to Fuller's Theatre down on the
corner of Wilson Street and Erskineville Road. It was
called The Majestic Theatre, and in fact it was used
later on for the Elizabethan Theatre and Opera. But
in those days, there was a regular dramatic company
that used to do melodramas, and the actors were
well-known to everyone. They put on plays with
names like, *The Girl Who Took the Wrong Turning*. I
think they used to do a different play every week.
Elsie's husband was a violinist, and he used to play

Mo (Roy Rene), a notorious vaudeville character.
(Greater Union)

1 See Janette Beard, 'The Municipality of Newtown, 1892–1922: A
Social Sketch', BA Hons. Thesis, 1983, University of Sydney.

THERE'D BE A BIT OF A SONG AND DANCE IN THE PARLOUR

in the orchestra at the theatre. Everyone went. The tickets were very cheap and the whole place was always full. I think it was called Frank Neill's Company. There was a comedian, and there was a villain. Lots of those people later went into radio. There was a man who was always the hero, he was so handsome, Maurice Toohey, and women used to call their babies after him, he was a real matinee idol! Then there was also the Vaudeville at Clay's, which is still a picture show down there opposite Newtown Station, with chorus girls, and dancing like a London music hall. One evening, I went into Clay's with a friend. We didn't have any money to pay, but we sneaked in, and we got in upstairs and these two grown-up girls let us sit with them and we stayed there and my mother was frantic. I remember feeling terribly guilty at the time. ZENA SACHS

One of the best buildings ever built was The Majestic Theatre in Newtown that was the greatest picture show of all time. The acoustics were that good, they didn't have to use a microphone and it had three storeys. They used to have plays and operas, but we went when it was the pictures. FRANK ALTOFT

Actually Clay's was the training ground for Williamson's, if you could get through Clay's on the stage, then Williamson's would consider you for their shows, but, if you couldn't go through Clay's, they wouldn't even look at you. After a show you came out and there was a hot-dog stand on four wheels and you could get pies and hot dogs and all that, they called it 'the poison cart,' you always referred to things derogatively, the more you enjoyed them the more you were willing to pan them. LES CROSS

Mr Ockleford was a local artist; he was a very clever, brilliant wood-turner and a lot of his work was in the Sydney Town Hall and buildings around town. But he was also a great bone man and also earnt his living playing the bones on the Tivoli and at Her Majesty's Theatre and on tours. We went to Her Majesty's Theatre a lot, it was on the corner of Bedford Street running down the side of the Newtown Town Hall. One Saturday night during a Cinderella performance suddenly the lights went out and they came on the stage to tell everybody not to be frightened, but a big fire at Marcus Clarkes in Brown Street was out of control and that part of Newtown was plunged into darkness. The artists stayed there singing with lamps and slowly people left the theatre, not one person was injured. My parents took us on a regular basis to Clay's Theatre, that was vaudeville. But Her Majesty's, that was usually light opera, musical comedy. I saw Gladys Moncreif perform there several times; Rio Rita, Nelly Collie was a very well-known artist in those days and she usually played the role of Prince Charming. She had this magnificent voice. You never forgot the well-known performers because they continued right up to modern-day television. GRACE SCHWEBEL

See, you could go in The Majestic and go upstairs in the gods for sixpence. So nearly ever Saturday night we'd be up at the gods. You had Mo one week, Ike Delavale another week, George Wallis another week, and Mike Conners and Queenie Paul another week. I saw Argus the Boy Wonder, the fellow that used to tell what a person had in their pockets. We had Cheffalo the Magician and his little midgets. Saw all those shows up there at The Majestic. HENRY BROWN

When I was young, my aunts used to go to watch all the girls coming from Clay's Theatre. All the chorus girls would be in their feathers and sequins, they used to have to run from the theatre, across the lane and into where the dressing rooms were, and that's where we used to wait for them. It was like waiting for all the fairies to come out, you know. There was a big vaudeville, The Majestic Theatre, on the corner of Wilson Street and Erskineville Road. We'd go in there and climb up all the back stairs until we were up about four tiers, right up in the gods, and lie on our stomach and see all the shows for nothing. We were coming down the stairs once and we ran into that very old famous comedian, Mo. I was about ten, there was always three or four of us, that would go up there. They used to leave the door open so we could, they never locked it deliberately, they knew there were kids there. I saw every play that was ever on at the Elizabethan when it was there. I was even in the audience when they came out and asked if there was a doctor in the house, Sir Ralph Richardson and his wife were in that play called *The Sleeping Prince,* and everybody knew that there was something wrong because she kept forgetting her lines, and the next thing she just collapsed on the stage, and that was that. I saw Larry Adler at the Enmore Theatre, I loved to go there. JEAN HENDY

Newtown was a very good centre, you had plenty of amusement, there was Hatties Arcade, which had three floors, with a dancing school in it. But there was lots of dances there, a lot of dances at the Newtown Town Hall, St George's Hall, the Manchester. The biggest charge of the lot was sixpence to get in, with thruppence half time, and of course half the time, half of us would have to wait until half time. We used to congregate a lot at the dances, where we used to meet and talk. We used to love dancing see, because we had such a lot of places to go to, like the Red Mill, if we were down in City Road, and that became known as the Surreyville, and then from there, you could go to the Albert Palais at Leichhardt on Parramatta Road, or you could go to the Strollers at Marrickville Town Hall. FRANK ALTOFT

People mainly met at church or at dances, at St George's Hall, and Newtown Town Hall. And then there was the Enmore Theatre and The Majestic Theatre which turned out to be the Elizabethan Theatre and then got burnt down. Grandma used to take us all to pantomimes at the Tivoli, Mum used to save up for those, and there was the old Victory Theatre in Erskineville Road, which is now the Police Boys Club. My aunt won a black bottom contest at The Hub one time. She made herself a costume out of black satin, with all black spangles on it, and a top hat, and it was like a small adaptation of a dinner suit with the tails, and she won the prize,

Dancers at the Surreyville Dance Hall on City Road, Darlington, in 1951. Like much of Darlington, the hall was demolished to make way for the expansion of Sydney University, in this case the Wentworth Building. (Courtesy of Bev Hunter)

then she came out in a frilly dress and did the Charleston and won that prize, so she was very, very good. LORETTO THURGOOD

When I was about eighteen, I loved dancing and we used to go a lot to the Surreyville dance hall.* I wasn't allowed to go out with boys, and I wasn't allowed to go dancing, but I had a boyfriend up the street, and his mother let me leave my shoes and dress there, and this night we came home very late, my father met me up the top of the street there, and belted me from the top of the street there down home. Dear, I was not allowed to go out you know, I was supposed to be doing other things. ANN RAMSAY

* Located at No. 4 City Road, Darlington.

The Surreyville maintained its popularity from the 1920s:

In about 1950, Surreyville was very popular down in City Road. Well, it was noted to have the best dance floor, because it was on springs, so it was jitterbug, jive, all that, so, I suppose as I was older I might have gone three times a week there. My first husband and I, when we weren't married used to go there and dance. It was the rock, rock and roll, jitterbug era, so everyone was into that by then. So that was good. JOSIE FOSTER

All of us young ones used to go to the Surreyville, and apart from that, the bigger kids used to teach us to dance in the street. We had a radio. I was mad into rock 'n' roll when we were about sixteen. When we were teenagers, our friends would walk from Chippendale, up through Darlington where there was plenty of people around and lovely houses, and we'd go up to the Surreyville Dance Hall. We'd walk up there, go to the dance, come out and have a drink at the milkbar, and then walk back home. Now that would be eleven, twelve o'clock at night, never anything to worry about. BEVERLY HUNTER

At Woolloomooloo in the 1960s:

The Cypriot community used to have functions quite often. They might have had a dance once a month. As children we used to go there and our parents'd want to get up and have a dance, and the kids'd just tear around the place and have a good time, play hide and seek or just be naughty. ANDREW LAZARIS

" We were glued to it, your ear practically stuck to the thing."

The establishment of commercial radio in the mid 1920s took the medium beyond the dedicated enthusiast to the wider community. Radio plays and serials became, in the 1930s, a way of life, and a marker of the time of day; in the evening children were required to be home for 'Dad and Dave.'[2]

I was about fourteen, fifteen when radio started. And you made coils and you scratched along until you found the right spot. It was a crystal set.[3] I'd read about it of course, and it wasn't a surprise when it come out. KEITH MULHEARN

The radio was around, and we used to listen to Radio Lux Theatre quite a lot, especially when Peter Finch was on, he was in it quite a bit. That was our main enjoyment of the night time. They used to have plays and serials. 'Dad and Dave' and all those. DARIO LO SCHIAVO

We had a radio, but it was connected to a car battery, we used to have to push it around to the garage and get it charged. JANE LANYON

Before we ever got a radio, I had a crystal set. They were simple to build. All you need is a coil and a little crystal, and a pair of headphones and an earth and you were in business. A big day at Camperdown School was when the Government allocated radios to Catholic Schools. The excitement when we went over, to carry this radio over to the school room. We eventually got a radio at home and I listened to all the stories, 'The Adventures of Jimmy Allen' and the like. LEO HANNAN

'Chandoo the Magician' was one serial and there were all sorts of spooky ones, they were rivetting. KATE DUNBAR

In the early '30s they bought a radio, those ones that had a great big horn. My father and uncle used to sit up all night listening to the test cricket from England and all you could hear was a crackle. JEAN HENDY

2 For further information, see Colin Jones, *Something in the Air, A History of Radio in Australia,* Kangaroo Press, 1995.

3 Crystal wireless sets were particularly popular with young people before the radio receiver was perfected and available to the mass market. See Lesley Johnson, *The Unseen Voice: A Cultural Study of Early Australian Radio,* Routledge, London, 1988, pp. 12-13.

One night my father and I nearly died. He wanted to listen to the test cricket in England. And we sat here by a little open four-gallon kerosene tin, full of smouldering coke, and we didn't wake up for two days. Carbon monoxide, nearly killed the two of us. And we sat up from eleven in the night till about five in the morning because Bradman had scored three hundred. MICK GREEN

My grandmother lived next door to us, and we used to go in there and listen to 'Dad and Dave' on the wireless. If we were naughty, we weren't allowed out, so we used to put our ears up to the wall and try and hear the wireless from my grandmother's place to hear the serials like 'Search for the Golden Boomerang'. BETTY MOULDS

You had serials and plays from morn till midnight pretty well on the radio. We had 'Martin's Corner', which was one of the original soapies, and 'Mrs Hobbs', which was quite funny. Mrs Hobbs was played by an old pantomime dame, I think his name was Dan Elgar or Edgar. We were amongst the last in our street to get a radio, it was about 1937 and we were glued to it, your ear practically stuck to the thing. Of course these radios sat in the corner of the room and you grouped your chairs around it and you looked at it. It was the centrepiece of conversation, it killed conversation, but we all sat looking at the thing, the idea of putting it aside just didn't dawn on people. They were quite splendid pieces of furniture, some of them, they had big cases, inlays and all that sort of thing. I remember songs like 'Waltzing Matilda,' 'When I grow too old to dream', 'The Isle of Capri', 'Ferryboat Serenade.' Then later on, we never had one, the radiograms came in, and they were even more bulbous than the old radio. PAUL HERLINGER

People went to bed early, most people were in bed by nine o'clock because most men's jobs started at seven in the morning, and they would have to get up about five or six to get there. Children went to bed about seven at the latest, so there wasn't a lot of evening time. But the radio was a big thing; we got enormous pleasure out of that. When I was eleven there was a serial called 'The Mysterious Mr Lynch', some sort of thriller. My father would put some of the lights out to make it creepier, and then we would have supper of cocoa and biscuits. When I was twelve and thirteen, when the war was on, there was a serial about the war called 'First Light Fraser—A Drama of War-Torn Europe', about this secret agent that was buzzing around eluding the Gestapo everywhere, and we were very keen on that. PORTIA FITZSIMMONS

In the evening we'd have the radio and a gramophone. Dad always had his favourite records, Richard Tauber and those type of things. And my mum had her favourite records which were more modern. I had a cousin who used to work on the Jack Davey show, Don Slater. He lived with us, and then there was 'Pick-a-Box'. BOB SLATER

In the evening we'd listen to the radio. We'd listen to 'The Argonauts' and 'The Search for the Golden Boomerang', and 'Nancy'. The door would creak 'eeeeeeee, this is Nancy the witch of Salem' — and we'd hear a horror story. 'Bobby Blue Gum', he used to sing 'Hello, Bobby Blue Gum, hello', there was a whole song, and there was drama, there were plays. And of course during the war we'd hear the war news. They'd always broadcast what was happening. JUDY CHAMBERS

In the evenings we'd listen to Caltex Theatre, and all the plays, and what was popular in those days was the 'Quiz Kids', and we'd listen to that, and the hit parades, and see who was popular. My father played a lot of classical music, and we used to listen to 2FC. JOSIE FOSTER

At Darlinghurst, the wireless was a very big part of our life; the serials 'First Light Fraser' and 'Jess', and 'Yes What', they were all very much part of our early life. When they started putting on serials about murder my mother got all uptight, saying we couldn't listen to that, and we found that very hard to accept, couldn't see anything wrong with it. CLIFF FOGARTY

THERE'D BE A BIT OF A SONG AND DANCE IN THE PARLOUR

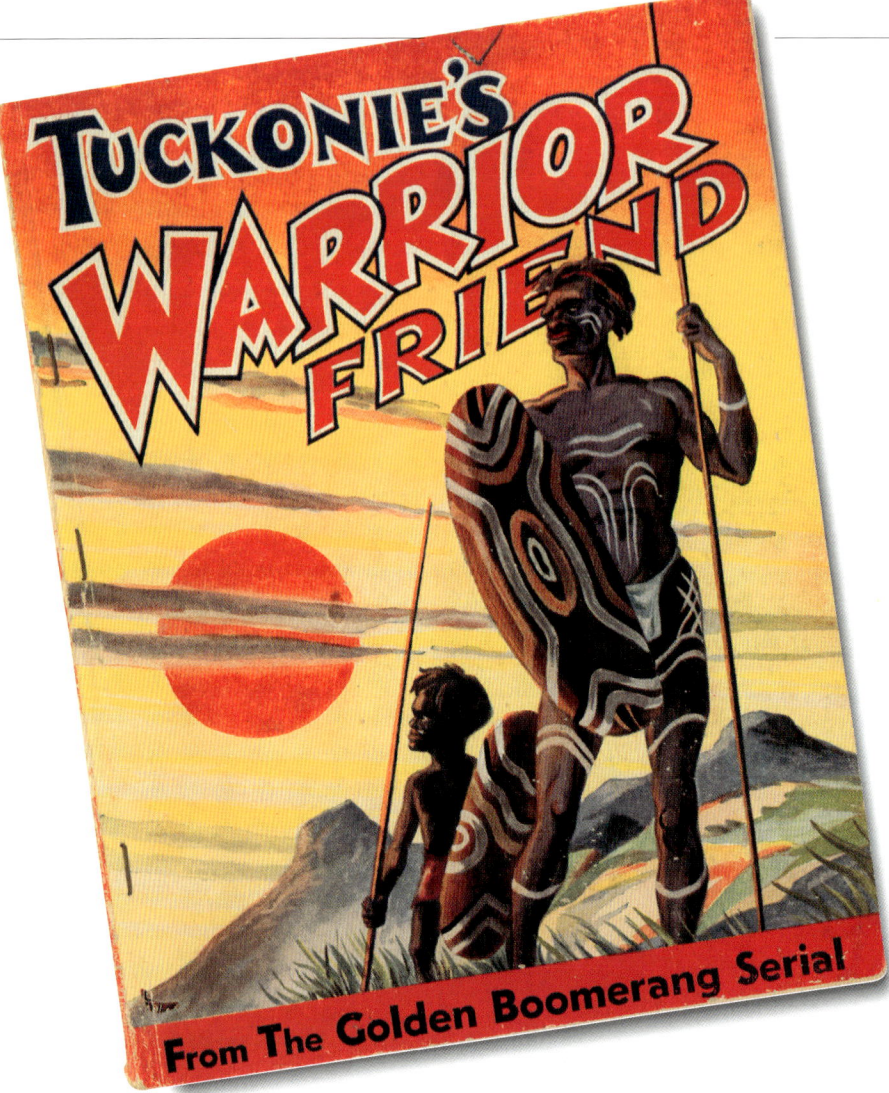

'The Search for the Golden Boomerang' became an extremely popular children's radio program. (Courtesy of Gerard Colreavy)

Tea was probably just a touch after six 'cause we used to go and often I'd meet Dad and we'd walk home together. And we'd sit down and he'd sit at the head of the table, and you had to be quiet because he used to put the news on. He used to turn on the radio and tune it in. You had to stop and listen to the news, no-one was allowed to talk while the news was on, and that's why everyone ate tea in silence. Virtually the whole room was taken up by this table and chairs and the fireplace and his radio, but no-one was allowed to touch it, only him. WARREN RICHARDSON

In the evenings we used to listen to Jimmy Shand and his band, and all the Scottish singers and 'Police Files' and 'Hot Harrigan' and 'Tarzan' on the radio. On a Sunday, you used to buy the paper, and they used to act out the comics on the radio. HARRY BRENNAN

" And then His Master's Voice put out a phonogram."

Before television the home was also an important place of communal entertainment with relatives and neighbours joining to have singalongs and to dance in front rooms. Even in suburbs, such as Redfern, that were being targeted under 'slum clearance' initiatives, many children learnt the piano and had dancing or singing lessons.

I remember when my auntie's family got their first record player, it was the cylinder with the big horn. And that was fantastic, that was marvellous and we would have an early tea and walk down all the way down to Darlington to listen to this wonderful new machine. And then His Master's Voice put out a

"WE NEVER HAD A HOTBED OF CRIME"

Johnny O'Keefe (National Archives)

phonogram and we were one of the first in the street to get a phonogram, and that was an upright one, and you wound it up and my father started buying records and that was when I knew a lot about the opera. Well-known singers, Nelly Melba, Essie Ackland, Caruso, all those great artists were very common in our home. And we got a lot of comedy shows, Billy Williams and they would have 'When Father Painted the Parlour', I could even sing it for quite a while and they had the English comedian doing 'The Census', that was a funny show, it was political satire. A lot of the neighbours who didn't have a phonograph would come in and listen to the records being played, having a laugh and a spin. And we'd push back the chairs and tables and there'd be a bit of song and dance in the parlour. Then there was E.J. Wilkes, big musical store in Sydney, and we got a gold Bransome pianola, and people would play that and stand around and sing. We'd have little community singsongs. Everybody would stand around and sing to the records and most of them knew the songs and the tunes, even the operas. GRACE SCHWEBEL

—

We were all very musically inclined. On a Sunday afternoon we used to get in the front room, which was street level, and my two sisters would play on piano, one on bass, one on treble. My brother on first violin, I was on second violin, my father with his squeeze box, accordion, and my mother on guitar, and we used to play there, it was really great fun. And after a while there would be quite a crowd of people outside, and they used to clap.[4] DARIO LO SCHIAVO

—

At twelve or thirteen I was going to different clubs. My mother used to take me to the girls' club at the Mission, and at St Paul's Church, and The Settlement. I was taught singing by a missionary, and how to read music, and my sister and I used to sing duets, and they had drama classes. We did a lot of singing in the church of a Sunday night. One of the people who came one Sunday night wrote and asked the minister if we could sing on Station 2CH, and my sister and I sang 'What a friend we have in Jesus' as a duet. We went back a couple of times.

Another happy time was when I won first prize in a singing competition at the Redfern Picture Show. I sang 'Thanks for all the memories', and I got a big block of chocolate. I ran home and I give it to my mother, and the look on her face was quite nice. JANE LANYON

—

From the age of eleven, mother used to take me to concerts. You wore white dresses, and we'd go to the concerts in the Town Hall. I heard Phillip Hargraves play and he was only eleven, he was a child prodigy. And my mother used to take me to *The Messiah,* always on Christmas Eve. We had a lot of family rituals like that, and my mother made things exciting always. There was Lottie Lehmann, who was a German pianist. We'd to go to the Conservatorium a lot; there was Jascha Heifetz, who was a violinist, there was a Muir Auld, he ran the conservatorium, and Mother also had a friend, Kathleen O'Connor, who was married to a well-known musician. My mother knew most of the musical world in Sydney. PAT ROSE

—

We had a priest up here at the time, a Father Brean; he was a lovely old priest, and it was the first year before the war that the Viennese Boys' Choir come out here, and Father Brean paid for all my class to go in to the Town Hall to hear them. And it was just magnificent, you know, to go in and hear a concert like that, it was beautiful. I never forgot that, and I never ever forgot how great it was to think that a priest in them days would've given us an opportunity to go and hear something like that. MAUREEN OLIVER

4 Pianos had been imported by company's such as Palings since the nineteenth century. With the home a popular entertainment venue, it was usual for families who could afford it to purchase a piano. See Eve Keane. *Music for a Hundred Years: The Story of the House of Palings,* Oswald Zeigler Pty. Ltd., Sydney, 1954.

Billie Black on 'Teen Scene' compered by Johnny Chester, on ABC TV in the 1960s. (National Archives)

"People were in an uproar about rock and roll."

The 1950s and '60s brought about a disjunction — a generational gap evident in youth's attraction to rock 'n' roll and groups like The Beatles, a preference generally not shared with their elders.

We used to like Chuck Berry, Little Richard, Bill Haley. Nat King Cole used to have a lot of soft songs, but we'd all sing 'em. Gene Vincent and his Blue Caps, Cliff Richards, but he was a little bit later. Oh, Buddy Holly was a favourite, Ritchie Valens, The Everley Brothers, Paul Anka... Oh boy, there was a lot! Bo Didley... WARREN RICHARDSON

We just used to play music, or listen to songs, sit around and talk. Rock and roll was in then. It was all right in the '60s. I got married in 1963, when I was eighteen. The Beatles and all that hadn't come onto the scene yet. People were in an uproar about rock and roll, there was a lot of things going on about it, they used to rouse about the music; it was too loud and you couldn't understand the words and this and that, and I know when we used to go out for drives or whatever in the car, you'd put the radio on, and we would want to put it on the rock and roll, and they'd get cranky, 'Oh you can't understand what they are talking about, it's all just noise'. I used to like the Everley Brothers, and I liked Connie Francis. Connie Francis, and Elvis were probably my favourites. KATHY INGRAM

There were big concerts in the stadium. The Beatles performed in Sydney Stadium. It's been demolished, it was at Rushcutters Bay. Oh, it was incredibly exciting. Big concerts would happen in the Stadium, say Johnny O'Keefe. The Beatles was the first concert I went to; I think it was the only big one. BRENDAN DOYLE

Once a month they'd have a dance at the playground [Woolloomooloo]. Of course the boys used to dance with boys, they wouldn't dance with the girls when we were kids. And then I used to always dance with my mate and the old Beatles' songs and that type of thing and if you'd won a dancing competition you'd get a Mintie each. We were eleven and twelve years of age and we'd dance together; like, yuk! you wouldn't dance with a girl. My dance partner was Big John, and we used to win lollies all the time. I can remember dancing to all the Beatles' songs, like 'She Was Just Seventeen' and all the old stomp, and wipeout, surfie songs and that type of thing, they were in our era. I can remember 'Rockin' Robin' and 'Let's Twist Again' and all those old songs. ANDREW LAZARIS

I remember Elvis well, I remember his early songs. For some reason I was addicted to him, and

*Olivia Newton-John was a guest artist on the first program of 'Teen Scene'.
Regulars included Johnny Chester and the Chessmen and the Thin Men. (National Archives)*

when he finally died — it was '77, June, July — I was overseas, I was in a little village in Greece, on an island, out the back of nowhere, miles from any civilisation. I had a little radio there, and I heard the news on the radio, and from where I was, to hear it, I mean, I cried. And I came back here, after my holiday, I don't know, I still didn't believe it had happened, I had to read it in an Australian paper first. GEORGE TOURVAS

I had one of those little trannies and I used to stick that under my pillow, especially Sunday night, 'cause that was when some American guy used to do the top forty. SHANE CAMPBELL

I remember the Bay City Rollers, terrible bunch, terrible bunch. But I remember them coming to town, and they stayed at The Boulevard. We were across the road 'cause apparently they were going to make a scene, a wave at the window or something and I remember standing there for hours and hours, with a little tartan neck scarf. A couple of girls climbed up the outside and I think they were rescued, I always thought they plummeted, but I think they were rescued before they plummeted. Yeah, that was a pretty big event, like there was crowds everywhere, it was just huge. ZOWIE CAMPBELL

One time they had a concert on the roof of the swimming pool at Victoria Park. I forget who it was, it may have been Skyhooks, someone like that. The park was just completely and utterly packed out, like you couldn't see the grass for the people, and they had huge speakers and a huge scaffolding construction sat up on top of it, you could hear it for miles, it was great. COLIN BELL

 ## Me father drank, me mother went to church and I went to the pictures."

The Saturday arvo flicks were, until recent times, virtually an institution. If parents didn't have the money, children could usually scrounge it, by selling bottles or doing messages. Picture shows were often local and were a significant place for both adults and children.

We saw plenty of movies, yes, it was only thruppence, that was your Saturday morning. When we were kids you got sixpence, thruppence to go in and thruppence to spend, that was your pocket money for the week. We saw pictures mostly at West's Picture Show, a great big place.[5] We'd go to The Majestic in Oxford Street, and The Australian on the corner of Wentworth Avenue, where that great big block of flats is now. We used to get in there for nothing, because you could walk up the stairs, and lay yourself down on a water pipe and then jump about another ten foot and you were in the toilet, so you got in for nothing. BILLY PASCOE

Every Saturday we used to go up to The Shell, a picture show in town, and we'd go and see this serial, *The Perils Of Pauline.* You have no idea what it was like! You'd sit in the middle of the pictures, and that finished at quarter past one or something; you'd move from the middle over to the other side. Sister Mary Alicoe[6] used to wait at the top of the stairs on a Saturday to see who the Catholic kids were that were going to the pictures at Kings Cross, and not putting the money in the poor plate. Of course, we used to go every Saturday afternoon. So the Catholic children couldn't go up the stairs, they used to have to walk up to William Street, and around. She was a dear old thing really, trying to keep everybody on the right path. She lived at St Vincents, up there in Victoria Street. But she worked at Columbkille's, in McElhone Street. JOYCE HIGGINS

It was threepence to go in to The Hub to the silent pictures and you would go every Saturday to watch the serials. The kids'd be queued up. The serials would end up in some very dramatic thing, and you'd have to go the next week to find out what happened. There'd be cowboy ones, *Tom Mix,* and *William S. Hart* and earlier on, a women named Pearl White, who got into the most marvellous situations; she used to do the most extraordinary feats, lying on railway lines and the train'd be coming. Then it'd

say, 'See next week' and of course, next week she'd be nowhere near the railway line, she'd have got off in the interval. They all had their own orchestras of about two people, which died away when talkies came. ZENA SACHS

There was three picture shows, there was the Douglas Social Hall, the Prince of Wales at St Peters, and then there was Newtown Hub, number one and number two and Hoyts up in King Street. FRANK ALTOFT

We went to the theatre every Saturday. We had our sixpence to go in, and we saw such things as Jackie Cougan and Rin Tin Tin and all these serials. And we'd have community singing; they would put up on the screen the words of songs and the organist would play the music and we'd sing along. All the children around us used to go, like from all areas, went to the theatre. And some of the boys'd misbehave and throw things and you'd think, 'those rotten kids,'* you know; you'd sort of look down on them, they didn't know how to behave, and they stopped you from hearing properly, or there'd be a scuffle in the aisle or something like that. GLAD WILLIS
* The Woolloomooloo kids!

We would go to the pictures a lot as kids, and it only cost you sixpence to get in. At Christmas they used to have a free matinee at all the different picture shows. You'd go to see St Peter's one day, the Enmore Hoyts another day, and Newtown Hoyts another day. Where the Police Boy's Club is in Erskineville Road now, that was the old Victory Silent Picture Show, and when I was at Erskineville School, when I was about seven or eight, they took a party from the school up there to the pictures. First of all it was the Victory Theatre, then they used it as

5 For an account of T.J. West and West's pictures in early Australian cinema, see Eric Reade, *Australian Silent Films,* Lansdowne Press, St Kilda, 1970. It was West who introduced the newsreel, which became a standard feature at the pictures.

6 Sr Mary Alicoe was a Sister of Charity who taught at their little school, St Columbkille, *Australian Catholic Directory, 1888–1933,* Sydney Archdiocesan Archives, St Mary's Cathedral, Sydney.

a stadium for fighting and wrestling. Then they made it The Hub No. 2 and I saw pictures like *Holiday Inn* with Bing Crosby and then later on they turned it into the Police Boys' Club. But the thing that still sticks in my mind was one of the first Felix the Cat cartoons, *Felix the Cat at the Circus.* HENRY BROWN

▬

Me father drank, me mother went to church and I went to the pictures. I'd pay my own way. I remember seeing *Gungadin* and I first developed a love for music the first time I heard the 1812 Overture. There was a conductor at the Regent Theatre named Jan Ribini who had a full orchestra. There was a second movie and a newsreel on for sixpence. Even if you didn't get a full orchestra playing the 1812 Overture or something akin to it, you got an organ recital like at The Capitol or The Lyric. In Newtown there was the Hoyts and there was the Enmore Theatre. The orchestras and the organists were mainly in the city. LEO HANNAN

▬

My mother had posters for the local cinema, and they got a couple of free tickets for that, and we'd go to the local movies, up to what is now the Enmore Theatre, and around the bridge at Newtown there was The Hub. We all used to go, Mum, Dad and me. I used to get a piggy back home from Enmore and I can remember the saddest day of my life when I was told I was too big to have piggy backs any more, I had to actually walk. At one stage they had a mini golf course next to Enmore Theatre which was great fun, and we used to go up there and play a round of mini-golf after the pictures came out. On Saturday afternoons there were the matinees and serials, *Tom Mix* was great, the cowboys in the afternoon and all the various things that left you hanging till the following week. I liked anything with animals in it and I can remember seeing the most awful film called *The Return of Doctor Foo Man Chu,* which caused me to be afraid of the dark until I was about fifty years old. I believe my father took the other family to see *Dr Jekyll and Mr Hyde,* and my sister was carried screaming from the theatre. Children had to be tough in those days. KATE DUNBAR

I'd go with my friends to the picture show, up at King's Cross. It was sixpence into the picture show, and if you had a penny to spend you were lucky, if you didn't you ran in the shop and stole a chocolate and ran out the other door. He'd have to be quick to catch me, they never could. So you'd see the pictures: *Tom Mix, Hop A Long Cassidy,* all those Western two-bit movies that they had; serials that you couldn't wait to get there next week to see what happened, like *Roy Rogers.* And of course idols were Judy Garland, Deanna Durban, Shirley Temple, and all those beautiful young girls that you went off into a fantasy about because it was so beautiful, they wore all these beautiful clothes and they could sing *and* dance. JEAN JURD

▬

We used to go up to the pictures of a Saturday afternoon and take all the kids with us; I suppose that was to get them out the way while Mum and Dad did the betting. *Ming the Merciless* was a serial; it was like an outer-space type of thing. And, you know, they say about the great movies of yesterday, well I don't remember all that many of them to be quite honest. There was one, *The Blue Danube* or something like that. And Sonja Henie used to be the skater, you know. Shirley Temple, I couldn't stand her, she was so bloody good and perfect. MAUREEN OLIVER

▬

We'd go to the Saturday afternoon matinee at the Lawson at Redfern a lot. They used to call the one in Botany Road the 'Bug House,' that used to be the old Plaza.* I think it just got its name because everyone used to start scratching because originally it was a disused warehouse. ROBERT HAMMOND

* *Also referred to as 'The Redfern Empire'.*

▬

It was funny, we used to go down the Five Ways pictures and one kid would have sixpence to get in, and we'd gather all the little kids, and say, 'Do you want to go to the pictures?' And we'd take them all down there, or go round the back lane, and then somebody would pay in, and they'd go down and you'd be waiting at the door, and they'd say, 'Are you ready?' 'Yeah' and they'd lift the bar off the

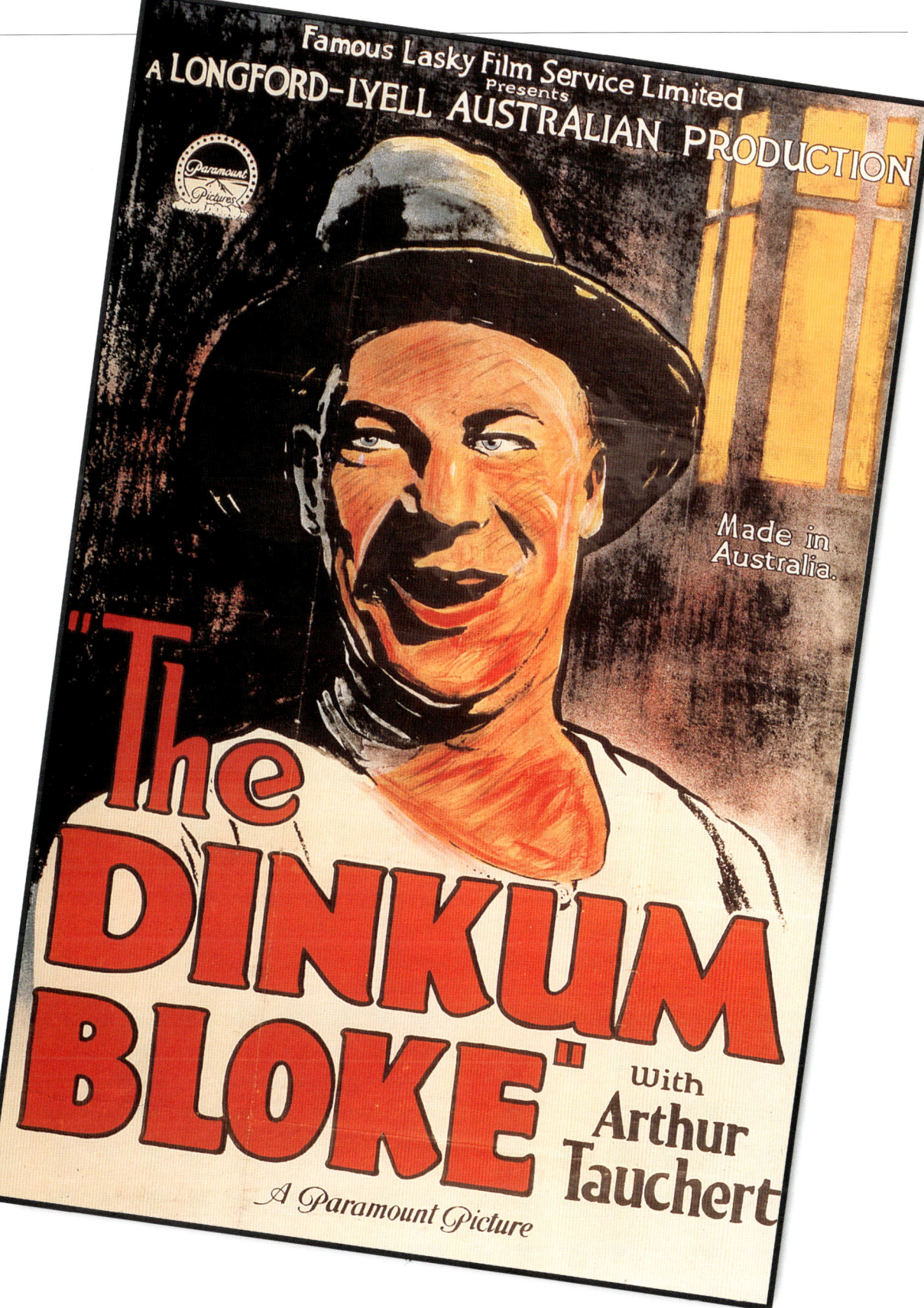

(National Film and Sound Archive)

THERE'D BE A BIT OF A SONG AND DANCE IN THE PARLOUR

door and they'd throw the door open and we'd all run in, and the ushers would catch all the little kids first and by the time they're caught, you're all sittin' down. KEVIN RYAN

▬

We used to go to the flicks of course at King's Cross Theatre, you'd have a film, then the serial, and then you would have another film. But the serials! Oh they were marvellous, absolutely marvellous! Almost pantomime in the way that everything was high drama. When you went to the pictures, the first two hundred kids got a present, and there was only two hundred kids that went to the pictures, but you'd get a present, and I got a bucket and a spade, can you imagine this? And my sister got a beautiful enamel brooch. One movie I remember is *Blood and Sand* with Tyrone Power, but the MGM musicals were the favourites. BRENDA HUMBLE

▬

On Saturday arvo we'd go to the pictures at the Cross,[7] and watch the villain with his black hat, and the hero in his white hat gets blown up, and he comes out without a hair out of place, 'To be continued next week!' Every Saturday afternoon just children would go, and we'd scream and stamp our feet on the wooden floor, and cheer for the hero, and boo the villain! Oh it was wonderful. We'd roll Jaffas down the aisle. We used to get sixpence, and it cost thruppence to get in, and we had thruppence to spend, and that was enough for an ice cream, and probably either Columbines or Fantales or Jaffas and chips. And you always asked for a packet of Smith's, because that was the only chips there were, and they were unsalted, and in the bag was a little twist of paper with salt in it. There were two shows and you'd be away four hours, so you'd take your lunch, you know, a packet of sandwiches and some fruit, and eat it in there. The pictures were wonderful. They had an organ, and in the middle they'd have a band that played songs, instead of just an interval, they'd have items. They'd rise up from the ground, the whole band there playing. And the best thing they had was the newsreels. Where the State Theatre is now, next door, was the State Newsreel Theatre. It was

continuous, it never stopped, you'd go in say, and it was in the middle of something and you'd stay right through until you came back to where you came in, so people were coming in and out all the time. It used to be about an hour, because you could fill in an hour while you were shopping or waiting for your mum or something, because it was quite safe. And they had cartoons and shorts and news reels. JUDY CHAMBERS

▬

When we got older, even up until I was going to work, we'd go three nights a week to the pictures, because Monday and Tuesday was one, two movies actually, and Wednesday, Thursday, Friday was different, and Saturday night was another different one. BEV KARONIDIS

▬

We went up to the Kings Cross Theatre. I wasn't one of those kids that was fortunate enough to go up of a Saturday afternoon; that again was money. Also, my mother was really against the films that were on at the theatre. I mean, in the late '40s and early '50s, even for a Saturday afternoon, there was a lot of propaganda: anti-communist, terrible films. But some of them were musicals and I would've loved to have gone to see them. All Saturday morning the girls would be getting all their hair done up in curlers and putting on their best dress to go to the picture theatre. BETH THORPE

▬

Favourite movie stars, of course Elvis, you had to go for him. And then we had all our singers, you had them pinned up. I mean I loved Cary Grant, all the older ones. Yeah, we used to go to the cinema all the time: *Ben Hur, My Fair Lady, Paint Your Wagon.* Of course *The Sound of Music,* definitely *The Sound of Music,* I must've seen that eleven times. CHERYL LINDO

---

7   The Minerva Theatre at Kings Cross opened in May 1939 and became extremely popular. In 1981 after a varied history, it reopened as the Metro International Food Fair after the building was rejuvenated under National Trust supervision. See Barry Sharp, *A Pictorial History of Cinemas in New South Wales: Showcases of the Past,* n.p., 1983, p. 80 and John Stephen Clark, *The Minerva,* (Art Deco Cinema Series, Pt. 1: The Minerva) Australian Theatre Historical Society.

It was alright to go to Kings Cross and watch a movie on a Saturday afternoon. It used to cost us one and thruppence, which is about twelve cents these days, to see a movie. And there was a serial that was on every week and if you didn't go one week you'd miss what was happening, because it was a continuing story; *Spiderman* or something like that it was, as I recall. And they quite often had good old Elvis movies on there; Elvis was one of my favourites as a kid. We went to the Newsreel and around the corner from there was the Metro Theatre, we used to quite often go to the Metro Theatre. I remember seeing John Wayne in *Hitari*. I was only a little boy and I used to like John Wayne, and *The Guns of Navarone* and *The Battle of The Bulge*. All the Westerns were great. Andrew Lazaris

—

Movie stars, they don't seem to compare now, to what they used to, you know, you can't get a Gregory Peck or a Cary Grant, or Rock Hudson. Tom Cruise or Richard Gere or whoever, they don't stack up, and none of the girls ever stacked up to Marilyn Monroe anyway. George Tourvas

Once we had the TV it was a big event."

The first television stations came on air late in 1956. There were two commercial channels (7 and 9) and the ABC. Initially they only broadcast for two or three hours a day, with Channel 7 managing six hours of programming. Despite this, within three years sixty per cent of Sydney households had a TV.[8]

In the early 'fifties, watching television in the store windows, that was really something to see. Walking along George Street, for example, seeing Palmer's window TV and thinking, 'Wow, that's really something'. And going to pick up my girlfriend, who lived up in Paddington at the time, and stopping and just staring at the television in the store window and being late. Terry Glebe

—

TV was probably the biggest impact. That was 1956. It didn't have much impact on us because we didn't have a TV, but those that did have it wouldn't want to come out any more, they stayed in and watched TV. Beth Thorpe

—

When we got a television, it was a seventeen-inch Admiral, we had to put all the blankets up at the window to make the place as dark as possible for the TV. The last show was 'Superman' at eight-thirty. It closed at nine, it didn't open until four. There was no such thing as an outdoor aerial at first, they were all indoors. But if we did happen to go anywhere, after my father died, an uncle of ours used to come down and take us to the mountains or for a drive, and we would count the TV aerials as we drove past; we would be lucky to count a dozen all day. Harry Brennan

—

We used to go and watch TV down the road at a friend's place. Mainly we went up to Dawn Keeler's. She was the daughter of John Keeler, who had the funeral business, and they're still in Newtown. They

---

8 *Something in the Air...*, p. 66.

got television as soon as it came to Australia and fortunately, you know, we were friends and so we got to watch television from the very start. The earliest shows I can remember were 'The Mickey Mouse Club', that was one of the very first shows, and that Johnny O'Keefe show, 'Rock Around the Clock'. BRENDAN DOYLE

Before TV we were all little kids and we were all playing up and down the street until it was dark, and then we'd come in and go to bed or whatever. But once there was TV, a typical evening would be dinner and then TV, and then we'd all drift off to bed. Before we actually had TV, I used to go to other people's places, and one of the things that I used to like watching was 'Cheyenne', which I think was on Saturday nights. And I used to go next-door to this elderly couple, that we called Auntie Pearl and Uncle Deak, and sit in there with them watching TV. We'd all sort of wander off to different places, you know, do our TV watching before we got it. I can't even remember the year that we got television; I think I might've been about eleven or twelve, so that was early '60s. CATHI JOSEPH

Once we had the TV it was a big event. The room would be full of people, we'd be glued to the TV. We'd be sitting on the floor and there might've been a dozen people watching. Not everybody in the area could afford one, but between the family they had managed to buy one and the neighbours would be over having a look as well. I remember Mickey Mouse, yeah, Mickey Mouse Club. I used to like 'Batman', and 'Man from U.N.C.L.E.' and 'Superman' was probably my favourite show at the time. There were a lot of cowboy shows, 'Cheyenne' and all that type of thing; I remember 'Rin Tin Tin'. ANDREW LAZARIS

I don't remember before television. I used to love watching Zoro, making the sign of the Z, that was a lot of fun, and then you'd go out and play Zoro of course. GEORGE TOURVAS

We had dinner in the evening, around five, then we'd watch the box for a bit and then get sent to bed. We'd sit around and watch TV, if the coins lasted, because it was one of those coin-operated numbers and you'd get like two hours or something. ZOWIE CAMPBELL

Favourite television programs? 'I Dream of Jeannie', 'Bewitched', 'Good Times', 'JJ', 'M.A.S.H'. We used to have to watch football, even though I didn't like it, because my brothers were into it, that was dreadful. They followed South's or East's, or probably Balmain, but it was mainly South's, because everybody follows South's, and they were doing really well at that stage too. On Saturday morning, about five o'clock in the morning, the cartoons were on. ESOSA EQUAIBOR

When I'd get home from school I would go and play and run to the park or whatever. We had to be home about 5 or 5.30 for dinner. Once we'd have dinner, I remember I would have to go straight and have a bath, get into my pyjamas and then was allowed to watch TV until 8.30. Then we had to go to bed, unless 'Prisoner' was on, then I was allowed to stay up till 9.30. I remember some of the shows that were always on at home, like 'Sons and Daughters', and 'Prisoner' was one of the main ones, I'll never forget that one. DEAN INGRAM

Opposite: There were many celebrations, but one of the big years was 1938, the 150th anniversary of the establishment of the first white settlement on Australia's shores, and when Australia hosted the British Empire Games. (National Library)

"WE NEVER HAD A HOTBED OF CRIME"

British
Empire
Games
5-12 Feb. 1938

AUSTRALIA'S
150TH ANNIVERSARY CELEBRATIONS
SYDNEY · 1938

Particulars of Travel and
Bookings at Shipping Offices
and Travel Agencies.

Issued by the Australian National
Travel Association.—Offices:— London;
Los Angeles; Toronto; Wellington; Batavia;
Shanghai; Tokio; Paris; Cairo; Sydney
(Endeavour House, Macquarie Place)

THERE'D BE A BIT OF A SONG AND DANCE IN THE PARLOUR

"We'd go to the Royal Easter Show and you used to get your show bags free."

The Easter Show and circus were eagerly anticipated every year. Even when times were hard, fun could be had for little money. The show was popular as kids were allowed in for free and in the early days, sample bags were given away. If the circus was a little more expensive, ways could be found to take a look without paying, by doing odd jobs or sneaking under the tent.

Everyone went to the Show. They'd start up College Street and there'd be a big parade, they used to throw samples everywhere, before you got out of the show you might've picked up ten or fifteen bags, for naught, zero, nothing. And the circus, there's always the free circus down what they call the Capitol Theatre. Wirth's Circus, that was a free day, for kids. Circus day, when the Show's on. BILLY PASCOE

In those days the samples were free, you would go in there, you could gorge yourself on beautiful chips, and you'd get hot dogs and things, you know, for practically nothing, then you got your samples. You got home and you stuffed yourself full of those, and then you lost the lot later on, but who cared! DARIO LO SCHIAVO

We'd go to the Royal Easter Show and you used to get your show bags free. I think you used to get Pick-Me-Up Sauce bags, Gartrell-White bags with the cakes in, Arnott's biscuits, Vita-Brits, and lolly bags. That was our big event because it used to be only about two shillings in. We always saved up for it. BETTY MOULDS

Another thing that we used to do for entertainment was go to carnivals. These were held on a vacant allotment on the corner of Georgina Street and King Street.* There'd be a merry-go-round, and a razzle-dazzle; it was very exciting, it was a round thing with seats on it and the man used to run around and set it off, and it would go round and round and up and down, and you'd be hanging on by the skin of your teeth. And I vaguely remember a man walking on the tight-rope, and me looking at him, being terrified. There was also Housie, that was very popular and the chocolate wheels they used to have at these carnivals. Wirth's Circus came every Easter, to what was called the Hippodrome, it became the Capitol. I remember my father taking me once to the circus there. ZENA SACHS

* This vacant block of ground was known locally as 'The Stadium' as it was formerly the site of a stadium which had been burnt

Lost at the Easter Show in 1938. (SLNSW)

down. Grace Schwebel lived opposite the stadium and refers to the political rallies and social events that occurred there.

—

We had a friend from Sole Brother's Circus, Jack Sole, who always stayed with us when he was in Sydney for the Sydney Show, he used to sometimes bring show people with him. One in particular was a chap named Mick St Leon[9] and he'd turn somersaults up and down the footpath. There were carnivals that used to come and go, and they would set up on any vacant allotment that was about. They would have hoopla, and merry-go-round rides. My uncle had one of these bagatelle machines that you play, and I think if they got a certain score they won a prize, and the police came and had a go at him, or so I was told, that it was a game of chance and it wasn't allowed, and he said, 'No, it's not a game of chance, it's a game of skill'. Luckily, when he pulled the lever to send the ball up, it went where he said it would go, and they walked away and left him. FRED FOREMAN

All the cattle used to come down from the country for the Royal Easter Show and they'd drive them down Mitchell Road and over the top of Raglan Street, down through Moore Park and into the showground. Every year, when the circuses came in, they used to bring them in by train there. Used to get the elephants going up there and they used to put up the shutters and let you see the tigers. That used to be a real day out. My father managed to often get passes to the circus for us because he knew a chap in Belmont Street, he had a butcher shop, he'd give Dad about five double passes because he was the New South Wales manager for Wirth's Circus, so we often got to the circus when it was in town. ROBERT HAMMOND

—

In Goulburn Street, where the CID is today, was vacant ground, and that's where the circus came to every year, just across the road from my house, and we got enormous amounts of fun out of hanging around and watching the elephants. At Easter they gave out free hot-cross buns and ginger beer to all the local children. I queued up for that and was so excited I was sick and missed out. Once my father

got enough money to take us to the circus, and we sat on a blanket on the ground in front of the seats. The Depression wasn't as much stress for the children as it was for the parents, because the parents had to struggle with trying to feed the children, but, as far as we were concerned, everybody was in the same boat and we didn't feel deprived. But looking back on it there wasn't much fun, there was just no spare money, and so the circus was really a big thing to go to. Another man in the audience bought ice-creams for us; you know, a better-off man; we thought it was a gift from God. PORTIA FITZSIMMONS

—

We'd wake up, probably about five o'clock in the morning, we'd hear the rattling noises, so you'd get up and rush and look out the window, and it would be Wirth's Circus, coming down George Street, Redfern, from the Alexandria Goods Yards, and then the elephants would pull the other animals and all the equipment up to Exhibition Park. There was no water down there apparently, because they'd bring up the horses and the elephants twice a day to the trough across the road and there was another trough outside Cleveland Street School. So we'd get sort of a free show. Then every night after tea you would go for a walk down the park and look at the animals, and talk to the circus people who we thought were rather wonderful. Then on Good Friday you would take a mug with you, and line up, and you'd get ginger beer, and a free hot-cross bun, and then they'd put on a small circus for you. Just for the locals. I remember it being said they thought we were deprived. I think Mrs Wirth used to come down and speak to you. BEV KARONIDIS

9 The St Leon photographic collection now in the National Library extensively documents this family's circus life and travels. See also Mark St Leon, *Spangles and Sawdust: The Circus in Australia,* Greenhouse Publications, Richmond, 1983.

Fortunately, where the big police station is down in Goulburn Street now, was a big open paddock at the time and occasionally a circus would come by like Bullen's Brothers or Wirth's Circus. That was big time, and by helping out, going and doing odd chores around the place you could get in to see some of the circus, or you'd sneak under the tent and make yourself as inconspicuous as possible. They realised that kids didn't have much money at that time and they made it possible for you to do things, which was quite good. I once got kicked in the backside for being under the tent. TERRY GLEBE

▬

Used to go out to the Easter Show a lot because it was walking distance and you'd save all your beer bottles up to get in 'cause once you got in you'd walk around all day. You wouldn't really have many rides, because of the money, but just to walk around you might have enough to buy one or two bags and if you bought one bag that was good. They used to be about two and six and you probably got about ten bob's worth of stuff because I remember the Fountain's bag, you'd get all the little bottles of tomato sauce and you'd have your chutneys, and your sultanas and flour and all things... it was worth *buying.* Oh, the licorice bag was my favourite, but I suppose I'd get one of them every year being the baby. Lucky. WARREN RICHARDSON

" That night was like a Wonderland to kids."

The first Empire Day on 24 May 1905 was to be an 'outward sign of an inner awakening of the peoples who constitute the British Empire'.[10] With the decline of the Empire after World War II, as colonies fought for and attained independence, the name was changed to 'Commonwealth Day' in the mid 1950s. By that time the original meaning had been all but forgotten and the real significance of the day lay in the half-day school holiday, bonfire building and crackers. In 1967 the celebration was moved by the Department of Education to the June Queen's Birthday weekend. Controls on the sale of fireworks in the mid 1980s brought an end to some of the tantalisingly dangerous, illicit and sometimes tragic high jinks recounted here.

10 'Empire Day to Cracker Night' in Peter Spearritt & David Walker (eds.), *Australian Popular Culture,* George Allen & Unwin, Sydney, 1979, p. 18 and passim.

THERE'D BE A BIT OF A SONG AND DANCE IN THE PARLOUR

And the wonderful times were... Empire Night; everybody shared their crackers. 'Cause I had no crackers, we couldn't afford crackers even, I mean this was getting into the Depression. And that night was like a Wonderland to kids. GLAD WILLIS

For Cracker Night families used to buy us all the crackers, or they'd give us spending money. We used to buy what they call a basket bomb. It was a square one, wrapped in cane, and we used to run around whacking them in everybody's letterboxes, they'd just go 'Boom!' and blow them apart. And they used to chase us, abuse us for weeks. And the big bonfires, we used to light them in the middle of the road in Walker Street, Redfern, and all the streets. All day they'd be piling on the bonfire, and they used then just set her away, there would be crackers and Tom Thumbs and starlights, and sparklers, and jumping jacks and, oh it was a big night, big night. Everyone in the street would be out there. TED McDERMOTT

Cracker Night was a big thing there. Used to have bonfires everywhere in the middle of the street. And down Woolloomooloo the fire brigade would come down and they'd chop their hoses and everything so they couldn't put them out. And they used to have a big one down in Sutherland Street, Paddo. Basket bombs were about three inches cubed, they were frightening things, and you'd put them in a garbage bin upside down and it would throw it up over the lights. They stopped them making them. And the skyrockets, oh it was a real big, real big thing. And Guy Fawkes was another night, kids used to get dressed up, and they'd go round and knock on the door, they used to say, 'Christmas is here, the ducks are getting fat, please put a penny in the old man's hat, if you haven't got a penny then a ha'penny will do, if you haven't got a penny, well God bless you.' KEVIN RYAN

We used to have Guy Fawkes Night on the fifth of November. We'd get dressed up in costumes, and of course in Woolloomooloo there is nowhere you can light fires, except in the middle of a crossroad, so they'd light fires and they'd put a guy on top, and we'd go around shaking a can, calling, 'A penny for the guy'; people'd put pennies in. Along would come the fireman with their hoses to put the bonfires out, because it was dangerous, all these old houses everywhere, and the older boys'd come out, and get tomahawks and chop through the hoses. I can still see it: the flames leaping up in the dark, and the silhouettes of the people around it, and the firemen, and their old-fashioned brass helmets, these kids just chopping the hoses in half. And then they'd call the police. JUDY CHAMBERS

On Cracker Night out here in the middle of Ann Street, just at the junction of Reservoir Lane, Surry Hills, we used to have big bonfires. Skyrockets would be let off, everyone had their bungers and their Tom Thumbs; that was a big ritual. A friend of mine, Brucie Hughes, had a pocketful of crackers and someone dropped a lit one in his back pocket and they all went off in his pocket and he received enormous burns. He was taken off to hospital and ultimately had skin grafts and so on; it just did enormous physical damage to him. But apart from that, for the most part it was quite a lot of fun, big spectaculars. And then ultimately, the Fire Brigade would show up, and the water outlet was on the other side of the street, so we used to always sit on top of that and the fireman would be looking around trying to find the damn thing. Round about the night the war ended, there was a huge bonfire out here and people brought tyres, there were huge billows of black smoke going up and some effigies of Hitler and Tojo being burnt on top of it. TERRY GLEBE

Cracker Night was a very big night. You'd save as much money as you could, for as long as you could; you'd cash in bottles or you'd scrape together something to get these crackers, and there might be two or three bonfires down at Woolloomooloo. There'd be one in Brougham Street, there was another one in Dowling Street, and there was probably another one closer to the wharves. In fact, one year I can remember the fire was so ferocious that it actually burnt the tar off the road. Everybody, even mums and dads you never saw from one year to another, would all come out on Cracker Night. It was wonderful. I suppose probably the best part of Cracker Night was saving all the wood up and going around to the factories and asking them for wood. So even the preparation was just as exciting as Cracker Night itself. BETH THORPE

There was always a bonfire every year, and there was a paddock in Wyndham Street. And we built a bonfire and my brother bought a truckload of timber for us, and we built this. And they interviewed us the day before, and someone lit it that night, so the bonfire was lit a night before; someone from another area I suppose. We were only interested in the noise. If we had ten bob to spend on crackers, we would buy double happies, bungers and twopenny bungers. We used to put a skyrocket in the tram line and light the skyrocket, and it would shoot up Redfern, up the hill and turn

right into Redfern Street, sssssshhhhhhhhuuuuuu! HARRY BRENNAN

On Cracker Day we used to build big bon-fires and like we'd all go out and gather wood and set it up in the car park next door; we'd have a big sort of teepee thing of wood and rubbish and whatever else. That'd be me and Dad. He used to light them all, we'd have to stand back and he used to light them all. Cracker Day was a big one when we were kids, it was the highlight of our year. A week leading up to Cracker Day we'd be collecting wood and sometimes you'd get a pile six foot high. ZOWIE CAMPBELL

9

I had a freedom for which I was very grateful

Most kids from South Sydney weren't confined to their own neighborhoods or even to South Sydney. Family outings or organised group activities were a regular part of life. And whether on foot, bike, tram, bus or ferry, children roamed South Sydney and beyond. If they didn't have the fare, boys particularly would scale the trams. Girls tended to be more restrained and there is a sense that parents exercised more control over their peregrinations. But parents didn't always know exactly where their sons or daughters were.

" We'd be out everywhere."

We'd go to the city occasionally, go to Manly now and again, and we used to go bushwalking out to mostly the other side of Enmore. You'd take your billy and your potato, you'd make a fire and cook your potato, and go out there to La Perouse. And we used to go a lot to Willoughby. Tony Maloney, he lived at Willoughby before coming here. We would catch a tram down to the Quay and then the boat and the Chatswood tram, get off at Willoughby. There was the fort at Castlecrag with a moat round it and all that sort of thing. We could see every kind of a bush flower growing there. KEITH MULHEARN

We'd go to Menangle, or Douglass Park or Picton on a Friday night. You'd go to George's Biscuits and buy a pillow slip full of broken biscuits, ninepence, you'd go and get eight saveloys, they were a penny. We'd catch the train up Menangle and walk to wherever we were going, you'd camp there for two nights, we had a little 22 rifle too. We'd swim in the Nepean River, fresh water, no clothes on, naturally, because there was no-one up there. Might be eight or ten of us kids. Eleven or twelve, up to fourteen, fifteen years old. BILLY PASCOE

We used to go to University Park, where we played around. Went down to Alexandria, there were dairy farms down there, also chicken farms, and the Chinese had their gardens down there. Long before it became an airport there was the Brighton Golf Course, and I was there one Sunday when a fella from Randwick that bought one of Kingsford Smith's planes, and the wings used to fold back and this plane came down, and only one wing folded down, and both he and the pilot got killed. BILL SCHWEBEL

I'd go for hikes with my friends too, down in the Royal National Park. We'd go by train to Sutherland, then we would hike down to a place called Burning Palms and go for a swim. Oh, but it was beaut. Sometimes we used to go out to La Perouse on one of those open drays. The chap down the street was a fruit marketer, and on Sunday he'd collect us all, there'd be about twelve, fifteen of us on the back. We'd have a picnic out there, Mr Marsh, and a couple of mothers and my parents. ANN RAMSAY

We'd go for a walk over to the aerodrome, because in those days you could wander through the hangars, and there was Clancy the Sky Baby that the Clancy Brothers built, which was a little plane that had a motorbike engine. When Bert Hinkler landed we went over there and had a look over his plane, Amy Johnson's plane, Kingsford Smith's plane. When they made Mo's picture, *Strike Me Lucky,* Reggie McLeod and myself had wandered over the airport there and Goya Henry was a famous stunt pilot in those days, and he was supposed to be Mo landing the plane, so we started running across to the movie cameras and the next thing, my mate says 'Down!' And we dived down and the plane just sort of skimmed over us. Well, they left that scene in the picture but the lousy so and so's wouldn't even give us a free pass to go and see it. HENRY BROWN

We mostly walked, we walked to the Botanical Gardens a lot. Faith and I would go around in Elizabeth Bay, we could get down on that beach, in front of Boomerang. It was a lovely little beach, beautiful little shells, sort of iridescent shells, like pearl, and we were always collecting shells on the beach. We'd also go to Nielsen Park a lot. The trams

Four little girls at Trumper Park, Paddington, in February 1935.
(SLNSW)

and buses and everything went through there, The Cross was such a busy intersection. It was on the way to Watson's Bay, so we went out there, on the tram. PAT NICKS

—

With my friends we'd go out to the beaches or the show, or walk across the Harbour Bridge. We'd go to Manly or Bondi because you could scale the trams from here. Nobody had a penny to pay the tram fare, but we thought nothing of getting onto the tram on the wrong side between stops, and when the guard came along you'd just drop off and grab the end of the tram as it went past. Those people that had a penny wouldn't pay it because the rest of the mob didn't have a penny to make the trip. LES CROSS

—

Generally we didn't go away on holidays as such, but we'd be out everywhere. Rushcutters Bay, The Domain, and down to The Quay and up around Paddington, and over to Manly, and Clifton Gardens. There was a big resort at Clifton Gardens. Later, we used to go over there, and have dances there. This was before the war proper, the Second World War. When the war started it was a naval base and it got very run down. And there was Bronte Beach, Bondi Beach, as we got older we went there; Maroubra, any of those beaches we went to. ROSE CLEMENTS

—

Down in Rushcutters Bay Park you could play cricket. It was safe in those days for kids, although I remember once one of our friends being almost molested by some fellow at the far end of Rushcutters Bay. It was a big spot for us when we were young. We could also go to Elizabeth Bay, Elizabeth Bay Crescent. As we got older we'd go as far as Darling Point, later on we'd catch trams out to Watson's Bay and attempt to walk back to King's Cross along the edge of the bay … When we were about twelve, thirteen, we'd catch trams out to La Perouse, that was a fairly lengthy trip, or better still a tram trip out to Ryde, that was exciting because there were cows out there, and sheep. PAUL HERLINGER

—

Once I went round through Waverley cemetery

and down the cliffs between Bronte and Tamarama and got caught on the ledge there, and ultimately I was helped up by a few fishermen. When we were about fourteen we actually rode all the way to Parramatta and back; that was quite an adventure, just the sheer experience of going that far from home on a bike. One of the other exciting things was riding around Centennial Park on your bike. TERRY GLEBE

—

I was very fortunate in a very broad upbringing. I had a lot of influences, over those years. My mother always told me that if I was out somewhere, and I was having difficulty getting a bus, get a cab. I remember horrifying people by the fact that I was coming home from scouts club at Paddington and there was no buses and I was getting a bit concerned so I hopped into a cab, and the cab driver had somebody else, so he took me all around Clovelly and Coogee and eventually I came back, and then he gave me two bob, just for the company. And I wasn't unduly disturbed by that, so I had a freedom about me, for which I was very grateful. CLIFF FOGARTY

—

Sunday afternoon the pubs weren't open, so my dad was sober enough to walk us — there was none of this get in the car — we'd walk to Botany Bay from here, and we'd have our swim. It's all been wrecked now it's all been dredged and that for the airport but it was lovely out at Sir Joseph Banks Park, and we'd swim and the sand was as white as anything, and the bottom of the sea bed was beautiful and we'd walk home. Oh, it'd probably take an hour and a half, two hours, wouldn't worry us 'cause as we were going along my dad would tell us all the different plants and why this was this. And we'd take all the neighbourhood kids with us, that wanted to go. JILL EDWARDS

—

Gee, I rode a fair way when I got my bicycle, we went everywhere, you know. We went to Vaucluse, the Gap, and we used to ride everywhere. I had a couple of real good mates that I used to kick around with, one was Jack Slade, who I grew up with, and an Alan Sharp who lived up the street, they're no

The Royal National Park was one of many favourite recreation areas frequented by South Sydneysiders.

longer living there, Ronnie McFaden, yeah quite a few guys. When I was about ten or eleven, we went to the big extent of making sandwiches and everything else, and we'd pedal off on our pushbikes, about four of us, and pedal out around Mascot, and down through Brighton, and down to Taren Point, where there is now the Captain Cook Bridge. In them days there was a punt there, and we got across on the punt. That was a big adventure, and we made our way back, without our parents knowing. STEVE FENNELL

▬

I roamed, well, from where I lived, gees I remember going up to Edgecliff, and up the other end of Darlinghurst, towards The Cross. In those days, even The Cross was safer, because during the day, it had more of a bohemian atmosphere about it and you felt safe walking around. But we used to go to Rushcutters Bay Park which was just down the bottom, and stay there until all hours. We would go for a swim out at Redleaf Pool, and stay there until five, or six, seven o'clock at night and come back home. It didn't matter, you weren't going to get taken off the street, you weren't going to get attacked, so things were fine. GEORGE TOURVAS

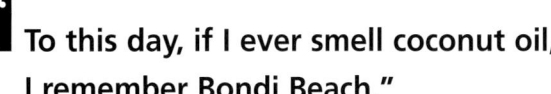

" To this day, if I ever smell coconut oil, I remember Bondi Beach."

Going to the beach or pool was an almost compulsive summer ritual — both accessible and cheap and everybody else was there. These iconic aquatic institutions (both natural and the concrete variety) lured one and all.

In summer time we'd go down to the surf at Manly or, more often, Coogee. And sometimes at night time we'd go down to The Domain Baths. We'd go by tram or walk. It was a tidal pool. The sand around the Quay and around the Gardens there was all white, of course when they started to use oil-burning ships it went black. All around the Quay and the Gardens and Woolloomooloo was sort of sandy beaches you could even see fish, and men catching fish, good fish. KEITH MULHEARN

▬

Everyone was sailing mad down here, they were mostly what they call sixteen footers. Actually my father sailed, Saturday and Sunday, everyone in Woolloomooloo sailed. You went as a crew, they used to put at least twelve, up to twenty in a boat. BILLY PASCOE

▬

We used to go to the beach quite a bit. I'd go with the older ones. My other sister met her husband at the beach. He was a great surfer in those days. I don't think she ever went in the water, but she used to go and sit on the beach fully clad, with hats and gloves and everything on. You could get a locker or a cabin, lock your clothes in there, and pin the key somewhere, hoping you didn't lose it, and then go off and swim, and sit on the beach. You'd stay there all day and cook! You'd simply bake! And you'd think this was wonderful. ZENA SACHS

▬

My father used to take us out to the beach, mostly to Bronte Beach. Patsy and I used to go to Bronte about seven o'clock in the morning, and get one of those houses, and then we'd wait for Mum to come out with the rest of the kids. There were five kids at that time and we'd be all out. There was what they called the Bogey Hole at Bronte, and it was safe for children. Now I look back, the sewer outlet came through there, but we never noticed that. The natural rocks made this little swimming pool, and that's where all the kids used to play. Oh it was good fun, and we spent our lives there in the summer, either there or down at The Domain Baths or Rushcutters Bay. The baths were segregated: women and girls in one, and men and boys in the other. ROSE CLEMENTS

▬

Dad used to always take me to Bondi with him. And he used to go out there surfing with, you know, mates of his from Erskineville. I suppose they were only young men at the time; to me they seemed terribly old. We'd catch the tram from the railway and go out to Bondi and they'd all surf. If I got

Schoolboys playing cricket in Trumper Park. (SLNSW)

sunburnt, Mum used to put on a tomato on me, cut a tomato and rub it on you. And to this day if I ever smell coconut oil I remember Bondi Beach, isn't it funny? MAUREEN OLIVER

–

Mum and Dad used to pack us up to go out to Bronte a lot, because the area was good for swimming and it had a big park with plenty of huts, the trams used to go right to the beach. We also used to go swimming in the North Sydney pool. A tram used to run to Circular Quay and we'd catch the ferry across, which I think was a penny down in the tram, and a penny in the ferry, and a penny into the pool, so for sixpence you'd have a good day out. We went to Manly as often as we could. We'd go to Bronte mainly, sometimes Coogee or Tamarama, but mainly Bronte, because it was good access for Mum and all us kids off the tram. ROBERT HAMMOND

–

We used to go to Chinaman's Beach, which is near Balmoral. It was called Chinaman's Beach because they had long shells, they were like Chinamen's fingernails, and we used to stick them on our fingers and pretend we were Chinamen. We picked blackberries near Balmoral. Sunday School picnics were always there, with the egg and spoon races and three-legged race. JUDY CHAMBERS

–

On Sunday, we always went for a swim out to Bronte. That was our favourite swimming place. In those days they had Coogee Aquarium going, which was a great big luxurious pool at Coogee. And they had Wylie's Baths which was a rock pool. So you could go out to the rock pool, and you could go to the aquarium, or you could go over to North Sydney to the Olympic Pool. JOSIE FOSTER

–

We used to go to the Botanical Gardens, or to Nielsen Park near Vaucluse, we'd catch a tram for a picnic, even if we just had sandwiches, and for a swim. And we used to go down to The Domain Baths, it was deep — it was natural — water from the harbour, washing in and out, the harbour was pretty clean. There was night swimming there and on hot

nights we were allowed to go. Lot of kids down here used to swim a lot. There's been two Olympic champions from Woolloomooloo: Etty Robinson (I was only a little kid when she lived here), and Bonny Mealing. They both won when they had the Olympic Games in Germany in those days. We'd go to Lady Macquarie's Chair and fish on the rocks and listen to the band in the gardens on Saturday and Sunday. NELL LEONARD

–

We used to go check out behind the Art Gallery, to see who'd been playing up in the grass. You'd find all these French letters. We'd go swimming on Saturdays and Sundays down The Domain Baths. Sometimes we'd get on a tram and come down to Bondi, swimming. We used to swim at Seven Shilling Beach, at Double Bay. We'd go on the train to National Park and hike down to the Woronora River and go swimming. This'd be when I was fifteen. JEAN JURD

–

Summers were good times. We used to all go to the beach: we'd all meet together on a Sunday morning at about eight o clock, and Mum would give you thruppence or something and it used to cost a penny there and a penny back. It'd take about an hour to walk, but we'd all pool our money. We'd go to Bondi. But Coogee we seemed to like because they had the big tower there, the shark tower, you know. It wasn't as rough and when we were young we didn't like the rough surfs and Coogee, 'cause of the island out there, always seemed to be a bit quieter. Plus they had pools there and a couple of us used to have the goggles and the snorkel. WARREN RICHARDSON

Bondi Beach, March 1957. (SLNSW)

All the Unions and the Councils used to have picnics once a year."

We'd go to Clifton Gardens a fair bit too, stayed there overnight, when we were kids, fourteen or fifteen. That's where all the union picnics were, and they used to have a lot of huts down there. We'd go down there Friday night and get what they call a hut, put our clothes in it, then when your parents or whoever it was came down on the Saturday or the Sunday they had a hut for the day. They had what they call Dixie Land, that was a big dance hall, that was a day out, Clifton Gardens. BILLY PASCOE

We used to go over to the railway picnic over at Clifton Gardens, the railway used to put on a big picnic for all their employees. Mum never went, my aunt used to take us. They used to have a little row boat there and they'd sing 'A penny a ride on the row boat', and of course the hit of the day was if you were invited to take all the pennies off the kids. So you'd be on the boat and you'd go round and pick up the pennies. And they used to have dancing there in the afternoon. And you'd all get a bag, and have an apple and orange, lollies and all that, and sports, you know, they'd have running and that was a great day. Everybody used to love to be invited to the railway picnic. MAUREEN OLIVER

When I was a boy scout, and we went away for the weekend with the scouts, up to Woronora River, the scout master had a little put-put boat, and we thought it was fantastic. We thought we were Vikings, that was terrific. TED McDERMOTT

The ALP would go on horse and carts to picnics and there was always some activity, it was the hub of which they all gathered around. We'd go to Yarra Bay, Sans Souci. MICK GREEN

The Eureka Youth League were the sons and daughters of the Communist Party. We used to go on camps once a year; the first one I attended was at Corrimal, then after that up at Springwood. So we would learn a lot about the bush: the trees and the animals; go on bushwalks. And for somebody that came from a treeless suburb, like Woolloomooloo, it was a totally different environment, it was wonderful. They would even have bushwalks at night. We'd sit round and light a fire of logs and sing songs in the bush of a night time. Probably the majority of the leaders were men, but it was also made up of women as well. It was probably not as sexist as our mothers and fathers. Because we basically went to school in the community, that's when the male was dominant, in the schoolground. But in the Eureka Youth League there were attempts to make no difference between the two sexes. So it made me very aware at a young age that women or girls were being treated differently than boys. BETH THORPE

We used to often go camping of a weekend, you know, like, if a long weekend come up. The playground used to have tents made. That was at Woolloomooloo: there was a sail maker and he used to make tents for us. When we were at school, we'd tell Mum, we'd have our bags packed and we'd jump on the train, go down to Cronulla, ferry across to Bundeena, and we'd walk from Bundeena all the way down to Stanwell Park, just stopping and surfing. The first night we'd all stop at Wattamolla, then stop at Garie, have a little surf here and there and everywhere, Burning Palms, and you'd get down to Stanwell Park would be the last day and then you'd catch a train home. WARREN RICHARDSON

*Clifton Gardens — the site of many union,
work or church picnics. (National Library)*

1926.

❝ We went on family outings.❞

Sundays were traditionally days for quiet and somnolence. The pubs and clubs were closed. These were the days reserved for family outings: visiting relatives; walking as a family to the Botanical Gardens; or meeting, as the Lazarus family did, other members of the Cypriot community for a picnic at Nielsen Park.

W e were very close my mother, my sister and I and I'm very sentimental about the Botanical Gardens 'cause Sunday afternoon we often walked into town from Kings Cross, and we'd walk to the gardens, and then always the treat at the end was to go to the little kiosk for afternoon tea. And that was very unglamorous, it had wooden floors, and marble tables, but the ice creams were served in little silver dishes. PAT ROSE

—

When I was probably twelve or fourteen, my grandmother used to live at Manly, and we used to always go to Manly. We'd get on a ferry, and go over to Manly and spend the day on the beach or spend the weekend down there with my grandmother, and the rest of the family. My mum's five sisters and her brothers, and all the kids, we'd all go down then. TED McDERMOTT

—

We used to go to places like Waverley Cemetery and play, and we were taken to the Gap. Now the Gap might sound funny to be taken there for an outing, but you didn't hear of people jumping over it, you went out there for afternoon tea. JOSIE FOSTER

—

We went on family outings, my cousins and that mostly. There was Lai Chee Hui, a social club. They had dances, picnics. On New Year's Eve they would hire a launch, go to one of the islands in the harbour, have dances. As a family, we'd go to picnics at Bronte, Clovelly or Nielsen Park by tram with the

Above: The World Scout Jamboree of 1956 held at the Royal National Park. The first Woollahra–Paddington Scouts are in the foreground. (Courtesy of Kevin Ryan — in the foreground wearing glasses)

Right: Allen's Sweets in Pine Street, Chippendale, was according to Bev Hunter where 'all the locals worked'. Bev, who later became a councillor on the South Sydney City Council, is pictured front row centre. (Courtesy of Bev Hunter)

Opposite: The Fitzroy Hotel Woolloomooloo Cricket Club Annual Picnic, 1926. (Courtesy of Joyce Higgins)

Paddington Council Tug-o-War Team at the Trumper Park Municipal Council's 1940 Picnic. Mr Tom Ryan, father of Kevin, is at the end of the line wearing a hat. (Courtesy of Kevin Ryan)

cousins. The kids went swimming, there'd have been six, seven of us children. FRANK W.

—

I remember we went fishing with my father because my father was really an avid fisherman, and so he had a boat, and he used to take us with him, and teach us how to do it, and we used to catch some squid and octopus, especially round Spit Bridge. My father would go fishing practically every weekend with his friends, and we had fresh fish which was really great. VIVI GERMANOS KOUTSOUNADIS

—

Every Sunday in summer we used to go to Nielsen Park at Vaucluse and have a barbeque there. A lot of my father's friends from Cyprus, and other friends he knew from here. Quite often he used to just load the boot up and go up there of a Sunday and have a barbie and a swim. There was always a lot of family activity like that. ANDREW LAZARIS

❝ Going for a drive was the big thing."

Cars made possible travel further afield and they added another dimension to leisure time. Families would go for a drive with no particular purpose in mind. For some, the Sunday afternoon drive became a custom. It provided an opportunity to 'sticky beak' at the residences and circumstances of people off the main tram, train and bus routes.

Quite often we went out around La Perouse, and we used to go to Yarra Bay. La Perouse would be quite a distance to go and have a picnic. You'd go down to Manly or somewhere like that, it was a big day. Quite a few times we went by tram, but if my dad didn't have a car, he nearly always had a truck. He bought his first new motor car in 1937, and it was a Chev, and he was the only

The Botanical Gardens and the Conservatorium were important venues. Pictured is Pat Rose with her mother and sister in the early 1930s. (Courtesy of Pat Rose)

one in Walker Street, Redfern, that owned a car at that time. TED McDERMOTT

—

We rather liked La Perouse, particularly on a
Sunday because they had a ventriloquist on the beach, and these were down and out theatricals. We had fellows with dancing dogs and the snake charmers, I think the snake charmer is still there. That seemed quite exciting to us. PAUL HERLINGER

—

In those days, the family was close, and I had an
auntie at Auburn, and an auntie in Wollongong. When we were children, we always went for drives, we always had a car, and so we used to go to Wollongong a lot. Or we'd meet half way, and have picnics. It was mostly on Sundays going for a drive. My father could drive around a suburb just looking at houses. You didn't have to go anywhere in particular, he would just drive round, up the streets, down the streets and looking. BEV KARONIDIS

—

Going for a drive was the big thing. We'd go to
places like Kurnell; it's on Botany Bay, there's a bit called Silver Beach which is quite nice. There wouldn't of been as much industry then in the early '50s. Royal National Park, we'd go there, Audley, you know; a place called Carr's Park, which is in the Kogarah municipality, it's on the George's River. I think it was East Hills, Picnic Point, that's the place. That seemed to take ages to get to because, you know, you didn't have the bridges that we have now, so you had to sort of go via Liverpool or something to get to Picnic Point. Whenever we got the chance, we'd swim. So I was a bit familiar with the beaches and the inner city. We hardly ever went to the North Shore, and well, Picnic Point was as far as we'd go west. BRENDAN DOYLE

—

" It was a palace of wonders for me."

The Art Gallery of New South Wales, the Australian Museum and the City Library in the Queen Victoria building were all places of escape from the everyday, and provided a glimpse of the world beyond the immediate.

O nce they were having inspectors from the Education Department come out to school to see a big marching day and teacher had said that anybody that was late wasn't to come. Well my friend had a dairy down the street, and she had to wait till her father came home before we could go to school and I waited for Ann. Well, when we got down there it was well and truly late, so we went to the old war memorial, the one that has been shifted to Canberra, it was near Chalmers Street, and next door to the Railway Institute. We stayed in there all day. Oh, it was a huge building and it had all the relics of the 1914 war in it, the old aeroplanes and everything. The smell of the must! For a long, long time my mother didn't know. And then I got belted! ANN RAMSAY

—

My parents did what they could to give us cultural
experiences, we had books, and I think the biggest discovery I had as a kid was finding the old Municipal Library, I used to get myself down there as often as possible. It used to be in the old Queen Victoria Building, and it was above Penfold's Wine Cellars, and you'd have this marvellous smell of vintage wine in the cellars seeping up through the building. The building itself inside was quite decrepit. It was a palace of wonders for me, it was marvellous to discover that. We'd go to the Art Gallery in wet weather, it was not as exciting as it is now, it seemed to be filled with things like *Rorks Drift,* a picture about the South African War, things like the *Arrival of the Queen of Sheba,* the *Sons of Clovis,* great gloomy, Victorian masterpieces, and of course plenty of the Gum Nut School, the Streeton's, and the Tom Roberts' and so on, but I always enjoyed going to the Art Gallery. And of course the Museum was there too, and that was another useful place. The Museum

Tom and Lillian Ryan with two of their younger children on the way to Manly in 1940. (Courtesy of Kevin Ryan)

I HAD A FREEDOM FOR WHICH I WAS VERY GRATEFUL

was much the same as it is now, perhaps the exhibitions weren't quite as exciting, but it still has that cold tomb-like atmosphere that I remember as a kid. We also used to like the Technological Museum very much, particularly the Strasbourg Clock, which we'd go and look at, and wonder at. I suppose an advantage of growing up in such an area was you were handy to the Library, you were handy to the Museum, you were handy to the Art Gallery, you knew where these were, where as numbers of kids who lived in the suburbs never had that. We knew all about the State Library, we used it. PAUL HERLINGER

Phillip Park Library and Craft was the best thing in the whole area, plus The Domain on Sundays. You heard everything from communism to salvation. Anyone could go up there, and stand on a soap box, and say what they liked. And there were the trees there, we used to call them vinegar berry trees, it's sort of an oval fruit with a big stone in it, like a prune stone, and you'd peel off the skin and suck them, they're just a slightly sour-sweet taste. And there were swings up there and Robby Burns' rose garden, and a fellow used to demonstrate how to do somersaults, and all the money used to fall out of his pocket into the sand, so we'd wait until he'd gone; we didn't actually think of it as stealing. You crossed over from Woolloomooloo and went through into The Domain down this lovely long path, with all flowers and bushes, and it was like being in the country. You couldn't see any buildings. If you went the Art Gallery way, you'd come to the Boy Charlton swimming pool. We swam there except I had a bad experience there with a flasher, and luckily someone came along. And then you'd come to Mrs Macquarie's Chair. And then if you went straight across, you walked into the Botanical Gardens themselves. They had an aviary there and a big wishing tree, a big fir tree, and you had to skip around it three times and make a wish. At the Art Gallery we'd sit on the lions, and try and climb up on the man on the horse. I went to The Australian Museum a lot. I liked it better than the Art Gallery because of all the animals and dioramas. JUDY CHAMBERS

 We used to rent a cottage at Kincumber for six shillings a week."

For most, holidays away were rare. However, places like Katoomba and the central coastal were popular. And, in the first half of the century, accommodation in guest houses was affordable for families of modest means.

We'd travel by steam train up to the Blue Mountains a lot. We used to stay a couple of weeks with my auntie at a guest house off Katoomba Street. I would go down and look at the falls... go for a walk down on me own, go down, right down to the bottom of the falls. IRENE WEBBER

We sometimes used to go to the Hydro. Mainly in the good years before the Depression. I always did bushwalking, and my sisters would play tennis, they were great tennis players. They used to play at White City. GLAD WILLIS

And we'd go up to the hotel Medlow Bath, that used to be quite a deal. We'd go up there and then we'd go down to Jenolan Caves, and stay at Caves House. It used to belong to the Government. Then we had relatives down in Bega, that's where all my relatives came from. I can remember going down there and staying with my relatives on their dairy farms. BOB SLATER

We used to rent a cottage at Kincumber for six shillings a week, and there were about eight of us, boys from the school, and we just rowed in the boats, and fished and swam, looking after ourselves. DARIO LO SCHIAVO

I only ever went on holidays with the school - we'd go away weekends but not very often. They'd take us up to Liverpool to the orphanage up there and we'd take some food with us, and we'd have our lunch and share it with the kids in the orphanage. NELL LEONARD

We'd go to the Blue Mountains, we would go on holidays to Lake Illawarra, camping. Dad used to drive us down, install Mum and us in the tent, and he'd have to drive back to Sydney to go to work, and we wouldn't see him until the next weekend. We would sometimes be down there for a month, and he'd come down every weekend, Friday night or Saturday and Sunday. I had my first ride in an aeroplane down there. On the beach there used to be a Tiger Moth, that was a two-seater plane, open plane, and it used to land and the guy used to give joy rides. And of course, when you went to a camping area like that, you were going there year after year, and you used to find that nearly all the same people were there, every time you went down, and everybody got to know everybody, like in Redfern. And they used to have a campfire of a night and we used to sit around the campfires and sing songs, swap yarns. All the older people seemed to have a little tale they could tell you. TED MCDERMOTT

You couldn't have many holidays. There was no money to go away on. I envied everyone who used to go Nambucca Heads. It's a place I always used to hear the kids talk about, they went to Nambucca Heads. I used to go to my aunt's at Glossodia, which is just out of Windsor, because we couldn't afford to go anywhere else. SIR NICHOLAS SHEHADIE

I went to Stewart House when I was nine or ten, it was sort of a holiday home and it was funded by the teachers of New South Wales. It was in with the Far West Children's Home thing. You went for a month and it was supposed to fatten you up. I'd been getting a lot of flu and colds, and the teachers had to recommend you, and I was chosen to go, and I did put on weight, I put on six pounds. The food was good, but I was terribly, terribly homesick of course, I'd never been away from my family at all. PORTIA FITZSIMMONS

The Sunday School had a place that we'd go for holidays at Cronulla. And we were given holidays away at Curl Curl, at Stewart House through the schools. We used to collect rags, and they'd sell the rags and the money then supported children from the city who needed a holiday. You were only supposed to go once, because there were so many children to get through. It was lovely because you could hear the surf pounding on the beach. I loved it there. I went twice with about three years in between. It was supposed to be for children who are a bit sickly and need a bit of a holiday by the sea. Really in Woolloomooloo, we were near the water anyway, but I was asked to go. JUDY CHAMBERS

We had a holiday home down at Bulgo, which is down the south coast. I think my father was part owner in it. We used to go down there for holidays. We also used to go to Bundeena, and we'd have holidays, maybe four or six weeks over there. It was called Bonneville, which is just out of Bundeena. We went on a lot of holidays, but we had the place down the south coast, actually Otford, and I think my father and his friend built it, and we went down there a lot, and it was a lot of fishing and swimming and surfing. We were never short of holidays. Also, my grandmother had a place at Woy Woy. It had a big verandah on the outside which probably half a dozen people could sleep on. We went up there, and they used to play cards, the adults, nearly all the time, card games for money. It had a boat with it, a rowing boat, and we were taken fishing and swimming. Every Christmas we'd go up for six weeks, my cousins, aunts, uncles and grandmother. Everybody would go on the old steam train, and buy oysters and that, and away we'd go, and in those years they used to catch very big flathead and that in the Hawkesbury. We'd have lovely times. JOSIE FOSTER

We did go away a bit. Relatives of ours had a bit of a cottage at The Entrance, and we'd go up there sometimes, but mostly we would go to Wollongong to stay. But I'm a funny person, and my mother wasn't much different, I don't move from Redfern, I don't like to go on holidays, I don't like to sleep away from home. And the funny part is, my Wollongong relatives didn't live very far from the railway station, and they had a big yard. It was big enough to build a tennis court at the end, and they had a big garden as well, and they used to keep chickens and my uncle used to go out rabbiting, and he would have the skins all stored there. He kept goats across the road, and I hated it. You'd lay there at night, and you'd hear these goats 'baarring,' and it was like country, and I don't like that. I like to hear cars going past. I used to hate staying down there because I like to hear movement. Bev Karonidis

We used to go away every year together, Mum and Dad and myself. We would go to Coffs Harbour or somewhere like that, or up the coast; we travelled a fair bit across Australia together, in caravans and things like that. We've done a few overseas trips together, the four of us. I went off to Japan and Hong Kong, Singapore, places like that. Dad was fortunate enough, he took us all on a boat cruise, and it took about eight weeks, it was a really good little trip. It would have been a bit unusual, yeah. Wasn't many people did trips like that, you know. Steve Fennell

My gran lived at Orange and my pop lived at Orange and she was bedridden, so we used to go up there. Mum bought a dodgy old car, a Hillman I think it was, and it was grey. And I remember when we got to the railway tracks near Orange, where the road goes over the railway tracks, we'd all have to get out and push because it didn't make it over the railway lines. My pop and gran used to have a cherry orchard, so we used to bring back boxes and boxes of cherries. So, I guess that was our holiday. We used to go up there 'cause Dad used to like to see his mum. Zowie Campbell

It was always known we had an Aboriginal background and we had an Aboriginal culture and heritage there. We would often go back to Yass, where my dad grew up as well. He grew up on the mission in Yass, and we used to go there for holidays quite a lot, and I remember one year we went up to where the missions used to be, and you could still see where the houses used to be, and there was an old well thing there. It was way, way, way out of town, right up over the hills out of Yass. One of Dad's brothers who lives down in Nowra, he's a net fisherman, takes the boat out with the nets, so we would go down there. We'd leave at four o'clock, early Saturday morning, and get down there about seven, and drive out to the beaches, and they would have tents and things set up. We would stay out at the beach for the weekend, and go out fishing and pulling in the nets and getting the crab baskets in, and just sort of live off the beach for the weekend, which was great. Down there, the sand is white, and the water is crystal-clear and it's just beautiful, beautiful. Colin Bell

On their return, the suburbs of home waited for more adventures and the resumption of the daily routines and weekly rituals that made up a child's life in South Sydney.

Cahills restaurants were well-known into the 1960s. This menu cover shows many of the sites referred to by South Sydney residents as being important to them.

List of Interviewees

YEAR OF BIRTH	CHILDHOOD SUBURB	NAME
1904	Newtown	Keith Mulhearn
1906	Newtown	Claire Mulhearn
1909	Surry Hills	Irene Webber
1911	Erskineville	Bill Schwebel
1911	Woolloomooloo	Billy Pascoe
1912	Woolloomooloo	Joyce Higgins
1913	Newtown	Zena Sachs
1913	Newtown	Frank Altoft
1914	Redfern	Anne Ramsay
1916	Newtown	Les Cross
1917	Kings Cross	Glad Willis
1917	Newtown	Grace Schwebel
1918	Potts Point	Dario Lo Schiavo
1919	Newtown/Erskineville	Loretto Thurgood
1919	Alexandria	Cliff Noble
1919	Erskineville	Henry Brown
1920	Chippendale	Jane Lanyon
1920	Kings Cross/Darlinghurst	Pat Nicks
1920	Kings Cross	Pat Rose
1920	Woolloomooloo	Nell Leonard
1921	Darlinghurst	Rose Clements
1923	Surry Hills & Roseberry	Fred Foreman
1923	Newtown	Leo Hannon
1923	Newtown	Iris Gower
1923	Newtown	Jean Hendy
1923	Newtown	Kate Dunbar
1925	Alexandria	Betty Moulds
1925	Potts Point	Paul Herlinger
1925	Surry Hills	Frank W.
1925	Woolloomooloo/Darlinghurst	Jean Jurd
1925	Redfern	Ted McDermott
1926	Beaconsfield	Mick Green
1926	Erskineville	Maureen Oliver
1926	Redfern	Sir Nicholas Shehadie
1927	Alexandria	Robert Hammond
1927	Darlinghurst	Pat Wright
1929	Surry Hills	Portia Fitzsimmons
1929	Alexandria	Sydney Fennell
1930	Darlington	Mervyn Jordan
1931	Paddington	Kevin Ryan
1931	Erskineville	Terry Murphy
1933	Potts Point	Brenda Humble
1933	Paddington	Bob Slater
1935	Woolloomooloo	Judy Chambers
1935	Darlington	Beverley Hunter
1935	Erskineville	Josie Foster
1936	Redfern	Bev Karonidis
1936	Surry Hills	Terry Glebe
1939	Kings Cross/Paddington/Potts Point	Cliff Fogarty
1939	Kings Cross/Potts Point	Geraldine Ohlsson
1939	Woolloomooloo	Beth Thorpe
1939	Woolloomooloo	Sam Donato
1943	Redfern	Vivi Germanos Koutsounadis
1944	Surry Hills	Warren (Whacker) Richardson
1945	Waterloo	Kathy Ingram
1949	Woolloomooloo	Cheryl Lindo
1949	Alexandria	Harry Brennan
1949	Newtown	Brendan Doyle
1950	Redfern	Cathi Joseph
1952	Waterloo	Jill Edwards
1952	Alexandria	Stephen Fennell
1953	Woolloomooloo	Andrew Lazaris
1957	Darlinghurst/Paddington	George Tourvas
1961	Darlington	Susan Alloway
1962	Woolloomooloo	Jackie Gratton-Wilson
1966	Surry Hills	Shane Campbell
1968	Surry Hills	Zowie (Gail) Campbell
1970	Chippendale	Colin Bell
1970	Waterloo	Esosa Eguaibor
1975	Waterloo/Redfern	Dean Ingram

Index